THE INSTITUTIONS OF COMECON

THE INSTITUTIONS OF COMECON

Giuseppe Schiavone

First published 1981 by
THE MACMILLAN PRESS LTD
London and Basingstoke
Companies and representatives throughout the world

Printed in Hong Kong

British Library Cataloguing in Publication Data

Schiavone, Giuseppe
The institutions of Comecon
1. Sovet ékonomicheskoĭ vzaimopomoshchi
I. Title
338.91′47 PC244

ISBN 0–333–28302–3

Comecon is like the bumble-bee which,
according to the laws of aeronautical
engineering, cannot fly because its wings
are too small for its body; but,
never having heard of aeronautical
engineering, the bumble-bee flies anyway.

Arthur J. Smith

Contents

Introduction

The legal and institutional aspects of international economic cooperation among socialist countries [1] – even though, in various forms and on various levels, such cooperation has now been in progress for more than three decades – have not been closely studied in the Western world. Indeed, the main legal features of the cooperation which is developing in a substantial section of the socialist camp form a subject which, on the whole, is comparatively little known in the West. In particular, the major works about Comecon, hereafter CMEA (from the initial letters of its full name, Council for Mutual Economic Assistance), with the exception of a few studies in German and French, have taken a strictly economic, historical or political perspective. The main areas of interpretation and assessment have often tended so far to be concerned with a handful of principal themes in economic integration and interdependence in order to evaluate, *inter alia*, the performance of CMEA in terms of the implications for Soviet political and economic control of Eastern Europe. In the last few years, on the other hand, the body of Eastern legal literature concerning socialist economic integration has been growing in size and improving in quality.

One cause of this state of affairs is, at least to a certain degree, the continuing difficulty for Western lawyers in obtaining detailed and up-to-date information about the evolution and regulation of the relations between members of the socialist 'system'. It should also be stressed that, as regards more specifically the field of international law and organization, in certain periods the socialist countries have agreed upon permanent actions of an international nature devoid of any legal form.

The present book is intended to serve as a 'guide' or 'handbook' to CMEA, providing a compendium of information with special reference to the most recent developments on the institutional level. All but two chapters of the book deal with CMEA and its principal and subsidiary organs; the two final chapters concentrate on 'functional' issues such as monetary and financial cooperation, and payments and capital flows. Overall, the aim is to provide a balanced summary rather than an exposition of the author's own viewpoint.

It is not uncommon, in works of this kind, to make comparisons between CMEA and more or less corresponding Western bodies such as the OECD (formerly OEEC) and the EEC.[2] In fact, the view is widely shared that CMEA cooperation and integration emulate that of Western intergovernmental organizations and of the EEC in particular. The very foundation, thirty years ago, of CMEA appeared essentially as a Stalinist riposte to the Marshall Plan and the OEEC.[3] Since that time several major changes in CMEA have occurred, but the success of cooperation and integration policies in Western Europe still serves as a powerful incentive for the strengthening of CMEA and the move towards some form of enhanced supranational authority. It is nevertheless to be doubted that comparisons which are important for a political or economic appraisal of CMEA are equally meaningful from a legal standpoint. On a strictly formal level, certain alleged similarities and analogies may more often than not prove misleading and stand in the way of a fuller understanding of organizational phenomena which are a distinguishing trait of the socialist camp. More substantially, consideration of the peculiar socio-economic structures of the socialist countries should be approached with caution and superficial comparisons avoided – the more obvious the more deceptive.

Furthermore, it is important to bear in mind the major role played by the Communist and workers' parties of the socialist countries, and especially by the Communist Party of the Soviet Union, in promoting and directing the various forms of cooperation, both bilateral and multilateral. The relations between the parties, and the differences and disagreements that occasionally arise on different issues and at different levels, therefore assume an overriding importance, and give cooperation among socialist countries a marked political character.

Despite continuing and significant conflicts within the socialist world, which originate both from historic and traditional rivalries and economic interests and antagonisms, Soviet scholars claim that international relations between socialist states are of a *new and higher type*, being based upon the harmony of national interests with those of the 'system' as a whole. The Marxist-Leninist principle of socialist internationalism, which allegedly governs the mutual relations of socialist states is said to be considerably richer and more complete than the principles governing cooperation among Western countries. Along with specific national interests, socialist states are claimed to have more general and 'international' interests which call for mutual support and assistance. More precisely, the principle of mutual assistance is defined as the legal right to receive assistance from other socialist states and the corresponding legal duty to render assistance to other socialist states. These principles obviously provide an institutional basis for interference in internal affairs 'in the greater interest of the socialist camp'. Economic cooperation and integration, for their part, are said to be the most important aspects of this mutual assistance inherent in the principle of socialist internationalism. Therefore, it is not by chance that the most important organization of the socialist countries for economic cooperation and integration bears the name of the 'Council for *Mutual Assistance*.'[4]

When the CMEA Charter was amended in 1974, explicit mention was made of the principle of socialist internationalism in paragraph 2 of Article I. It must nevertheless be stressed that the reference to the said principle was accompanied and counterbalanced by the introduction, in the same paragraph, of the principles of independence and non-interference in internal affairs.

Despite such a careful blend of principles and counter-principles, some small CMEA members, and especially Romania, are deeply concerned at the possible dangers of loss of national sovereignty and economic independence that can result from fairly comprehensive integration plans. The very principle of socialist internationalism is, in fact, now being openly discussed within the Communist movement and a trend towards its substitution with a much looser concept is gradually emerging. Although it is far from easy to foresee how important its impact will be, such a tendency will undoubtedly affect the basic principles governing relations within CMEA and the broad issues of cooperation and integration. In any event, it is the small CMEA countries which are apparently destined to reap the most substantive benefits from the decline of socialist internationalism.

A brief survey of some recent documents may help bring out

the progressive developments of the new 'solidaristic' conception and the consequent changes which have occurred to date. As a first example, one can cite the statement of 24 November 1976 about the further development of cooperation and fraternal friendship between the Soviet Communist Party and the Romanian Party, the USSR and Romania.[5] After stressing that Soviet-Romanian cooperation takes place in 'a climate of strict respect of the principles of equality of rights, of independence, of sovereignty, of non-interference in internal affairs and of mutual fraternal assistance', the declaration makes reference to relations with the other states and parties. In the very context of the definition of these relations, one significant point appears to be the substitution – consecrated only a few months earlier by the Berlin conference of the European Communist and workers' parties, which will be discussed later – of the principle of 'international solidarity' for that of socialist internationalism. Indeed, the declaration stresses 'the steady improvement of relations between socialist countries, sovereign and having equal rights, on the basis of the principles of international solidarity'. Furthermore, the Soviet and the Romanian parties declare their firm intention to contribute to the strengthening of the unity of Communist and workers' parties 'on the basis of the principles of Marxism-Leninism and of international solidarity, with full respect for equality of rights and of the autonomy of each brother party and of non-interference in internal affairs'.

'Fraternal and voluntary international cooperation' as a basis for relations between the two parties and countries is repeatedly cited in the Soviet-Yugoslav communiqué of 17 November 1976, in which no reference whatsoever is made to proletarian internationalism, while solemnly reconfirming 'the respect for autonomy and freedom of choice of different ways of socialist development', in conformity with the historical, national and international peculiarities of each country.[6]

The gradual evolution of the meaning and content of internationalism may be seen more clearly by comparing the ritual formulas used in various declarations by the conferences of representatives of Communist and workers' parties. As an example, in the declaration of the conference of the Communist and workers' parties held in Moscow in November 1957, explicit reference is made to socialist internationalism, citing full equality of rights, respect for territorial integrity, independence and state sovereignty, and non-interference in internal affairs as basic principles governing relations between socialist countries; such relations are said to be characterized by mutual fraternal assistance, the fundamental expression of socialist internationalism.[7] Similar statements are contained in the declarations issued on the occasion of other meetings until the late 1960s.

One year after the Prague Spring and the subsequent invasion of Czechoslovakia, at the June 1969 Moscow conference of the representatives of Communist and workers' parties significant differences emerge between the advocates of the doctrine, which might be termed traditional, of internationalism and the supporters of the solidaristic conception, designed to safeguard the distinguishing features of the theory and practice of individual parties and states. The latter approach found a solemn consecration on the occasion of the conference of twenty-nine Communist and workers' parties of Europe held in Berlin from 29 to 30 June 1976.[8]

In the remarkable document adopted at the conclusion of the Berlin conference and entitled 'For peace, security, cooperation and social progress in Europe', proletarian internationalism is not mentioned at all, while reference is made to 'friendly and voluntary cooperation and internationalist solidarity, with strict observance of the equality of rights and of the sovereign independence of each party, of non-interference in internal affairs, of respect for the free choice of different paths in the struggle for progressive social changes and in favour of socialism'.[9]

It should be stressed at this point that, quite naturally, a strong defence is still made by the Soviets of the principle of socialist internationalism in its traditionally accepted form. This happened during the Berlin conference, with an address by the head of the delegation of the CPSU who reconfirmed the paramount importance of the principle and categorically ruled out the possibility that the pressing appeals for a strengthening of internationalist ties are aimed in practice at the re-establishment of a Soviet-dominated 'centre' for guiding the international Communist movement. Similar concepts had been expressed on the occasion of the XXVth Congress of the CPSU, held in February–March 1976, just a few months before the Berlin meeting.

In spite of Soviet denials and the concessions made in Berlin by the CPSU and 'loyalist' parties on proletarian internationalism, the actual danger of a new 'institutionalization' of relations between Communist parties is repeatedly emphasized by analysts and policymakers. In his report to the XIth Congress of the League of Communists held in Belgrade from 20 to 23 June 1978, President Tito openly referred to the negative tendencies towards the 're-emergence of centres for guiding the workers' movement'.[10]

Although it is still too early to measure the impact of Eurocommunism on East European theory and practice, the available evidence indicates that this evolutionary process is causing no small concern to existing leaderships while encouraging, on the other hand, cautious attempts to assume independent postures in domestic and/or foreign affairs.

The transition to a solidaristic conception is fairly clearly apparent also in the communiqué issued at the end of the meeting of the secretaries of the parties of Eastern Europe, the USSR, Mongolia, Cuba and Vietnam, held in Budapest from 27 February to 1 March 1978, to discuss ideological and international policy problems. In the communiqué, the traditional reference to proletarian internationalism is replaced by the formula of internationalist solidarity.[11]

Of outstanding importance in highlighting the changing features of the relations between socialist countries are certainly the declarations of the Warsaw Pact members and the communiqués concerning the sessions of CMEA.

From the standpoint of international politics, the Warsaw Pact's Political Consultative Committee is a major coordinating and policy-issuing body which has been performing over the years a fundamental role in stressing Soviet views on European problems. Among the latest documents, mention should be made of the declaration adopted at the PCC's meeting held in Bucharest on 26 November 1976, entitled 'For new goals in international détente, for the strengthening of security and the development of cooperation in Europe'. In this declaration the Pact's member-countries express their firm resolution constantly to strengthen cooperation 'on the basis of the principles of Marxism-Leninism and of international solidarity, of respect for the equality of rights and for the sovereignty of each state, of non-interference in internal affairs and of fraternal mutual assistance'.[12]

Socialist internationalism retained until 1977 a prominent place in the communiqués issued at the end of CMEA sessions. Also in the final communiqué on the 31st session (Warsaw, June 1977) reference is made to the establishment among member-countries 'of international relations of a new type, founded on the principles of Marxism-Leninism, of socialist internationalism, of full equality, of respect for the sovereignty of each state, of non-interference in internal affairs, of reciprocity of advantages and of mutual fraternal assistance'.[13] In the communiqué of the following session, held in Bucharest in June 1978, clear mention was made of 'the principles of Marxism-Leninism and of internationalist solidarity'.[14] Any reference to either Marxism-Leninism or internationalism is omitted in the final communiqué on the 33rd session (Moscow, June 1979).[15] On the other hand, the declaration on the 30th anniversary of the organization, adopted by the heads of the delegations at the end of the said session, contains a comprehensive list – entirely reproducing the relevant provisions of the CMEA Charter – of the principles governing the 'international economic relations of a new type' among member countries.[16]

Finally, the constitutional provisions recently introduced in some Eastern countries with reference to cooperation with the other socialist states and to mutual assistance are worth mentioning. An important example is provided by the new Soviet constitution, which the Supreme Soviet approved in October 1977. Article 30 of the constitution states that the USSR, as an integral part of the world system of socialism and of the socialist community, shall develop and strengthen friendship, cooperation and mutual fraternal assistance towards the other socialist countries 'on the basis of socialist internationalism' and shall actively participate 'in economic integration and in the international socialist division of labour'.

The above-mentioned rules – which the Albanian press immediately labelled a new proclamation of the doctrine of 'limited sovereignty'[17] – could but raise serious problems.[18]

The constitutional amendments adopted in Poland in February 1976 led, *inter alia*, to the insertion of a formula recognizing 'friendship and cooperation with the Soviet Union' and the other socialist countries, while solemnly reaffirming the 'independence and sovereignty of the Polish nation'.

Not unexpectedly Albania followed a basically different course proclaiming, in the revised constitution of December 1976, a policy of full and complete independence *vis-à-vis* any other country be it socialist or capitalist.

It would be premature to conclude from the examples offered above that the gradual shift from socialist internationalism to a doctrine taking into more adequate consideration national interests will substantially alter the patterns of intra-CMEA cooperation in the very near future.

Be all this as it may, the decline of socialist internationalism appears to be the product of a long historical trend which affects all East European countries to a greater or lesser degree and, to a certain extent, the USSR itself.

The significance of this trend appears the greater when one looks at recent developments inside CMEA marked by piecemeal approaches to integration while overall plans (such as the Comprehensive Programme of 1971) are shelved and replaced by selected programmes concerning specific branches of production and a handful of joint industrial projects. Consequently, intra-CMEA coordination in the next few years will presumably affect only a fairly limited set of products – especially fuels and primary goods – and national planners in Eastern Europe will retain substantive authority on major economic policy issues, despite persistent Soviet efforts at strengthening CMEA planning apparatus. It is not unlikely that some CMEA members such as Hungary and Poland will introduce significant changes in their planning and steering mechanism thus further contributing towards the differentiation of the economic systems of the area and to keeping multilateral planning on a minimal scale. The new wave of economic and institutional reforms initiated throughout the USSR and Eastern Europe in the late 1970s will doubtless affect the future prospects for intra-CMEA cooperation. Moreover, Vietnam's recent entry into CMEA and the consequent growing importance of non-European 'developing' members will make even more difficult any real progress toward effective coordination.[19]

On the legal plane, Romania, adhering closely to the 'interested country' principle, has been successfully resisting any project intended to increase the powers of CMEA and to alter in a supranational perspective the decision-making process.[20] Also, on the very sensitive issue of the Warsaw Pact's defence expenditure and military integration, Romania strives to pursue an independent policy.

Additional food for thought is being provided by the conflicting and contradictory behaviour of East European regimes towards the increasing willingness of some parties and states to challenge Soviet authority and to question the Soviet model.

Throughout the East European area major departures from the Soviet line in domestic or foreign affairs remain confined at the moment within rather definite bounds. No one move by itself has been conclusive but the global course of events may eventually bring forth a remarkable change in the balance of forces and consequently in the pattern of cooperation and integration. How and how much only time will tell.

NOTES TO INTRODUCTION

1. For a review of the various definitions of 'socialist' countries see M. Lavigne, *The Socialist Economies of the Soviet Union and Europe*, London, 1974, p. xiv ff.
2. See, among others, the comments by J. Caillot, *Le CAEM: Aspects juridiques et formes de coopération économique entre les pays socialistes*, Paris, 1971, pp. 47, 58, 72, 77. See also N. Faddeev, *Sovet ekonomicheskoi vzaimopomoshchi, 1949–1974*, Moscow, 1974, p. 62 ff. For a broad comparative synthesis, see Iu. Sdobnikov, *Ekonomicheskaia integratsiia v usloviiakh dvukh sistem*, Moscow, 1976.
3. M. Kaser, *Comecon: Integration Problems of the Planned Economies*, 2nd edn., London, 1967, p. 9.
4. For a recent stand on this issue, see N. Faddeev, *Sovet*, op. cit., p. 44 ff. *et passim*; A. Talalaev, 'Kritika burzhuaznykh pravovykh kontseptsii otnositel'no SEV i sotsialisticheskoi ekonomicheskoi integratsii', in *Sovet ekonomicheskoi vzaimopomoshchi. Osnovnye pravovye problemy*, Moscow, 1975, pp. 345–99; A. Talalaev, 'Kritika nekotorykh sovremennykh burzhuaznykh kontseptsii otnositel'no printsipov i organizatsionnopravovykh form sotsialisticheskoi ekonomicheskoi integratsii i roli SEV v ee osushchestvlenii', in *Pravovye voprosy deiatel'nosti SEV*, Moscow, 1977, pp. 172–91.
5. *Pravda*, 25 November 1976.
6. *Pravda*, 18 November 1976.
7. *Programmnye dokumenty borby za mir, demokratiiu i sotsializm*, Moscow, 1961, p. 10.
8. The Berlin conference undoubtedly marked a milestone in the evolution of 'Eurocommunism'. For a thorough discussion of this subject, see R. Godson and S. Haseler, *Eurocommunism: Implications for East and West*,

London, 1978; G. Urban (ed.), *Eurocommunism: Its Roots and Future in Italy and Elsewhere*, London, 1978; J. Valenta, 'Eurocommunism and Eastern Europe', in *Problems of Communism*, March–April 1978, pp. 41–54.

As a very recent illustration of the importance of the said conference for the definition of the basic rules that the Communist parties must follow in their mutual relations, one may cite the joint declaration on the further development of friendship and cooperation between the Soviet Party and the Hungarian Party, the USSR and Hungary issued in Budapest on 1 June 1979 (*Pravda*, 3 June 1979). While stressing that the friendship between the USSR and Hungary is based on their 'fidelity to the principles of Marxism-Leninism and socialist internationalism', a significant reference is made to the Berlin conference. Indeed, the two parties are said to be struggling to develop 'the fraternal cooperation among all Communist and workers' parties on the basis of universally accepted rules . . . elaborated during bilateral contacts and international meetings, *including the Berlin conference of 1976*' (italics supplied).

9. *Pravda*, 1 July 1976.
10. *Yugoslav Survey*, Vol. XIX, No. 3, August 1978, p. 11 ff.
11. *Pravda*, 2 March 1978.
12. *Pravda*, 27 November 1976.
13. *Pravda*, 24 June 1977.
14. *Ekonomicheskaia Gazeta*, No. 28, July 1978.
15. *Pravda*, 30 June 1979.
16. Ibid.
17. *Zëri i popullit*, 1 November 1977.
18. Had some of the proposed amendments been accepted, the Soviet right to intervene in other countries 'to defend socialism' would have been expressed even more clearly. See, for example, the proposals set forth in *Krasnaia Zvezda*, 21 and 25 August 1977.
19. In addition, there seems to be a competition among CMEA less developed members in order to get a larger share of much-needed aid. At the CMEA Executive Committee meeting in Ulan Bator in September 1978 Mongolia's appeals for more help apparently received a halfhearted response while Vietnam was being promised – both bilaterally and multilaterally – a substantial aid to make up for the cancellation of Chinese assistance. See A. Sanders, 'Mongolia takes second place', in *Far Eastern Economic Review*, 8 December 1978, p. 62.

    A stronger and more clearly defined commitment to help the reconstruction and development of Vietnam was taken at the following (88th) meeting of the Executive Committee (Moscow, January 1979).
20. According to a Romanian leak, Soviet proposals for changing voting procedures in CMEA were put forward, without success, at the 32nd Session of the Assembly in June 1978.

1 The Historical Framework

1. EAST EUROPEAN COUNTRIES AFTER WORLD WAR II

The origins, developments and forms of economic cooperation within the framework of CMEA could not be understood without reference to the events which marked the relations among European socialist countries at the end of World War II.

For a long time, these relations were regulated on a bilateral basis, through agreements between the Soviet Union and each of the minor countries, as well as through agreements between the latter. There was thus formed, from the early postwar years, a close network of mutual relations which created the necessary preconditions for subsequent multilateral cooperation.

As is well known, the postwar period was characterized in Eastern Europe by the establishment of regimes following the Marxist-Leninist ideology, and consequently by far-reaching economic and social reforms, usually patterned after what had been done in the Soviet Union.

During the period from 1945 to 1948–9, the people's democracies of Eastern Europe concluded a number of bilateral treaties of friendship, cooperation and mutual assistance both with the USSR and between themselves, as well as trade agreements.

Indeed, during this early postwar period, cooperation among these countries was achieved largely through exchanges of goods under trade agreements, and only in a few instances did it develop within a broader context. With respect to the latter, mention should be made of the agreements concerning economic assistance, extended mainly by the Soviet Union. As reconstruction proceeded, cooperation was also extended to science and technology and to many other sectors.

To the initial rapprochement of the economic structures there corresponded, on the political plane, the establishment of Cominform which was set up in Warsaw in September 1947. This body, which included the Communist parties of the USSR and of the East European countries (as well as the French and Italian parties), was intended to ensure stable and close contacts among the national parties. Cominform, even though it remained in existence only until April 1956, did perform the important function of politically strengthening Eastern Europe by consolidating the system of bilateral agreements between the USSR and the people's democracies, upholding the role of the various parties (and especially of the CPSU), in promoting cooperation and laying the foundations for its future institutionalization.

After 1948–9, the process of transformation of the economies in the people's democracies became more marked, moving away from the Western socio-economic structures. The extension of nationalization to cover almost all industrial and service activities, the beginning of collectivization in agriculture and the adoption of long-term plans to regulate every aspect of economic life, were associated with a substantial decline in trading with the West and with an increasing degree of dependence on the Soviet Union.

In the meantime, the relations between the USSR and the USA were becoming increasingly strained and the cleavage between Eastern and Western Europe was growing deeper.

In June 1947, at Harvard University, Secretary of State Marshall delivered a speech which was to go down in history, announcing that the United States intended to offer to all European countries economic and financial aid to solve the problems involved in postwar reconstruction. As is known, the East European countries declined to participate in the Marshall Plan (Czechoslovakia, which had formally accepted, withdrew), maintaining that this would have seriously threatened their independence.

The Soviet Union, making this very charge, caused the failure of the tripartite Anglo-Franco-Soviet Conference held in Paris from 27 June to 3 July 1947, to define the details of Europe's acceptance of Marshall Aid. Stalin himself, in July 1947, told the members of a Czech delegation in Moscow that the true purpose of Marshall Aid was to isolate the USSR from Europe.

During 1948 the international situation took a turn for the worse because of a further deterioration of the relations between the two blocs.

The February 1948 *coup d'état* in Czechoslovakia and the Berlin blockade in July of the same year were countered by the West with the adoption of controls on exports to socialist countries. The United States adopted the initial export controls in March 1948 and was followed by other Western countries; of particular significance was the embargo imposed on goods of primary strategic importance. Subsequently, a special working committee (the so-called Cocom) was established, made up of fifteen Western countries, for the purpose of coordinating control measures and promoting common action against the various forms of embargo evasion.

Meanwhile, on 16 April 1948, sixteen countries of Western Europe signed the Treaty establishing the Organization for European Economic Cooperation (OEEC) which, by ensuring the implementation of the Marshall Plan, laid the foundations for permanent cooperation.

The year 1948 also saw a landmark in the postwar history of Eastern Europe: the formal condemnation of Yugoslavia which, alone among East European countries, was resisting increasingly heavy Soviet interference in its internal affairs and, at the same time, was seeking a national and autonomous road to socialism.

On 28 June 1948, Cominform released a resolution, adopted unanimously by all other Communist parties, condemning the leaders of the Yugoslav Party and asking the 'healthy forces' of the latter to force on the leadership a new political line. The Yugoslav leaders stuck to their positions and won this trial of strength, but they had to pay a heavy price in the isolation of their country which, on the one hand, was excluded from the process of integration of the people's democracies and, on the other, remained in a difficult position *vis-à-vis* the West. Yugoslavia's exit from the Eastern bloc, it need hardly be said, produced appreciable effects on the development of economic cooperation between the socialist countries, resulting, among other things, in that cooperation, under marked Soviet influence, assuming more rigidly authoritarian features.

Against the background of the events briefly outlined above, January 1949 saw the birth of the Council for Mutual Economic Assistance, intended to promote multilateral cooperation among the European socialist countries. With 1949 began, in effect, a new and important chapter in the political and economic history of the Soviet Union and Eastern Europe.

2. THE ESTABLISHMENT OF CMEA IN JANUARY 1949

Unlike the OEEC, which had kept the world fully informed about the preparatory proceedings, its purposes, charter and institutional machinery, very little is known about the beginnings of CMEA.

A Tass Newsagency release of January 1949 was the first document relating to the new organisation created by the socialist countries.[1]

The Soviet Union, Poland, Czechoslovakia, Hungary, Romania and Bulgaria were the founding countries; Albania joined on 21 February 1949 and the German Democratic Republic on 29 September 1950.

The Tass release confined itself to giving summary and rather general indications about the outcome of a meeting held in Moscow:

'In January of this year an economic Conference was held in Moscow attended by delegates from Bulgaria, Hungary, Poland, Romania, the USSR and Czechoslovakia.

'The Conference noted considerable success in the development of economic relations among the countries concerned and above all the great rise in the turnover of trade.

'As a result of the above-mentioned economic relations and the implementation of economic cooperation between the countries of people's democracy and the USSR, conditions have been created to accelerate the restoration and development of their national economies.

'The Conference further observed that the governments of the United States of America, of Great Britain and of certain Western European states had boycotted trade relations with the countries of people's democracy and the USSR because these countries did not consider it appropriate that they should submit themselves to the dictatorship of the Marshall Plan, which would have violated their sovereignty and the interests of their national economies.

'In consideration of these circumstances, the meeting studied the question of the possibility of organizing wider economic cooperation between the countries of people's democracy and the USSR.

'To establish this wider economic cooperation between the countries of people's democracy and the USSR, the Conference considered it necessary to create the Council for Mutual

Economic Assistance between the countries represented – on the basis of equal representation and with the task of exchanging economic experience, extending technical aid to one another and rendering mutual assistance with respect to raw materials, foodstuffs, machines, equipment, etc.

'The meeting decided that the Council for Mutual Economic Assistance would be an organization open to other countries of Europe sharing the Council's principles and desirous of participating in the widening of economic cooperation with the above-mentioned countries.

'The Council for Mutual Economic Assistance would take a decision only with the agreement of the interested countries. The Council shall meet periodically in the capital of each of the signatory countries in turn under the chairmanship of the representative of the country in whose capital the session takes place.'

It is important to stress from a legal standpoint that CMEA 'was the first formal assembly of the Soviet Union and its associates as states'.[2]

The Soviet Union appeared to be the promoter of the new organisation, since it was interested in establishing closer economic relations with the countries of people's democracy and in opposing to the OEEC a body formed by socialist states. Furthermore, the establishment of the Council should have made possible the adoption of effective measures against Yugoslavia, whose conduct had caused not only a diplomatic break, but also economic sanctions which had to be tightened with the aid of the new organisation.

3. THE CREATION OF CMEA: CAUSES AND CIRCUMSTANCES

Before going into a description of the main stages of the Council's activity in the field of economic cooperation, it seems useful to look into two questions which are posed, more or less directly, by a reading of the communiqué quoted above.

The first and rather controversial question concerns the set of causes – both political and economic – which led to the creation of the Council. The second question, of a more properly legal nature, originates from the absence, which continued through more than one decade, of a written agreement about the establishment and operation of the organization.

As regards the causes, both disclosed and undisclosed, which led to the creation of the Council, one should in the first place call attention to the almost general consensus that CMEA was essentially conceived as a response, more political than economic, to the Marshall Plan and to the OEEC.

In this connection, it would not seem questionable that, at the time of its creation, the Council was conceived as a response to the Marshall Plan rather than as a real instrument for the promotion of economic cooperation. This, however, should not lead one to underestimate the continuity of Soviet policy for the integration of the economies of the East European countries. From this angle, the establishment of the Council might be considered as a natural step in the evolution of relations between the USSR and the people's democracies. By early 1949 the system of bilateral agreements between these countries, creating the conditions for a substantial increase in trade and for a further strengthening and widening of cooperation had been completed.

It should also be recalled that, between 1946 and 1948, some East European countries had proposed plans for economic union, such as the Yugoslav and Bulgarian plan for the establishment of a Balkan union and the more or less similar plans propounded by Poland and Czechoslovakia. The establishment of a multilateral organization like CMEA could satisfy, at least to a certain extent, the aspirations of some people's democracies for a closer cooperation, without affecting, but rather strengthening, the pre-eminent role of the Soviet Union.

On the basis of the foregoing, it seems that the conclusion can be drawn that the causes of the creation of CMEA were various and complex, and certainly not solely reducible to the Soviet desire to oppose to the OEEC an East European organization. The establishment of the OEEC certainly served as an incentive, but it seems to have provided no more than an occasional prompting for the establishment of a multilateral cooperation body, the need for which was already felt.[3]

Also to be stressed is the close connection existing between the multilateral cooperation operating within CMEA's own sphere and the bilateral or multilateral cooperation formally or substantially outside that body. It is not always easy to draw a precise line of demarcation between forms of cooperation decided and carried out essentially within the Council and forms of cooperation decided and carried out on other levels and with different instruments. In any event, it is within CMEA that the bases for multilateral economic cooperation were created and that the guidelines for this cooperation have been and still are laid down.

The second question that seems worth investigating briefly concerns the protracted absence of a written agreement concerning the establishment and operation of the Council. Indeed, the actual Charter of the organization, which codified the principles deriving from practices covering more than ten years, was approved by an international treaty concluded in Sofia on 14 December 1959 and entered into force on 13 April 1960.

The absence of a written agreement relating to the establishment of the Council is admitted by many authorities, who also tend to rule out the possibility of the Council having been governed, for the first ten years, by a secret agreement. Some maintain, however, that the Tass communiqué of January 1949 is itself an international treaty, so that it would be reasonable to wonder why such treaty was not ratified by the appropriate bodies in the signatory countries. This thesis, however, appears unacceptable: admitting that the communiqué contained the basic principles which were to guide the organization is a quite different proposition from maintaining that the communiqué constitutes an international treaty. In all likelihood, the establishment of the Council resulted not from a written agreement, of which no trace can be found, but of a tacit agreement under which the states concerned took voluntary and concrete actions. Indeed, a written agreement is not a necessary condition for the creation and operation of an organization: a tacit agreement and given associative behaviour is all that is needed. This actually seems to have been the case of CMEA until an explicit agreement was concluded late in 1959.

4. THE COUNCIL'S ACTIVITY: FROM ITS CREATION UNTIL 1954

The activity so far carried out by the Council for Mutual Economic Assistance can be divided – by way of rough approximation and in order to simplify the analysis – into six main periods: the first from its foundation in 1949 until 1954, the second from 1954 to 1958, the third from 1958 to 1962, the fourth from 1962 to 1969, the fifth from 1969 to 1974, and the sixth, which began in 1974 and is still in progress.[4]

The reasons for such a subdivision will be clear from a discussion of the most significant events which have characterized the various periods of CMEA evolution.

The first period of the organization's life, generally referred to as 'bilateral', was characterized mainly by the conclusion of long-term trade agreements between member-countries (a system, however, which had been adopted even before CMEA's creation) and of conventions for the promotion of technical-scientific cooperation.

The first meeting of the delegates of the Council's member-countries was held in Moscow from 26 to 30 April 1949, and was devoted mainly to the working out of a rudimentary organizational structure.

It is important to note that until 1954, the conference of the member-countries' delegates – which will hereafter be referred to as the 'Assembly'[5] – holding periodical plenary sessions, was in practice the only organ of the Council, if one excepts an office with strictly organizational functions, assisted by a secretariat located in Moscow, with a very small staff.

Besides organizational problems, the first Session of the Assembly defined the general goals of CMEA in the fields of trade and technical assistance.

Of significant importance was the 2nd Session of the Assembly, held in Sofia from 25 to 27 August 1949, which concerned itself with the drafting of the standard form to be used for the agreements on scientific and technical cooperation.

Very little is known about the 3rd Session, held in Moscow from 24 to 25 November 1950, which again probably discussed problems relating to the expansion of inter-regional trade.

No meetings were held by the Assembly between the end of 1950 and the spring of 1954, and very little is known about CMEA's activities in those years.[6]

It is worth mentioning, however, an important form of cooperation which gradually took shape during the first period of the Council's life, namely technical-scientific cooperation, mainly in the form of the organization of scientific research, of the development of plans, of technical documentation exchanges, of participation in and technical assistance to the building and installation of industrial plants and in the development of mineral resources, of exchange of patents and technological know-how, etc.

From a general standpoint, it should be noted that, while the cooperation promoted by the OEEC was making significant progress, economic coordination among European socialist countries encountered serious obstacles, due to the particular features of their economic and social structures.

Following the Soviet – and more precisely Stalinist – notion that industrialization at any cost, especially through the creation of a heavy industry, is the best way to socialism, the East European countries began a period of forced industrialization, during which each of them aimed to have its own steel, engineering and other industries. These self-sufficiency policies resulted in the same branches of industry being developed in all countries, causing a shortage of raw materials in the area as well as, particularly in the case of machinery, serious difficulties in disposing of the surpluses on foreign markets, with the resulting accumulation of large stocks.

The errors committed by the people's democracies in creating autonomous and completely isolated planning systems became especially evident during the Korean crisis, when the first five-year plans had to be drastically revised. Following this, the Council began a major effort to coordinate the economic plans of the member-countries. The success of the international organizations of Western Europe spurred CMEA to step up its efforts. Moreover, Stalin's disappearance had significant consequences on the development of real cooperation among CMEA countries.

5. 1954 TO 1958

The Council's organization, ill-suited to the new tasks, was radically changed and substantially strengthened during the second period of CMEA's life which – according to the subdivision adopted here – started with the Assembly's session held in the spring of 1954.

It should be noted, from a general standpoint, that the change in policies made in 1954–6 took place during a period of serious political and economic crisis, especially in the German Democratic Republic, Poland and Hungary, and therefore adjustment to the new principles proved particularly hard. This is apparent from a quick glance at the subjects discussed in the Assembly sessions held during this second period.

The 4th Session of the Assembly, held in Moscow from 26 to 27 March 1954, considered the possibility of coordinating plans for the period 1956–60. The 5th Session, also held in 1954 (Moscow, 24–25 June), tackled in a more practical manner the problem of coordinating the five-year plans for 1956–60 and discussed the most effective measures to be adopted to promote specialization in the production of certain types of farm machinery.

In the meantime, the Warsaw Pact, concluded on 14 May 1955 (and entered into effect on 5 June of that year) between the Soviet Union and the East European countries (Albania, Bulgaria, Czechoslovakia, Poland, the German Democratic Republic, Romania and Hungary) on the basis of 'friendship, cooperation and mutual assistance', completed in the political and military field the system of relations established by CMEA.

During the 6th Session, held in Budapest from 7 to 11 December 1955, the problem of the division of labour was discussed extensively and priorities were established for the production of certain member-countries.

In this session a new attitude emerged towards the economic integration of the area, to be achieved through coordinated planning. It was in 1955, indeed, that the first serious attempt to coordinate the economic development of the CMEA countries seems to have been made.

At the 6th Session, in particular, the main lines of the trade agreements for 1956–60 were developed and specific problems of coordination were tackled.

An even more important landmark in the Council's history is the 7th Session, held in Berlin from 18 to 25 May 1956, only a few months after the 20th Congress of the CPSU. The condemnation of Stalinism, the importance of peaceful coexistence, the possibility of following national roads to socialism – the basic themes of the Congress – could not fail to influence the future evolution of CMEA.

During the 7th Session measures were adopted to facilitate trade among member-countries and a call was issued for the conclusion of agreements that should be not only bilateral, but if possible tripartite. Of fundamental importance was the conversion – during this Session – of the temporary 'working groups', which had till then played a minor role, into twelve Standing Commissions responsible for developing practical measures designed to facilitate the work of coordination.[7] In the final communiqué of the 7th Session the need was also stressed to create a common electricity grid, to develop the hydro-electric resources of the Danube, to coordinate transport, as well as production and development in a number of industries – especially steel, engineering, chemicals, oil and natural gas, and coal mining. Special attention was also devoted to the problems of agriculture, such as grain and fertilizer requirements.

After the 7th Session, the organs of the Council became very active and made appreciable progress, among other things, in the field of standardization. The Standing Commissions widened their scope of action, going further into questions connected with specialization in the various branches of industry.

The 8th Session, which was held in Warsaw from 18 to 22 June 1957, adopted some decisions concerning the drafting and coordination of economic plans for a period of ten to fifteen years, while the Standing Commissions – the number of which was increased to fifteen – were assigned additional tasks. Furthermore, important measures were adopted in the field of trade among the member-countries, stressing the need for multilateral agreements. Problems of coordination in the energy sector were also discussed.

It is important to recall that during the 8th Session the members of the Council signed an agreement concerning the introduction of a multilateral clearing system, in which the USSR State Bank served as a clearing house. This agreement marked a significant step towards the 'multilateralization' of payments.

A goal of major practical importance was achieved at the end of 1957 within CMEA with the adoption of a standard set of rules for international sales among member-countries. On 13 December of that year the Standing Commission on Foreign Trade, meeting in Moscow, adopted the 'General Conditions for Deliveries of Goods among Foreign Trade Corporations of CMEA Members'. The General Conditions contained detailed regulations about this complex subject: rights and obligations of buyers and sellers, place and date of delivery, quality and quantity of goods, packaging, markings, checking the quality of goods, guarantees, shipment directions, payment procedure, arbitration, etc.

The General Conditions – entered into force on 1 January 1958, later amended and finally replaced, in 1969 and again in 1976, by new rules also going under the name of General Conditions – appeared particularly noteworthy not only because they substituted a single discipline for the bilateral agreements previously in force, but also because they automatically regulated all sales contracts, without it being necessary to insert into each contract an explicit reference.

The 'recommendation' adopted by the Standing Commission on Foreign Trade concerning the General Conditions gave rise to differences in interpretation about the regulatory powers of the organs of the Council. In any event, it should be stressed in this connection that, further to that recommendation, the Foreign Trade ministries of the CMEA countries issued directives requiring their dependent foreign trade agencies to conform, when entering into sales contracts, with the provisions of the General Conditions.

In substance, it may be said that the second stage of CMEA activity was characterized essentially by an effort to establish a direct cooperation among the various states in the drafting of the individual national economic plans, prepared in such a way that each took into account the others, so as to create the preconditions for an actual division of labour. In particular, the first specialization agreements, limited to the allotment of production within individual product classes (rolled steel, ball-bearings, tractors, etc.) were negotiated bilaterally between some CMEA countries as early as 1954. In 1957, on the proposal of the German Democratic Republic, a start was made on the joint drafting of material budgets and sectoral plans for certain important industrial products, although for agricultural products it proved impossible to achieve any solution acceptable for all Council members.

Finally, mention should also be made, again with reference to the period considered here, of the conclusion in Moscow on 26 March 1956 of the agreement setting up the United Institute for Nuclear Research at Dubna, USSR. The cooperation of scientists for the peaceful use of atomic energy was taken as an essential goal of the Institute, which showed considerable similarities with CERN. In addition to the countries that were then members of the Council, the agreement was also signed by the socialist nations of Asia (Mongolia, the Chinese People's

Republic, North Korea and, later, North Vietnam) which, among other things, in the latter half of the 1950s began sending observers to follow the activities of some organs of CMEA. The Institute cooperates with CMEA Standing Commission on Atomic Energy, but it is not subordinate to the latter nor does it appear to have any organic connection with the Council.

In conclusion, one of the major problems which emerged during the second period of the Council's life, was probably that created by the many difficulties experienced in pursuing the goal of the division of labour among member-states. The forced and isolated industrialization of the people's democracies had resulted in the creation of many branches of industry – out of proportion with the capabilities and requirements of the individual countries – whose coordination was prevented or retarded by serious obstacles. On the other hand, it was more than understandable that member-countries should hesitate to accept a radical restructuring of the industries created with so many sacrifices. Actually, specialization could not and cannot be achieved without profound changes, such as to involve the suppression even, or at least a substantial decrease in production, of certain branches of industry of a member-country.

The fact should also be considered that, from the early days of CMEA, many countries of Eastern Europe had taken – and are still taking – a cautious and reluctant attitude towards an advanced degree of integration of their respective economies, which would have tied them to each other too closely and therefore created an interdependence which would prove extremely dangerous in the event of serious tensions arising within the area.

The unenthusiastic attitude of the people's democracies towards a high degree of economic integration, in spite of the Council's recommendations on the implementation of coordination and division of labour, corresponded, on the other hand, with the attitude of the Soviet Union, which did not intend to give up its aspirations to self-sufficiency.

From the standpoint of organizational efficiency, it should be noted that the Council's activity was often adversely affected by the rigidity and complexity of the bureaucratic structures. The decisions adopted were not infrequently overtaken by events, and this called for adjustments and revisions involving the repetition of complicated procedures.

6. 1958 TO 1962

The Conference of the First Secretaries of the Communist and workers' parties of CMEA member-countries, held in Moscow from 20 to 23 May 1958, marked the beginning of the third period of the Council's life. It is important to stress that the meeting of the representatives of the Communist parties preceded by just one month the 9th Session of the CMEA Assembly which took place in Bucharest from 26 to 30 June 1958.

The Conference, according to the official communiqué, considered the feasibility of promoting economic cooperation on the basis of a stricter application of the principles of the international division of labour, that is, on the basis of a more advanced degree of industrial specialization. Emphasis was duly placed on the multilateral character of cooperation and on its conformity with the national interests of each country. The Conference, finally, reconfirmed the need for expanding the activities of the Council and informed the latter about the decisions adopted, so that it could take appropriate measures for their implementation.

As can readily be seen, the Conference did not say anything significantly new; the importance of the Conference and of its conclusions consisted in the introduction, in the Council's operation, of a new element: the summit of the Communist parties.

The 9th Session of the CMEA Assembly, held one month after the Conference, applied itself to the implementation of the latter's decisions and changed the number and responsibilities of the Standing Commissions, establishing *inter alia* a Commission on Economic Problems. During the Session a study was made of the possibility of increasing trade with the West and appropriate recommendations were adopted for the coordination of the national plans for the period 1961–5.

The 10th Session, which took place in Prague from 11 to 13 December 1958, adopted a number of recommendations on specialization; it also decided on the construction of the *Druzhba* ('Friendship') pipeline to transport Soviet crude oil from the Urals to Poland and the GDR; a branch pipeline was destined to supply Hungary and Czechoslovakia. The *Druzhba* pipeline was, in fact, one of the most impressive achievements of CMEA cooperation.

It should also be noted that the 10th Session decided to set aside

Romania's proposals to establish a common investment fund in order to finance joint projects.

The tenth anniversary of the foundation of CMEA was celebrated during the 11th Session, held in Tirana from 13 to 16 May 1959. The Assembly adopted recommendations concerning specialization, in particular for chemicals, engineering, steel and mining; the most important recommendation, however, concerned the erection of a CMEA electricity grid. The connection of the grids of the USSR and the people's democracies was substantially completed early in the 1960s and bears the name of *Mir*.

The 12th Session, held in Sofia from 10 to 14 December 1959, noting the growing importance of the Council in promoting economic cooperation among member-countries and in consideration of the opportunity of setting forth in an actual constitution the basic principles worked out through the resolutions and practices of the various organs, approved the Charter and the Convention on the Legal Capacity, Privileges and Immunities of CMEA. The Polish delegate Jaroszewicz stated on that occasion: 'The publication of the Council's Charter, registered with the UN, puts an end once and for all to the speculations of certain foreign economic circles about the alleged supranational character of the Council. The Charter is based on more than ten years of experience . . .'.[8]

The Charter, consisting of a Preamble and seventeen short articles, expressed the firm will of the governments of the member-countries to further develop their existing cooperation on the basis of the international socialist division of labour. At the same time the Charter expressed the desire of the CMEA countries to develop economic relations with all countries, irrespective of their economic and social systems, on a basis of equality, mutual benefits and non-intervention in internal affairs.

The most significant provisions of the Charter – which was later repeatedly amended – will be discussed further on, when the structure, functions, power and legal nature of the Council are considered more specifically.

The 12th Session also considered matters relating to agricultural production and to specialization in the production of machinery, as well as the coordination of economic plans, both for the period up to 1965 and that following.

On 2–3 February 1960, another conference was held in Moscow of the representatives of the Communist and workers' parties, concerned specifically with agricultural developments. In conformity with the directives issued by the Conference, the Council's 13th Session (Bucharest, 26–29 July 1960) carried out an in-depth examination of the problems connected with the specialization and increase of agricultural production, as well as with specialization in the construction of farm machinery. Also discussed were the many questions connected with the coordination of the national long-term plans to 1980. During the meeting the rules of procedure for the Assembly and the other organs of the Council, namely the Conference of Representatives and the Standing Commissions, were adopted.

The specialization of production, especially in chemicals, the conclusion of bilateral trade agreements for 1961–5 and the problems of maritime transport were among the main items discussed by the 14th Session of the Assembly, held in Berlin from 28 February to 3 March 1961. The Session also reviewed work on the coordination of plans to 1980.

The pressing need to establish guidelines on the division of labour and to solve the problems arising from diverging conceptions of future development led to the adoption of a rather vague and contradictory document in the course of the 15th Session of the Assembly which took place in Warsaw from 12 to 15 December 1961. This document – entitled 'Basic Principles of the International Socialist Division of Labour' – set forth the principles and methods that were to guide the division of labour so that efficiency would be increased without hampering the balanced growth of the poorest members.[9]

Coordination thus came to be turned towards promoting specialization of production among member-countries. Specialization was seen as the concentration, in one or more countries, of the production of homogeneous types of goods, in sufficient quantities to meet the requirements of all member-countries; more specifically, each country was to develop all branches of production, carrying out specialization within each branch, that is, engaging exclusively in the production of certain items or groups of items. Particular rules were laid down to regulate specialization in key branches of the economy, especially engineering, chemicals, ferrous and nonferrous metallurgy.

It should be noted that no delegate from Albania – whose

relations with the USSR had been deteriorating badly – participated in the activities of the 15th Session.

On the whole, the third period of activity of CMEA ended with good prospects for the intensification of cooperation in the fields of trade and payments; on the other hand, the climate in the area of economic and production integration appeared far less favourable. In the latter connection, mention should be made of the stubborn Romanian opposition, which was to come out into the open during 1964.[10]

7. 1962 TO 1969

The fourth period of the Council's activity, from June 1962 to March 1969, was characterized by an alternation of events. Alongside certain positive results, in the area of general economic cooperation, and in particular of the coordination of the national economic plans, sharp disagreements arose about the Soviet attempts to promote more intensive forms of investment coordination, production integration and division of labour through the creation of a central CMEA planning body.

During 1962, significant changes were introduced in the structure and operation of the Council, but proposals to shift some functions of economic management from the competence of the respective states to a supranational planning organ were successfully fought off by Romania.

The 'Basic Principles' – developed in the course of the 15th Session of the Assembly held in Warsaw in December 1961 – were explicitly approved by the Conference of the First Secretaries of the Communist and workers' parties held in Moscow on 6–7 June 1962. It should be noted that not only did the Conference approve the document containing the Basic Principles, recommending that CMEA member-countries conform with it when preparing long-term plans for economic cooperation, but also announced the admission of Mongolia – which for years had been present as an observer – as a full member of the Council. Thus, the Conference of the representatives of the Communist and workers' parties once again intervened decisively in CMEA's life, and also changed its Charter to allow the admission of a non-European country. On the same day (7 June) that the Conference ended, and also in Moscow, the CMEA Assembly held its 16th Session, which lasted only a few hours and was designated as an 'extraordinary' session.[11] At the meeting, measures were taken to implement the Conference's decisions and the Executive Committee – a new organ of the Council formed by the Deputy Prime Ministers of the member-countries and vested with important powers in all sectors of economic cooperation – , three other Standing Commissions, the Bureau for Integrated Planning Problems and the Institute of Standardization were established. In addition, the standardization of statistics and planning indicators was strongly recommended.

It is important to stress that at neither the June 1962 meetings nor at the following ones could any measure to increase CMEA powers in a supranational perspective be adopted because of strong Romanian opposition.

In the summer of 1962, Khrushchev, making reference to West European economic integration, proposed the creation of a single CMEA planning organ and consequently the adoption of a common mandatory plan for all CMEA member-countries. Such a project would have encroached on the right of each member-country to choose its own pattern of development and, in particular, would have confined Romania to the role of a large-scale raw-material supplier of the area. Romania's opposition to supranational modifications of the CMEA structure was to be made public only about two years later, in April 1964, probably as a political move rather than as a statement of strictly economic policy.[12]

Another Session of the Assembly, the 17th, was held in 1962 (Bucharest, 14–20 December) and discussed, among other items, some questions concerning the coordination of investment plans beyond 1965; it also dealt with the problems of energy sources and with those relating to expansion and specialization in agriculture.

In the course of the same Session, the Assembly began to give serious consideration to the possibility of creating an international bank among the socialist countries and, in view of that prospect, set up a new Standing Commission to deal with currency and financial questions.

The agreement on the draft charter of the Bank – which took the name of the International Bank for Economic Co-operation – was reached during the 18th Session of the Assembly, held in Moscow on 25–26 July 1963. At this Session, new

Standing Commissions were created and a review was made of the coordination of plans for 1966–70.

Almost simultaneously with the 18th Session (24–26 July), the Conference of the First Secretaries of the Communist and workers' parties and of the Prime Ministers of the CMEA countries was held in Moscow and confirmed the basic importance for mutual cooperation of the 'interested country' principle, thus setting aside supranational projects.

It appears that, from the latter half of 1963 until early 1965, the Council's activity, for various reasons, showed signs of a slowing-down.

The 19th Session, held in Prague from 28 January to 2 February 1965, noted that the work of the organs concerned with the development of economic cooperation had been carried out in conformity with the decisions both of the Conference of the First Secretaries of the Communist and workers' parties and of the Prime Ministers of the member-countries and of the 18th Session of the Assembly. Thus, the importance of the role played by the First Secretaries' Conference was once again stressed.

In the course of the Session, a discussion took place about the coordination of the national development plans for 1966–70 and various problems in the field of technical-scientific cooperation; the satisfactory results achieved by the International Bank for Economic Cooperation were confirmed. The Session ratified the agreement between the Council and Yugoslavia, making it possible for that country to begin cooperating with the Council in areas of common interest. Cuban observers were present at the 19th Session.

The Sessions held by the Council in 1966 and 1967 did not involve significant progress in the field of plan coordination and in the strengthening of technical-scientific cooperation.

More specifically, the 20th Session (Sofia, 8–10 December 1966) took into consideration preliminary questions concerning the coordination of plans for 1971–5 and discussed plans for joint investments in nonferrous metals and the possibility of closer cooperation in the field of research.

More concrete proposals, again concerning the coordination of plans for 1971–5, were considered at the 21st Session of the Assembly, which was held in Budapest from 12 to 14 December 1967.

Early in 1968, Czechoslovakia's new course appeared such as

to create serious repercussions on the development of cooperation, especially in the fields of planning coordination, production specialization and the division of labour. In particular, Poland and the German Democratic Republic, for economic as much as for ideological reasons, showed themselves to be firmly opposed to Czechoslovakia's approaches and reforms. Czechoslovakia, for its part, in challenging more or less openly the principles and criteria of the division of labour, gave new strength, although for different reasons, to the positions steadfastly held in this field by Romania.

CMEA, to cope with the new tasks created by the need for an effective coordination of the national economic plans of the member-countries, would have needed to wield those very 'supranational' powers which some countries viewed, and still view, with strong disapproval. Indeed, towards the end of the 1960s and of the fourth period of existence of the Council, a major crisis took shape.

The opposition of several East European countries to a more advanced division of labour, the severe political unrest which had its climax in the invasion of Czechoslovakia in August 1968 and the serious difficulties of the economies of various member-countries, caused the Council to become the target of bitter criticism.

Because of the complex political and economic situation, the celebration of the twentieth anniversary of CMEA – on the occasion of the 22nd Session of the Assembly held in Berlin from 21 to 23 January 1969 – took place without special solemnity. In a lengthy address, the Council's Secretary summarized the activities of the organization over the two decades of its life, stressing certain goals achieved by the member-countries in qualitative and quantitative terms, and noting the efforts made for the coordination of the 1956–60, 1961–5 and 1966–70 five-year plans, as well as other aspects of cooperation.

In the course of this Session the coordination of plans for 1971–5 was considered and proposals were made for closer cooperation, in spite of persisting major disagreements.

Hungary and Czechoslovakia – although for different reasons – showed little interest in strengthening and tightening cooperation beyond certain levels, while Romania, with frequent references to the non-supranational character of the Council, stressed the need for preserving independence.

The Soviet Union and Poland, for their part, backed in certain aspects by the German Democratic Republic, urged substantial progress towards plan coordination.

The role played by the economically less-advanced countries of the area, such as Bulgaria and Mongolia, appeared necessarily limited and of minor importance. Yugoslavia's participation was institutionally limited to certain specific areas of cooperation. The observers, finally, because of the continuing crisis in Sino-Soviet relations and other particular causes concerning the socialist nations of South-East Asia, were reduced to Cuba alone, whose representative had attended the celebrations for the Council's twentieth anniversary.

8. 1969 TO 1974

The widespread awareness of the need to give new impetus to CMEA and the resulting attempt to reformulate and clarify basic objectives and concrete forms of cooperation had their first expression on the occasion of the Council Assembly held in April 1969. Indeed a new period – the fifth, according to the subdivision adopted here – seemed to begin in the spring of 1969.

Because of the impossibility of framing a common plan, firmly opposed by those CMEA countries that enjoyed greater autonomy and regarded as extremely dangerous a further tightening of their relations with the Soviet Union, it was preferred to follow the way of the coordination of the plans of the individual countries, to the explicit exclusion of all supranational prospects.

The meeting of CMEA Executive Committee, held in Moscow in the first half of April 1969, concentrated mainly on the problems connected with the system of multilateral accounts in transferable rubles.

The Council's 23rd 'special' Session, held in Moscow from 23 to 26 April 1969, emphasized the urgent need for improving the forms and methods of coordination of the national plans, for broadening monetary, financial and credit cooperation, for developing the activities of the International Bank for Economic Cooperation and for the creation of a new banking agency, institutionally charged with investment financing.

The Assembly proclaimed the need for intensifying economic, scientific and technical cooperation and for developing economic integration, elaborating to this end concrete measures in the framework of a long-term plan. The task of working out such a plan was given to various Commissions.

On the whole, in the April 1969 Session an attempt was made to 'relaunch' the organization, stressing for the first time the need to create closer forms of cooperation, in a tendentially 'integrationist' prospect.

The following (24th) Session of the Council, held in Warsaw from 12 to 14 May 1970, considered the work done by the Commissions for the development of the long-term plan but failed to strengthen CMEA structures substantially.

The 24th Session is particularly memorable for the agreement reached – without Romania's participation – on the creation of the International Investment Bank; it was also decided to establish an International Institute for the economic problems of the world socialist system. Finally, measures were approved to step up cooperation in the planning field, in particular through periodic consultations on major economic policy issues, the exchange of experiences in the formulation of development forecasts relating to the main sectors of the economy, of science and technology, and the coordination of long-term plans in the leading economic sectors.

The events in Poland in late 1970 seemed seriously to affect efforts for the establishment of closer cooperation within CMEA.

In an attempt to reconcile, insofar as possible, and to overcome the conflicts and disagreements deriving from profoundly different conceptions of 'socialist integration' and of its medium- and especially long-term objectives, the 25th Session, held in Bucharest from 27 to 29 July 1971, approved an extensive document containing the 'Comprehensive Programme for the further intensification and improvement of cooperation and the development of socialist economic integration among CMEA member-countries'. This programme consisted of four chapters and seventeen sections and laid down the basic criteria and progressive steps that were to characterize cooperation and integration on a medium- and long-term basis (1971–80 and beyond).

In correspondence with the political and economic context briefly outlined above, the document was necessarily the product of a compromise between opposing tendencies: those aimed at the creation of a particularly marked form of integration among the member-countries, from which a further strengthening of the dominant role of the Soviet Union would have resulted, and those tending to promote economic, scientific and technical cooperation, but categorically ruling out any possibility of reaching an integration which, sooner or later, would have taken on supranational features.

'Socialist economic integration' – it is stated in paragraph 2, Section 1, Chapter I of the Comprehensive Programme – 'is conducted on a purely voluntary basis, is not accompanied by the creation of any supranational organs and does not affect internal planning problems or the financial and accounting activities of organizations.'

In addition, the document reconfirmed that cooperation and integration were to continue to be based on the principles of socialist internationalism, with respect for sovereignty, independence and national interests, of non-interference in internal affairs, of full equality of rights, of mutual advantage and friendly mutual assistance.

It should be noted that participation in the Comprehensive Programme, or parts of it, was and is open to states not belonging to CMEA but willing to accept the purposes and principles of the Programme.

The brief statements quoted above contained the reconfirmation of the non-supranational character of the Council, without any explicit reference to the principle of unanimity as an essential condition for the formation of the will of CMEA organs and, therefore, for the adoption of the resolutions concerning cooperation and integration.

Indeed, according to the CMEA Charter, both types of actions through which the Council exercises its powers, namely decisions and recommendations, may only be adopted by a favourable vote of all members, although any state not concerned with the matter at issue may abstain. The abstaining state, however, may subsequently adhere to the decision or recommendation. Now, the repeated references in the Comprehensive Programme to cooperation by countries 'interested' in individual programmes seem to reconfirm the possibility of certain decisions of the organization being adopted in practice on a majority basis, with the favourable vote of some member-countries and the abstention of one or more 'dissident' countries that declare themselves 'not interested'.

One might wonder in this connection, also in relation to the importance of the decisions adopted, whether the abstaining countries might not find themselves later forced, for various practical reasons, to bow to the will of the majority.

Besides cooperation in the development of forecasts and the coordination of the respective five-year and long-term plans for the most important economic sectors and types of production, the Comprehensive Programme explicitly provided for 'joint planning' in (unspecified) individual branches of industry by interested countries. In this connection, mention was made of the fact that joint planning would have constituted a new form of cooperation in the field of planning techniques, such as to enable the participating countries to pool their efforts, in order to achieve more quickly major technical-scientific goals, to increase labour productivity, to meet domestic demand more adequately and to improve competitiveness on world markets. Also, the coordination of investments on individual projects of common interest was to be carried out.

With regard to the improvement in currency and financial relations, the Comprehensive Programme contained a number of indications in Section 7, specifically concerned with such relations. In this connection, the preliminary statement was made that currency, finançial and credit relations were to play a more important and effective role.

After stressing the need for expanding the functions proper of the 'collective currency', i.e. the transferable ruble, as a measure of value, instrument of payment and means for capital formation in the relations among members, the Comprehensive Programme laid down, for the entire span of the 1970s, successive steps towards the interconvertibility of the currencies of the member-countries and the introduction of a single exchange rate of such currencies between themselves and relative to the transferable ruble for all payment operations.

From a general standpoint, one cannot help noting the vagueness of many of the indications contained in the document, which appeared, as a whole, an attempt to improve a system of relations still largely bilateral and bound to remain such for a long time, rather than a real step towards the multilateralization of economic relations among CMEA members.

Also during the Assembly's 25th Session, in order to facilitate and expedite the arduous task of planning coordination, a Committee for planning cooperation was established; another Committee was created to deal with scientific and technological cooperation.

The first opportunity to review the initial stage of the Comprehensive Programme was provided by the 26th Session of the Assembly, held in Moscow from 10 to 12 July 1972. In taking note of the progress made both in the fields of the theoretical study of the problems and of the adoption of concrete measures, the Assembly re-stressed the basic importance of the Comprehensive Programme and pointed out its manifold implications.

Of considerable importance, obviously more political than economic, was the announcement of Cuba's admission to full membership of CMEA.

In October 1972, the Executive Committee approved the 'Organisational, methodological, economic and legal principles relating to scientific and technological cooperation of the Council's member-countries and the activities of the Council's organs in this sector'. This long document consisted of as many as 158 articles, designed to regulate the many aspects of technical-scientific cooperation, which for too long had been forced into the narrow confines of bilateralism.

For its part, the Standing Commission for Foreign Trade adopted the standard articles relating to foreign trade agreement terms on specialization and joint production, recommending that member-countries and Yugoslavia conform with them when entering into agreements of this nature. These articles concerned, on the one hand, matters relating to prices in the field of industrial specialization and cooperation, and on the other certain problems of trade cooperation.

The 27th Session of the Council, held in Prague from 5 to 8 June 1973, reviewed the results achieved in the implementation of the Comprehensive Programme and adopted a number of measures concerning, in particular, fuels and energy sources, and, once more, the coordination of planning activities.

Also in 1973, the Executive Committee approved the 'Standard Rules concerning the conditions for the establishment and activity of international economic organizations in the countries of CMEA' to regulate what might, by way of rough approximation, be called the 'multinationals' of the socialist world. Among the Executive Committee's activities in 1973, mention should also be made of the revision of principles and general conditions of foreign trade and the drafting of new texts in this field.

In the area of CMEA external relations, of special importance was the conclusion in Moscow, on 16 May 1973, of a cooperation agreement between the Council and Finland, which constituted the first case of institutionalization of relations with a non-socialist country.

The many formidable problems connected with the first stage of implementation of the Comprehensive Programme and the basic guidelines of socialist economic integration were closely studied on the occasion of the meeting of the leaders of the Communist and workers' parties of the CMEA countries (excepting the Cuban representatives) held in the Crimea on 30–31 July 1973. The decisions adopted there concerning CMEA activities and prospects had prompt repercussions on the organization, highlighting once again the primary role played by the summit of the Communist and workers' parties. The road was thus gradually prepared for further moves towards strengthening the Council *vis-à-vis* the member-countries and the rest of the world.

9. RECENT DEVELOPMENTS IN CMEA ACTIVITIES

The 28th Session, held in Sofia from 18 to 21 June 1974, seems to have opened a new period (the sixth) in CMEA's existence. The Session, during which the 25th anniversary of the foundation of the Council was celebrated, approved a number of important amendments to the text of the Charter, with a view, *inter alia*, to adjusting CMEA's structures to the new requirements derived from the Comprehensive Programme and broadening the scope of the organization's activities on the international level. For example, the possible establishment of formal relations with the EEC and the conclusion of cooperation agreements with some developing countries were considered.

With regard to the specific aspects of cooperation within CMEA, the Session took up matters concerning the coordination of plans for 1976–80 and the drafting of a coordinated five-year plan containing multilateral integration measures.

As was to be expected, the problems of fuel supply and energy sources played a major role in the Session's activities; it should be noted, however, that the East European countries had not been seriously affected by the enormous increases in world energy prices that had taken place in 1973–4.[13] To the two existing Committees on cooperation respectively in planning activities and in the technical and scientific field, a third Committee was added to deal with material and technical supplies.

The Session also took into consideration the creation of several 'international economic organizations' intended to promote a greater degree of cooperation in specific sectors.

It should be noted that in the communiqué concerning the 28th Session, explicit reference was made to the meeting of the representatives of the Communist and workers' parties of the CMEA countries, that had been held in the Crimea in July of the preceding year.

At the 29th Session of the Assembly, held in Budapest from 24 to 26 June 1975, one observer was present, representing the Democratic Republic of Vietnam. Once again, special attention was paid to the work in progress for the coordination of the 1976–80 plans. The Session approved the 'Coordinated Plan of Multilateral Integration Measures for 1976–80', a plan defined as a 'new step' towards a further increase in cooperation and the development of socialist economic integration. The Coordinated Plan concerned the implementation of several joint projects and the creation of additional production capacities, over the five-year period, by the 'interested' member-countries.[14] Specific measures were contemplated to meet the particular needs of the two less-developed countries of CMEA, Mongolia and Cuba.

In the area of scientific and technological cooperation, the Assembly noted with satisfaction the progress made, of which clear evidence was provided, among other things, by the increasing number of multilateral agreements concluded to promote the development of science and technology.[15]

As regards CMEA international relations, 1975 saw some important progress, with the conclusion of economic, scientific and technological cooperation agreements with two developing countries which for some time had been showing interest in forming closer ties with the Council, namely Iraq and Mexico. The respective agreements were signed in Moscow on 4 July and 13 August.

A few days after the Berlin Conference of European Communist and workers' parties of June 1976 the 30th Session of the CMEA Assembly was also held in Berlin (on 7–9 July). Observers from Laos and Angola, in addition to those from Korea and Vietnam, were present.

The Session drew up a detailed balance sheet of the achievements and shortcomings that had characterized the first five years of implementation of the Comprehensive Programme.

From the political standpoint, it should be noted that the Session was held during a period of relative stagnation of the process of détente in East–West relations, a fact which, in principle, should have encouraged the tendency towards closer relations within CMEA.

In addition to all this, there were the economic difficulties characterizing the situation in various East European countries, of which the events in Poland during early summer were but one of the most troubling aspects.

In the course of the 30th Session, the need was stressed again to continue more resolutely the process of coordination of the national plans, improving methods and procedures. The progressive broadening of the sectors covered by joint projects of 'interested' countries constituted the other major guideline for socialist economic integration. In this context, the Coordinated Plan for 1976–80 assumed particular significance. In addition, a set of long-term programmes spanning ten to fifteen years was taken into consideration.

The Assembly adopted decisions of considerable importance for cooperation in such sectors as electric power and transportation. The supply of fuels and raw materials at fair prices and the development of the basic lines of a long-term energy policy continued to take up a considerable share of the Assembly's time. The utilization of resources and the expansion of infrastructures and production in Cuba and Mongolia was another of the main subjects discussed by the Assembly.

Some members also called for an effective coordination of long-term agricultural policies.[16] Special cooperation programmes, covering specific sectors, were to ensure the meeting of requirements of cereals, animal and other food products and consumption goods.

The decision to concentrate cooperation and integration efforts in a few key sectors involved, however, a significant revision of overall development prospects and of the time schedules laid down in the Comprehensive Programme, a lower priority being given to other basic objectives, such as those of a monetary and financial nature.

A review of the progress made in the drafting of specific cooperation plans in a number of key sectors was one of the major items discussed at the 31st Session of the Council, held in Warsaw from 21 to 23 June 1977. The Session noted the need for concentration, in the first place, on the development of draft agreements for cooperation in the area of fuels, electric power and basic commodities, on the expansion of food production and on the supply of related machinery and equipment.

Having re-stressed the importance of the programme for the development of the nuclear industry, the Assembly recommended that members conclude in 1978 an agreement on multilateral specialization, on the joint production and mutual deliveries of nuclear power plant equipment for the period 1981–90.

With regard to scientific and technical matters, a decision was adopted on specific measures to increase mutual cooperation, planning its development more rationally and linking it more closely with the requirements of production. The Assembly approved the programme concerning the coordination of the national economic plans for 1981–5; the intergovernmental agreements and other documents produced under such coordination were to be signed at the latest in the first half of 1980.

Particular attention was paid by the Assembly to specific measures to promote a faster growth of the economies of Mongolia and Cuba, on the basis of proposals made by those countries. The Assembly moreover emphasized the progress made by cooperation between CMEA member-countries and other socialist nations such as Yugoslavia, Vietnam, Laos and Angola. The prospects for relations with the EEC were also taken into account.

The 32nd Session of the Assembly, held in Bucharest on 27–29 June 1978, adopted three long-term (to 1990) programmes of cooperation in the fields respectively of energy, fuel and raw materials, of agriculture and the food industry, and of engineering. The Assembly called for more advanced specialization in the production of nuclear power plant equipment.

The admission of Vietnam to full membership in CMEA assumed a markedly political significance. Present at the Session were observers from Laos, Angola and, for the first time, Ethiopia.

Despite persistent attempts in the first half of 1978 at increasing the powers of CMEA, the purely voluntary nature of cooperation was stressed in the declaration adopted by the heads of the delegations present at the Bucharest Session and proposals for changing voting procedures were rejected.

Two more long-term programmes concerning industrial consumer goods and the development of transport facilities were approved during the 33rd Session which took place in Moscow on 26–28 June 1979. The Session also approved a number of multilateral agreements covering international specialization in production for various branches, including the production of much-needed equipment for nuclear power stations.

An important resolution of the Assembly concerned the introduction in the CMEA Charter of some amendments in order to improve the activities of the organization and to increase its efficiency. The status of observer was granted to the People's Democratic Republic of Yemen. Finally, the Assembly stated once more its readiness to conclude an agreement with the EEC and its member-countries on the basis of equal rights and in the interest of all-European cooperation.

The heads of the delegations adopted, at the conclusion of the 33rd Session, a declaration to commemorate the 30th anniversary of CMEA pointing out the landmarks of the joint work of the member-countries.

There is neither space nor need to discuss in detail the future prospects of CMEA after three decades.[17] It will probably suffice to mention here just a few issues which seem to cause no small concern to economists and politicians alike and which might seriously affect the successful development of integration and the internal cohesion of the organization.

One major controversial issue concerns the nature of the relations that should exist between specific cooperation programmes and projects and national interests and requirements, as outlined in the development plans of the individual countries. So far effective plan coordination apparently occurs only in a few key sectors and selected joint projects, since member-countries generally seem to place far more weight on the improvement of individual economic performance than on the collective achievements of CMEA as a whole. At the very least, it seems unlikely that an agreement on a new and more 'supranational' distribution of power in CMEA may be reached in the near future.

Other serious difficulties stem from the extremely limited degree of implementation of those basic parts of the Comprehensive Programme that concern monetary and financial matters. The plans for preparing the convertibility of the currencies of CMEA countries and of the transferable ruble seem to have virtually ground to a halt, so that any decision on a single exchange rate for these currencies – with all the consequences that would ensue at the various levels – will probably be long in coming.

On the other hand, some substantial achievements of CMEA during these last few years cannot and must not be underestimated. With regard to coordination of five-year plans, the available evidence indicates that several joint projects envisaged by the Coordinated Plan are going ahead. The first stage of construction of the 2,750 kilometre *Soiuz* gas pipeline starting from Orenburg (Urals) and continuing across the Ukraine to Czechoslovakia is over. When fully completed, the pipeline will supply Czechoslovakia, Poland, Hungary and Bulgaria with 14,000 million cubic metres of natural gas annually and Romania with 1,500 million. The 750 kv power line linking the Soviet grid at Vinnitsa with Albertirsa in Hungary has come into operation. Two major joint projects, the asbestos complex in Kiembai and the cellulose factory in Ust'-Ilimsk are making headway. Other projects are under construction to expand capacity for the production of iron-bearing raw materials and ferro-alloys. New capacities to produce nickel and cobalt are being built in Cuba. A copper-molybdenum complex is under construction at Erdenet, Mongolia. Several cooperation projects envisaged by the Coordinated Plan in scientific and technical matters are also being implemented.

In addition, tangible progress towards setting an institutional framework for long-term joint planning in the 1980s and beyond may result from the adoption in 1978 and 1979 of the five specific programmes of cooperation. These long-term programmes – which the Assembly had been actively discussing since 1976 – might prove to be a remarkable step in the direction of serious coordinated planning in areas which are of outstanding importance for the further industrialization of CMEA countries. Extensive efforts are currently being undertaken both bilaterally and multilaterally to work out the agreements on the implementation of the provisions of the said programmes. It is too early to assess what implications these developments will have; in any case it would appear that the CMEA-wide coordination of demand and supply for important groups of goods and services will inevitably affect the basic choices of national planners in vital areas.

NOTES TO CHAPTER 1

1. The communiqué was published in *Pravda* on 25 January 1949. The latter is usually regarded as the birth date of CMEA, even though the communiqué did not say anything definite about the exact date on which the Council was established. According to N. Faddeev, *Sovet*, op. cit., p. 34, the conference establishing the Council was held from 5 to 8 January 1949.
2. M. Kaser, *Comecon*, op. cit., p. 11.
3. F. Pryor (*The Communist Foreign Trade System*, Cambridge, Mass., MIT Press, 1963, p. 208) states that in 1949 in Eastern Europe 'a clear need for an international economic organ was obvious to all'.
4. The subdivision into periods is adopted here essentially for convenience of discussion. The number and the respective length of the periods vary depending on the criteria adopted by various authors. A subdivision into six periods – with, however, a duration different from that indicated here – is adopted, for instance, by K. Weisskopf, 'Progress of the COMECON Integration Programme', in *COMECON: Progress and Prospects*, NATO Colloquium held 16 to 18 March 1977 in Brussels, pp. 23–34. A recent Soviet publication (V. Meshcheriakov, B. Poklad, E. Shevchenko, *SEV: Printsipy, Problemy, Perspektivy*, Moscow, 1975, pp. 11 ff.) opts, instead, for a subdivision into three periods only.
5. It is thought appropriate to use the term 'Assembly', even though many authors, more faithful to the Russian language designation of this organ, prefer the expression 'Session of the Council'.
6. For some indications, see I. Agoston, *Le Marché commun communiste: Principes et pratique du COMECON*, 2nd edn., Geneva, 1965, p. 28.
7. For a thorough discussion of the institutional reinforcement of CMEA during the period 1956–60, see M. Kaser, *Comecon*, op. cit., pp. 69–91.
8. See I. Agoston, *Le Marché commun*, op. cit., p. 40.
9. See E. Hewett, *Foreign Trade Prices in the Council for Mutual Economic Assistance*, Cambridge, 1974, p. 3 ff.
10. A detailed analysis of the evolution of the Romanian attitude within CMEA up to the mid-1960s is carried out by M. Kaser, *Comecon*, op. cit.
11. The June 1962 meetings and all the following ones took place in the absence of the Albanian representatives.
12. M. Kaser, *Comecon*, op. cit., p. 115.
13. In 1975 the USSR made substantial adjustments in the prices of its supplies to the other CMEA members, causing them serious difficulties. The

dependence on the USSR for energy supplies is very heavy for all European members of CMEA, excepting Poland and Romania. For an up-to-date analysis see J. Haberstroh, 'Eastern Europe: Growing Energy Problems', in US Congress, Joint Economic Committee, *East European Economies Post-Helsinki*, Washington, 25 August 1977, pp. 379–95; J. Bethkenhagen, 'Joint Energy Projects and their Influence on Future COMECON Energy Autarchy Ambitions', in *COMECON: Progress and Prospects*, op. cit., pp. 37–57.

14. Apparently the most important section of the 'Coordinated Plan' – which has not been published – is devoted to ten joint projects, eight of which are contemplated for the USSR. For further details see E. Hewett, 'Recent Developments in East–West European Economic Relations and their Implications for US–East European Economic Relations', in US Congress, Joint Economic Committee, *East European Economies Post-Helsinki*, op. cit., pp. 188–91.
15. On the many aspects of this delicate question see J. Wilczynski, *Technology in Comecon*, London, 1974; M. Lavigne, 'Les transferts de technologie entre les pays socialistes européens', in *Mondes en développement*, 1976, No. 15, pp. 587 ff.; M. Boguslavskii, 'Pravovye voprosy nauchno-tekhnicheskoi integratsii stran-chlenov SEV', in *Sovetskoe gosudarstvo i pravo*, 1977, No. 9, p. 117 ff.
16. See, on this matter, R. Laird, J. Hajda, B. Laird (eds), *The Future of Agriculture in the Soviet Union and Eastern Europe: The 1976–80 Five Year Plans*, Boulder, Colorado, 1977.
17. Among the latest studies concerning the future of CMEA cooperation, see A. J. Smith, 'The Council of Mutual Economic Assistance in 1977: New Economic Power, New Political Perspectives and some Old and New Problems', in US Congress, Joint Economic Committee, *East European Economies Post-Helsinki*, op. cit., pp. 152–73; D. Lascelles, 'COMECON's Future', in *COMECON: Progress and Prospects*, op. cit., pp. 259–69; A. Zauberman, 'The East European Economies', in *Problems of Communism*, March–April 1978, pp. 55–70.

2 Principles and Purposes

1. BASIC DOCUMENTS CONCERNING THE EVOLUTION OF CMEA

Since CMEA was founded three decades ago, its guiding principles and purposes have undergone major changes as a result of a substantial evolution in the concepts and methods of cooperation on both the economic and the political level.

The evidence of such evolution is to be found in a series of documents which are the milestones on the road so far covered by the Council.

The first of these documents, in chronological order, is the Tass communiqué of January 1949, announcing the creation of the Council for Mutual Economic Assistance, in order to 'organize a broader economic cooperation among people's democracy countries and the USSR'.

The CMEA Charter, approved at the end of 1959, entered into force in the spring of 1960 and extensively amended in 1962 and 1974, is of paramount importance, since it sets forth the official principles and purposes of the organization.

The guiding principles of intra-CMEA cooperation formed, in the early 1960s, the subject of another document which should be taken into account in analysing the purposes of CMEA: the 'Basic Principles of the International Socialist Division of Labour', with the associated directives designed to carry out that division division of labour, mainly through the coordination of individual national production and investment plans.

Several events on different levels, from the general political to the strictly economic, in the latter half of the 1960s, necessitated a thorough revision and redefinition of the criteria and methods of economic cooperation, to measure up to the pressing and often conflicting requirements that had been emerging. This led to the approval in 1971 of the document containing the Comprehensive Programme, in order to improve cooperation and to develop economic integration among the members of CMEA.

The amendments to the Charter made in the summer of 1974 formally embodied the basic approaches adopted in the Comprehensive Programme and adjusted the institutional apparatus to the new requirements and tasks, endowing it with additional major organs and broader powers.

A listing of the most important documents to be referred to for the purpose of analysing CMEA principles and objectives is of itself evidence of a basic tendency, both conceptual and operational, towards closer forms of cooperation, such as to create at least some of the fundamental conditions needed to achieve, in the long term, the goal of integration.

Within this context, it is important to analyse the gradual transition from cooperation to integration, both on the plane of the Council's principles and basic goals, and that of its institutional organization.

2. PRINCIPLES OF COOPERATION IN THE COMMUNIQUÉ OF 1949

Explicit reference to the basic principles that were to govern economic cooperation between the Soviet Union and the people's democracies was made in the Tass communiqué of January 1949, announcing the establishment of CMEA. The communiqué provided that the new organization was to be 'open to other countries of Europe sharing [its] basic principles and desirous of participating in the widening of economic cooperation' with the six founding states.

A first basic principle can be derived from the passage of the communiqué reconfirming the refusal of the founding nations to 'submit themselves to the dictatorship of the Marshall Plan, which would have violated their sovereignty'. Thus, the protection of sovereignty was claimed to be one of the major concerns of the founders of the new organization, which also expressed the intention of safeguarding the 'interests of their national economies' against the dangers connected with the acceptance of Marshall Aid.

The statement of the sovereignty principle was associated with that of the principle of equality. The newly born organization was to be composed of an equal number of representatives from each participating country and could make decisions 'only with the consent of the interested countries'.

The implications of such statements – taken up again and specified a decade later by the Charter – will be discussed later on, when dealing with the CMEA institutional structure and the composition of its organs, as well as with the characteristics of its actions.

For the moment, it is important to call attention to the emphasis placed on the condition of equality among member-countries and the repudiation of the majority principle insofar as the CMEA decision-making process was concerned; no country could be bound by a decision adopted without its consent.

In listing the Council's tasks, the communiqué also spoke of the 'mutual rendering' of technical assistance and of 'mutual aid' in various sectors.

3. CMEA PRINCIPLES ACCORDING TO THE CHARTER

Beginning with the Preamble, the countries that signed the Charter declare their adherence to the principles of equality, mutual advantage and non-interference in each other's internal affairs as the criteria governing their economic relations with third countries, regardless of differences in social and political systems. It seems that these statements should also be borne in mind when assessing the guidelines of cooperation among socialist countries, even though they relate particularly to relations with third countries and – being contained in the Preamble – are valid only as regards the general interpretation of the purposes of the organization.

The definition of the purposes of CMEA and of the principles to be followed towards the attainment of such purposes, forms the object of Article I of the Charter, consisting of two paragraphs, one on purposes and one on principles. Both of these paragraphs were modified by the 1974 Charter amendments.

The principle upon which the entire activity of the Council is to be based, according to the first part of paragraph 2, Article I, is the sovereign equality of all member-countries.

The general principle of sovereign equality is developed and specified in the second part of the said paragraph 2 of Article I.

According to the text adopted in the first draft of the Charter in

1959, economic, scientific and technical cooperation between member-countries was to be carried out in conformity with the principles of full equality of rights, respect for sovereignty and national interests, mutual advantage and mutual assistance. When the Charter was amended in 1974, these statements were reworded and, in a certain sense, expanded in content. In the revised text of the second part of paragraph 2 it is stated that cooperation shall be carried out in conformity with the principle of *socialist internationalism*, with respect for state sovereignty, of *independence* and of national interests, of *non-interference in internal affairs*, of full equality of rights, of mutual advantage and of mutual fraternal assistance. Special stress must be placed on the importance of the references – introduced in 1974 – to socialist internationalism, to independence and to non-interference in internal affairs.[1]

4. BASIC PRINCIPLES OF THE INTERNATIONAL SOCIALIST DIVISION OF LABOUR.

The goals of CMEA were more precisely formulated with the approval in 1962, by the Conference of the representatives of Communist and workers' parties, of the 'Basic Principles of the International Socialist Division of Labour'. The particular nature of this document, however, involves, rather than a statement of general principles, the indication of criteria to be followed in the area of planning coordination and production specialization.

Among these criteria, listed in Chapter 2 of the Basic Principles, the 'steady elimination of historical differences in the levels of economic development' seems to call for special attention. These differences, according to the document, stem from the conditions created by the previous capitalist development. The concept is taken up again at the beginning of Chapter 6, where it is claimed that 'the very nature of socialism dictates the equalization of levels [of economic development]'.

This should involve – according to the statements contained in Chapter 6 – countries on a lower level of economic development developing more rapidly than other countries.

It is important to stress that the gradual equalization of economic development levels is not intended to lead, however, to the creation of artificial equalities, nor *a fortiori* to the adoption of a pattern of consumption and way of life standardized and valid for all members, irrespective of the peculiar features of each country.

5. PRINCIPLES OF CMEA ACCORDING TO THE COMPREHENSIVE PROGRAMME

The Comprehensive Programme constitutes a further step in cooperation between CMEA member-countries and, of particular interest to this study, the most recent definition of the goals that CMEA should pursue and of the operational lines to be followed towards the attainment of those goals.[2]

As regards the fundamental principles of CMEA, Section 1 of the Comprehensive Programme appears to be of paramount importance. The eight paragraphs that make up this section set forth and explain the guiding criteria, the goals and modes of action of the Council.

In paragraph 1, after referring to the great strides made by the member-countries on the road to the construction of socialism and of economic, scientific and technological development, it is stated that cooperation among socialist countries is based 'on public ownership of the means of production, on a uniform institutional structure (the power of the people, led by working class) and on a single ideology, Marxism-Leninism'.

It is then stressed that the development and growth of each socialist country individually considered constitute the essential precondition for the development of the world socialist system.

Thus, a restatement is made of the features common to all socialist countries and of the link that is claimed to exist between the development of each country and that of the system as a whole. In this context, mention is also made in paragraph 1 of an acceleration of the growth rate of the industrially underdeveloped socialist economies, so as to lead to the gradual 'equalization of levels of economic development' mentioned above with reference to the 'Basic Principles of the International Socialist Division of Labour'.

With regard to the division of labour, paragraph 2 states that it should be achieved through 'a process deliberately and consistently regulated by the Communist and workers' parties and by governments', thus stressing once again the highly important role which the periodical 'summits' of Communist Party representatives and heads of government can play – outside and beyond the institutional mechanisms envisaged in the CMEA Charter – in laying down the basic guidelines for economic cooperation.

Again according to paragraph 2, the process of the division of labour shall lead to the harmonization of the economic systems of the countries concerned and to the formation of a 'modern and highly efficient structure made up of national economic entities'. This statement, designed to safeguard, at least in principle, the independence and the vital economic interests of each country, while on the one hand serving the purpose of allaying the fears of the CMEA members less favourable or even hostile to an interconnection of the respective systems of production, on the other clearly marks the limitations of the cooperation process.

The concepts outlined above find their more complete formulation in the second part of paragraph 2. More specifically, it is stated that 'the further intensification and improvement of cooperation and the development of socialist economic integration of the countries of CMEA shall continue to be carried out in conformity with the principles of socialist internationalism, on the basis of respect for state sovereignty, of independence and national interest, of non-interference in internal affairs, of the complete equality of rights, of mutual advantage and of fraternal mutual assistance'.

These principles were incorporated into the new version of the second part of paragraph 2, Article I of the Charter, formulated in 1974 on the basis of the statements contained in the Comprehensive Programme.

Finally, paragraph 2 of Section 1 of Chapter I of the Comprehensive Programme concludes, to remove any possible doubt about the significance and scope of the cooperation process, that 'socialist economic integration is carried out on a purely voluntary basis, is not accompanied by the creation of any supranational organs and does not affect the problems of internal planning or the financial and accounting activities of organizations'.

As regards relations with third countries, CMEA members undertake to act, as stated in paragraph 3, in conformity with the principles of equality of rights, mutual advantage and respect for sovereignty. It is pointed out, in fact – going back to a concept already expressed in the 1962 Basic Principles – that the international socialist division of labour is carried out progressively, taking into account the world division of labour.

The correlation which, according to the Comprehensive Programme, exists between the division of labour carried out by CMEA members and the division of labour to be put into effect on a worldwide scale, reflects the increasing interest of the socialist countries in a broad cooperation with the rest of the world.

This concept, however, remains vague in many ways and should have been more fully developed so as to specify its practical implications. It should also be made clear how and to what extent such an approach can both theoretically and practically be reconciled with the basic goal – solemnly reconfirmed in the Comprehensive Programme – of the final victory of socialism in its competition with capitalism.

6. BASIC GOALS OF CMEA IN 1949

As regards the analysis of the objectives of CMEA in terms of their historical evolution, it seems appropriate to start with the Tass communiqué of January 1949 and to consider the general goals set forth in it. In identifying and evaluating such goals it is important, of course, to bear in mind what was said above about the reasons, spoken and unspoken, both economic and political, which led to the founding of the organization.

The protection of the sovereignty and of the economic interests of the member-countries appeared to be a first and basic goal of the new body, although the intention of repelling 'imperialist' penetration into Central and Eastern Europe reflected a defence and containment strategy in some ways more 'negative' than 'positive'. The very organization of 'a wider economic cooperation between the people's democracies and the USSR' was depicted by the authors of the communiqué as a countermeasure against the Western 'boycott' of trade relations.

For a more precise evaluation of the purposes of the Council, it should also be noted that, from the very first lines of the communiqué, there emerged – although in a framework which was intended to be multilateral – two major partners: the Soviet Union on the one hand and the people's democracies on the other. The economic cooperation intended to develop under CMEA auspices in practice materialised through a series of bilateral relations maintained by the USSR with each people's democracy.

In promoting closer relations between the people's democracies and the Soviet Union, it was the particular task of the Council, according to the communiqué, 'to exchange economic experience, to extend technical aid to one another and to render mutual assistance with respect to raw materials, foodstuffs, machines, equipment, etc'. The situation of most of the people's democracies, as a consequence of the war and of the tremendous reduction in trade with the West, placed on the Soviet Union most of the burden of rendering of technical assistance and aid and of the supply of raw materials needed to start reconstruction.

It has been stated in this connection that the text of the communiqué 'amounts, to a certain extent, to an actual international and moral commitment of the Soviet Union towards its new satellites';[3] in fact, the explicit reference to mutual aid concerning raw materials appeared to involve for the USSR 'an implicit obligation to supply, within the limits of its capabilities, the main essential products needed by the countries of Eastern Europe'.[4] Hence, the conclusion has been drawn that CMEA in its early years was simply 'an organization whose purpose was to promote trade among member-countries'.[5]

On the whole, such a conclusion does not seem correct.

Even though for a considerable length of time the activity of CMEA was mainly characterized by the conclusion of long-term trade agreements among member-countries, trade promotion was at no time the sole aim of the Council. The very wording of the communiqué, in spite of its undeniable generality, seems to call for more extensive forms of cooperation and mutual assistance, beyond the merely trading sphere. The statements of the Charter that will now be considered constitute, at least to some extent, the development of the basic approaches already contained in the 1949 communiqué.

7. GOALS ACCORDING TO THE CHARTER

The general goals of CMEA find a first extensive enunciation in the Preamble to the Charter and are further specified in paragraph 1 of Article I which, as indicated above, was amended in several respects on the occasion of the 1974 revision.

In the Preamble, after noting that mutual economic cooperation contributes to the most rational development of the national economies, to the raising of the standards of living of the population and to the strengthening of unity and solidarity, the firm intent is expressed to intensify that cooperation through the consistent implementation of the international socialist division of labour, towards the attainment of the general goal of the building of socialism and Communism in the member-countries and the establishment throughout the world of a lasting peace.

Moreover, the member-countries reconfirm their readiness to develop economic relations with all countries, regardless of their social and political structure, on the basis of the principles of equality, mutual advantage and non-interference in internal affairs.[6]

Paragraph 1 of Article I is specifically concerned with the goals. In its original version, in 1959, it was stated that the purpose of CMEA was to promote, by uniting and coordinating the efforts of the member-countries, the planned development of the national economies and the acceleration of their economic and technical progress, the raising of the level of industrialization in the less-developed countries of the area, a steady increase in the productivity of labour and a constant improvement in the welfare of the people.[7]

The 1974 Charter revision could not avoid involving the statements quoted above, which necessarily had to be reconciled with the formulations of the Comprehensive Programme. The new version of paragraph 1 of Article I therefore makes two significant additions to the 1959 version. The most important amendment concerns the insertion in the first place among the Council's purposes of the *further intensification and improvement of cooperation and the development of socialist economic integration.*

The other amendment consisted in the insertion of a reference to the *approximation and gradual equalization of levels of economic development* of the member-countries, in conformity with the indications of the Comprehensive Programme and of the Basic Principles.

8. GOALS ACCORDING TO THE BASIC PRINCIPLES

Chapter 1 of the Basic Principles states that the objectives of the division of labour are 'a more efficient social production, a higher rate of economic growth, higher living standards for the working people in all socialist countries, industrialization of these countries and gradual removal of historical differences in the levels of economic development of the socialist countries and the creation of a material basis for their more or less simultaneous transition to Communism, within one and the same historical era'.

The main instrument for the implementation of this division of labour is the coordination of the national economic plans. The international specialization of production must be harmonized with the overall economic development of the various socialist countries, so as to achieve, in each of them, the fullest and most rational utilization of resources.

According to Chapter 2 of the Basic Principles, coordination, to be really efficient, must take place not only on a bilateral level but more particularly on a multilateral level; it should be concerned, in the first place, with the forecasting plans and go on to develop during the stage of formulation of plans by the various countries. Within this context, it is undoubtedly significant that one basic goal of coordination should be that of ensuring, within the framework of the world socialist system, the production of 'staple goods in quantities sufficient to meet the needs of the socialist countries with due allowances for their ever-expanding trade with other countries'.

9. THE COMPREHENSIVE PROGRAMME AND THE NEW DEFINITION OF CMEA GOALS

The Council's goals were once again listed and specified on the occasion of the framing of the Comprehensive Programme. The extensive nature of this document allowed, in fact demanded, a detailed description of such goals.

In Chapter I, Section 1, paragraphs 5 and 6 of this important document outline the goals and practices with which the CMEA countries are to conform in order to achieve socialist economic integration.

More precisely, it is claimed that, in the CMEA area, economic, scientific and technical cooperation will be intensified and that socialist economic integration will be developed with a view to achieving:

a) the accelerated development of productive forces in all member-countries, the attainment of the highest possible scientific and technical level, and the maximum growth of the economic efficiency of socialised production, as well as the maximum growth of productivity of socialised labour

b) the improvement of the structure and enlargement of the scale of production as the level of technological equipment in the various branches of industry is systematically raised, and the introduction of advanced technology in accordance with the requirements of the scientific and technological revolution

c) the satisfaction of the growing long-term needs of the economies of the various countries with respect to fuel, power and raw materials, modern equipment, agricultural products, foodstuffs and other consumer goods, mainly through the production and rational utilization of member-countries' own resources

d) the raising of the material and cultural standard of living of the peoples of the member-countries

e) the gradual alignment and equalization of the levels of economic development of the member-countries

f) the raising of the capacity and improvement of the stability of the world-wide socialist market

g) the strengthening of the position of the member-countries in the world economy and the securing of their ultimate victory in the economic contest with capitalism

h) the strengthening of the defence potential of the member-countries.

The many goals assigned to CMEA by the Comprehensive Programme constitute, to a large extent, the translation into practical terms of the basic guiding principles of the organization. As is readily apparent, alongside goals formulated in rather general terms and that may be regarded as common to any experiment in international cooperation, the listing includes more specific objectives, concerning particular sectors and characteristic aspects of the integration of the socialist economies.

It should be noted that the document reiterates the resolution of the member-countries to reduce, in the long run, their dependence on non-CMEA countries, through a more adequate utilization of the area's resources and potential.

Furthermore – even though at the end of the list and in deliberately laconic terms – reference is made for the first time to an increase in the military potential of the CMEA countries. Therefore, the competence of the Council would seem to extend beyond the strictly economic sphere.

The listing of goals summarized above is logically followed, in the Comprehensive Programme, by an indication of the basic ways and means to achieve such goals.

In particular, explicit provision is made for:

a) multilateral and bilateral consultations on basic problems of economic policy

b) intensification of bilateral and multilateral cooperation in national planning activities, including cooperation in forecasting and in the coordination of five-year and long-term plans for the most important economic sectors and types of production, the joint planning by the countries concerned of certain agreed sectors of industry and individual branches of production, and exchange of information on the improvement of the national economic planning and management systems

c) the planned expansion of international specialization and cooperation in industry, science and technology and the unification of the efforts of the countries concerned in exploring and exploiting mineral deposits, in building industrial plant and in scientific research

d) the planned expansion of trade and the improvement of its efficiency, the improvement of its organizational forms on the basis of state monopoly, and the development of trade concomitantly with the improvement of currency and financial relations and the foreign-trade price system

e) the expansion of direct relations between the ministries, departments and other state organs and economic, research and design organizations of the member-countries

f) the expansion of existing international economic organizations and the creation of new ones by the countries concerned

g) the consolidation of the legal bases of economic, scientific and technical cooperation, particularly with a view to increasing the material liability of the parties for the non-fulfilment or unsatisfactory fulfilment of their obligations towards each other. Special note should be taken of this last item, which shows the growing awareness of CMEA members of the need for expanding and improving legal instruments and methods of integration.

The broad area embraced by the Comprehensive Programme reflects the evolution in time of the basic principles and objectives of socialist economic integration. The coordination of plans, with its manifold implications in operational terms, retains the central place in the context outlined above.

Major importance is attached by the Comprehensive Programme to the expansion of trade among members in connection with the development of currency and financial relations and with the improvement of the foreign-trade price system.

However, the element which, because of its novelty, stands out in the Comprehensive Programme is the repeated reference to 'integration' – a term formally embodied in 1974 in the revised CMEA Charter.

Indeed, at the very beginning of the Comprehensive Programme, and specifically in paragraph 2, Section 1, Chapter I, the claim is made that a number of factors connected with the evolution of the CMEA member-countries make it 'vitally necessary constantly to intensify and improve economic, scientific and technical cooperation and to develop socialist economic integration'. In other words, the significant developments in CMEA activities and the changes that have characterized the economic and social growth of the member-countries and their mutual relations, have necessarily led to a broadening of perspectives and hence to the tendency to move beyond the basic scheme of cooperation by the introduction of a new and more sophisticated instrument, integration.

This new instrument, of course, is not antithetic to cooperation, which retains full validity since its 'constant expansion and improvement' are explicitly envisaged, but constitutes a natural outgrowth, once cooperation has achieved, at least in certain sectors, its assigned goals. The transition to integration, therefore, appears to be closely connected with a specific degree of development of cooperation.

In any event, economic cooperation continues to be the goal that the CMEA countries intend in principle to achieve, while the 'development of socialist economic integration' is seen as a further and higher goal to be taken into account for activities in specific fields, within clearly delimited areas, strictly circumscribed to the 'countries concerned'. An important example in this connection is provided by the above-mentioned 'joint planning, by the countries concerned, of certain agreed sectors of industry and individual branches of production'.

Such a form of planning, however, assumes within the context of the Comprehensive Programme a wholly special character, which makes it an exceptional instrument for the pursuit of CMEA objectives. In effect, the drafters of the Comprehensive Programme have made a point of stressing that socialist economic integration is conducted in a purely voluntary way and is not accompanied by the creation of supranational organs. This statement may lead to a restrictive interpretation of integration, which apparently forms the object of 'negative' specifications mainly intended to point out what *it is not*, rather than what it is.

Of course, the purpose of the clear definition of the limits of integration and of the reaffirmation of the non-supranational character of CMEA institutions was and is mainly to reassure those member-countries – Romania above all – which for years have firmly opposed the increasing of the organization's powers and the framing of a common development plan, applicable to the group as a whole.

The explicit reference to integration in the Comprehensive Programme and in the Charter as amended in 1974 undoubtedly constituted a turning-point in the prospects of CMEA, whose documents had previously cautiously confined themselves to speaking of cooperation. However, the introduction of the integration concept did not involve any major change in the functions exercised by the organs of the Council in implementing the international socialist division of labour, nor did it have any significant impact on the principles governing relations among member-countries.

NOTES TO CHAPTER 2

1. The references to socialist internationalism carefully balanced by the references to independence and non-interference in internal affairs constitute significant evidence of the effort to reconcile – also on a level of general statements – different and opposing requirements. On the special relevance of socialist internationalism in the CMEA Charter, see E. Usenko, 'Printsipy sotsialisticheskogo internatsionalizma v Ustave SEV', in *Sovet ekonomicheskoi vzaimopomoshchi. Osnovnye*, op. cit., pp. 87–121. See also

H. Wünsche, 'Die Bedeutung des sozialistischen Internationalismus für die Festigung der Souveränität der sozialistischen Staaten und die Organisierung ihrer brüderlichen Zusammenarbeit', in *Rechtsbeziehungen der sozialistischen Länder*, Berlin, 1966, pp. 11–44.

2. With regard to the Comprehensive Programme and the basic role which CMEA is called upon to play to ensure its implementation, see E. Usenko, 'Kompleksnaia programma sotsialisticheskoi ekonomicheskoi integratsii i rol SEV v ee osushchestvlenii', in *Sovet ekonomicheskoi vzaimopomoshchi. Osnovnye*, op. cit., pp. 9–56; a shorter contribution by Usenko bearing the same title as that just cited is to be found in *Pravovye voprosy deiatel'nosti SEV* op. cit., pp. 7–28. On the legal aspects of integration, see also E. Usenko, 'Sushchnost' i printsipy sotsialisticheskoi ekonomicheskoi integratsii', in *Sovetskoe gosudarstvo i pravo*, 1971, No. 11, p. 50 ff.; A. Talalaev, 'Mezhdunarodno-pravovye aspekty sotsialisticheskoi ekonomicheskoi integratsii', in *Pravovedenie*, 1972, No. 1, p. 9 ff.; E. Usenko, 'Pravovye aspekty Kompleksnoi programmy sotsialisticheskoi ekonomicheskoi integratsii', in *Sovetskoe gosudarstvo i pravo*, 1973, No. 7, p. 63 ff.; W. Seiffert, 'Der Prozess der Herausbildung des Rechtssystems der sozialistischen ökonomischen Integration', in *Sozialistische ökonomische Integration. Rechtsfragen*, Berlin, 1974, pp. 11–42; V. Saifert (W. Seiffert), 'Uchastie pravovoi nauki GDR v reshenii pravovykh voprosov Kompleksnoi programmy SEV', in *Sovetskoe gosudarstvo i pravo*, 1976, No. 5, p. 105 ff.
3. J. Caillot, *Le CAEM*, op. cit., p. 18.
4. Ibid.
5. Ibid.
6. In this connection comparison is frequently made with the EEC which, according to socialist authors, is a tendentially 'closed' organization. See, for example, the 'theses on imperialist integration in Western Europe' published in both *Pravda* and *Izvestiia* on 26 August 1962. Among the most recent critical assessments of West European integration are N. Faddeev, *Sovet*, op. cit., p. 44 ff. *et passim*; Iu. Sdobnikov, *Ekonomicheskaia integratsiia*, op. cit., pp. 13 ff., 88 ff.

   For his part, a Western scholar (J. Caillot, *Le CAEM*, op. cit., p. 21) argues that 'les buts réels du CAEM et de la CEE sont semblables, surtout si l'on ajoute l'objectif politique qu'ils renferment: cet objectif est la création d'une unité économique homogène qui doit conduire à une unité politique.' Also, the facts are said to show that 'les difficultés que rencontrent ces deux organisations économiques régionales dans leur marche vers l'integration sont identiques', even though 'les moyens utilisés pour arriver à ce but ne sont pas les mêmes.' Once again it seems appropriate to stress the difficulties already referred to about the usefulness of making comparisons between experiences which appear profoundly different not only in the means used but also in the objectives pursued. In particular, doubts are created by the alleged similarities between the real objectives of CMEA and the EEC. In fact, from the investigation as so far conducted into the purposes of CMEA, it seems clear that the members have never seriously considered the formation of an economic entity as the logical and natural premise to political union. Moreover, the latest documents issued by CMEA firmly and explicitly reject any prospects of a merger of national economic and political entities.

7. In the opinion of J. Caillot (*Le CAEM*, op. cit., p. 20) there are considerable similarities between the objectives of CMEA now listed and those set forth in Article 1(a) of the Convention establishing the OECD.

3 Functions and Powers

1. FUNCTIONS

The functions of CMEA, in conformity with the purposes and principles set forth in Article I of the Charter, are defined in paragraph 1 of Article III, which outlines and specifies the main guidelines along which the Council's action is to be directed.

Article III, which deals specifically with CMEA functions and powers, was involved in both Charter amendments of 1962 and 1974, as befitted the importance and sensitivity of its subject-matter.

According to the original (1959) version of paragraph 1 of Article III, the Council was responsible, on the one hand, for organizing certain activities, and on the other for assisting the member-countries in elaborating and implementing measures to be adopted jointly in certain fields.

In 1962, this paragraph was re-worded and expanded in the light of the new and more definite lines of economic cooperation. On the occasion of the 1974 Charter amendments, further specifications were made, designed essentially to introduce an explicit reference to the development of socialist economic integration.

Among the functions vested in the Council, paragraph 1 of Article III indicates in the first place that of organizing all-round economic, scientific and technical cooperation, with a view to making the most rational use of national resources and accelerating the development of production capacities. Moreover, according to the amendment introduced in 1974, the Council *contributes to the development of socialist economic integration*. Thus, the goal of integration was also written into the Article dealing with the Council's functions.

In this context, special importance is assumed by the function assigned to the Council, also by paragraph 1, of fostering the improvement of the international socialist division of labour through the coordination of national economic plans and specialisation and cooperation as regards production in member-countries. Another function of the Council is to study economic, scientific and technical problems of interest to member-countries.

Paragraph 1 then spells out the areas in which the Council is to assist member-countries in elaborating, *coordinating* (a term inserted in 1974) and carrying out joint measures for

a) the development of industry and agriculture

b) the development of transport with a view to ensuring priority for increasing import, export and transit shipments of goods

c) the most efficient use of investment funds allocated by member-countries for the development of the mining and manufacturing industries and for the construction of major projects which are of interest to two or more countries

d) the development of trade and exchange of services between member-countries and between them and other countries

e) the exchange of scientific and technical knowledge and advanced production experience.

The broad listing contained in paragraph 1 provides a necessarily general but on the whole fairly comprehensive idea of the many functions which CMEA is called upon to perform. The main lines of cooperation and integration, in the context of the international socialist division of labour and in the light of the basic guidelines laid down in Article I and analysed above, are therefore clearly enough defined.

2. MAIN FEATURES OF POWERS

Paragraph 2 of Article III is divided into two sub-paragraphs, concerning respectively the actions of CMEA and its power to make international agreements.

More precisely, paragraph 2*a* empowers the Council to make recommendations and adopt decisions through the agency of its organs; the characteristics of the two types of actions are discussed in Article IV, which deals specifically with this subject.

In 1974, for the purpose of strengthening the Council's position, again from this viewpoint, another sub-paragraph (marked *b*) was added to paragraph 2 of Article III, in which it is explicitly stated that the Council may conclude international agreements with member-countries, with other countries and with international organizations.

The 1974 revision also involved Articles XI and XII (previously numbered X and XI), concerning respectively the participation of other countries in the activities of the Council and relations with international organizations.

According to Article XI, the Council may not only invite non-member-countries to participate in the activities of its organs, but may also cooperate with them in other ways, generally through the conclusion of agreements.

Article XII, in its new version, states that the Council may maintain relations with the organs of the United Nations and with specialised international organizations, regulating such relations especially through the conclusion of agreements.

3. DECISIONS

Article IV deals specifically with recommendations and decisions, defining the conditions and effects of these two types of actions by the Council.

In this respect, it should be noted in the first place that while all organs of the Council may make decisions, recommendations may be made only by the main organs (Assembly, Executive Committee, Committees and Standing Commissions).[1]

Under paragraph 2 of Article IV, decisions are adopted by the various organs of CMEA on organizational and procedural matters; the decisions come into force on the day of signing of the minutes of the meeting of the competent organ that has adopted them, unless otherwise provided therein, *or because of the nature of the subject-matter*. The provision in italics and relating to the specific nature of certain decisions was introduced on the occasion of the Charter amendment of 1974 and constitutes the only amendment so far made in the original text of Article IV, dating back to 1959.

Decisions are required to be unanimous. According to paragraph 3 of Article IV, abstention is permitted when a member-country declares that it has no interest in the matter considered by a given organ of the Council. The decision will then be binding on all countries that have assented to it, but the abstaining country may subsequently join in the decision. In practice, the country that declares itself 'not interested' is kept informed about the developments of the decision adopted by the other members, so that it can adequately evaluate the possibility of subsequently joining in it.

From a practical viewpoint, it should be stressed that decisions, as well as recommendations, are not the outcome of a formally cast vote; the organs of CMEA follow in their decision-making the consensus procedure.

Particularly important among the decisions on organizational matters are those of the Assembly concerning the admission of new members, the participation of other countries or international organisations in the activities of the Council, the determination of the contribution of each member to the organization's budget and the creation of new organs.

The Assembly also appoints the Secretary of the Council, while Deputy Secretaries are appointed by the Executive Committee.

From the procedural standpoint, mention may be made of the decisions by which the organs of the Council set the dates for the respective meetings and adopt the agendas thereof. The Assembly, the Executive Committee, the Committees and the Standing Commissions adopt their own rules of procedure.

4. RECOMMENDATIONS

Recommendations, under paragraph 1 of Article IV, are adopted by CMEA on questions of economic, scientific and technical cooperation.

It is unnecessary to stress that recommendations constitute the action *par excellence* utilised by CMEA to achieve its substantial purposes and are therefore – as mentioned above – reserved for the major organs of the Council.

Recommendations may be general, addressed to all member-countries, or particular, when they relate to certain members only. The form of the recommendations varies according to circumstances and to their subject-matter; the substance of such actions may be clearly specified or confined to the indication of general directives, or to declarations of intent or of political conduct.

In this matter the drafters of the Charter operated in pragmatic spirit, leaving to the major organs of the Council a broad margin of discretion. On the other hand, it should be noted that, since in practice a single category of actions was entrusted to those organs, these actions had necessarily to be indicated with a high degree of flexibility, without rigidly fixing their distinctive features. This actually may give rise to certain perplexities and difficulties of interpretation, which will be discussed later.[2]

The said paragraph 1 provides that recommendations are to be 'submitted for consideration' to the member-countries; the recommendations accepted by the member-countries are put into effect by decision of the governments or other competent organs of such countries, in conformity with the provisions of the respective national legislatures.

Paragraph 3 of Article IV lays down also that the adoption of recommendations requires the consent of all members, but that any country not interested in the question may abstain, with the possibility of joining in at some later date.[3]

As can readily be seen, one difference between decisions and recommendations lies in the scope of application: decisions relate to matters of organization and procedure, while recommendations are concerned with questions of economic cooperation and integration. A further and no less important difference lies in the fact that decisions enter into effect virtually immediately (the day of the signing of the minutes of the meeting at which they were adopted, with due exceptions), while recommendations are first submitted for consideration to each member-country and then, if accepted, are put into effect by action of the competent state organs.

Attention should be called in this connection to the provisions of paragraph 4 of Article II, to the effect that the member-countries agree to ensure the implementation of the recommendations of the organs of the Council accepted by them, and to inform the Council about progress in such implementation.

Some authorities have maintained that the provision of paragraph 1 of Article IV, concerning the submission of the recommendations to the member-countries for consideration, has no practical significance, since a member-country whose representative concurred in the adoption of the recommendation by a given organ is required in any case to comply with such recommendation.[4] To support this contention, reference has been made to paragraph 4 of Article II, requiring members to ensure the implementation of the recommendations accepted by them.

This interpretation, however, does not seem acceptable, for it disregards specific provisions – contained in paragraph 1 of Article IV – designed to allow the country which considers the recommendation submitted to it to accept or reject it, thus guaranteeing the sovereign equality of the members and excluding any form of supranationality. Furthermore, the very provision of paragraph 4 of Article II seems to relate explicitly to those recommendations that were *accepted* by the various countries *after* considering them as provided for in paragraph 1 of Article IV.

In conclusion, the content of a recommendation becomes binding on a member-country only after the latter has formally accepted that recommendation.[5]

This procedure is further specified through the provisions contained in the rules of procedure of the various organs of CMEA.

The first stage is obviously that of the submission of the recommendation to the member-countries for their consideration. This is done by the Secretary or by the appropriate section of the Secretariat, who arrange for a copy of the protocol containing the recommendation to be sent to all member-countries, and not only to those which participated in the formulation of the recommendation and which, from one point of view, would be the only natural recipients of it.[6] Thus, the 'non-interested' countries are immediately given an opportunity to make a careful study of the measure adopted by the other members and to evaluate its implications.

The states which participated in the drafting of the recommendation are required to submit the latter for consideration to their respective government or responsible body and to give notice, within 60 days, to the Secretariat or its competent section, of the results of such consideration.[7]

The 60-day time-limit runs from the day of the signing of the protocol at CMEA headquarters. In special cases and when the particular characteristics of the recommendation require it, the Council may allow the member-countries a longer time for consideration.

As soon as the Secretariat or its competent section have been informed of the outcome of a member's deliberation, they are required to give immediate notice to the other members.

It should be noted that the recommendations – as well as the decisions – of the various organs may concern not only the member-countries but also Yugoslavia, which has concluded an agreement allowing it to participate in certain activities of the Council and which will be discussed in detail later. In the cases in which a recommendation is adopted with the concurrence of the representative of Yugoslavia, the latter is required to conform with the same procedures applicable to full members.

5. LEGAL NATURE OF RECOMMENDATIONS

On several occasions the legal nature of recommendations has formed the object of analysis and debate by Soviet and East European scholars.

As pointed out above, the mere adoption of a recommendation by the competent organs of the Council does not involve for the countries whose representatives participated in such adoption any legal obligation to implement the recommendation. At this stage the recommendation merely expresses the 'unilateral will of CMEA as an international organization':[8] this is indeed the expression of the Council's own will, intended to achieve a goal set forth in the Charter, clearly distinguished from the will of the 'interested' members.

The conduct of the representative of a state on the Council cannot be taken as an act legally binding on that state, but merely places on the latter a moral and political obligation.

The legal obligation arises only from formal acceptance, in cases where consideration of the recommendation – as usually happens in practice – has a favourable outcome.

The procedure of consideration and acceptance of recommendations by the 'interested' members has induced some authorities in Eastern, and also in Western, Europe to hold that what is involved is not decision-making acts by organs of an international body, but an actual contractual arrangement. In other words, they argue that recommendations – or at least some of them – are not collegial actions but international agreements.[9] More specifically, the international agreement constituted by the recommendation enters into force on the day when the Council Secretariat receives notice of acceptance by the last of the 'interested' member-countries.

These contentions have formed the object of thorough discussion and have been criticised by other authorities in the socialist camp.

Historically, the dispute began with the already mentioned adoption in 1957 – through a recommendation made by the Standing Commission on Foreign Trade – of the 'General Conditions for Deliveries of Goods among Foreign Trade Corporations of CMEA Members'.[10] The very particular circumstances attending the adoption of the General Conditions and their subsequent introduction into the legal systems of the Council member-countries seemed to provide adequate grounds for the contention that the recommendation containing the General Conditions amounted to an international agreement.

Other important documents, such as the 'General Conditions for Assembly' and the 'General Conditions for the Technical Service', both adopted in 1962, showed characteristics similar to those of the 'General Conditions for Deliveries of Goods' cited above. In these cases, too, some authorities spoke of recommendations having the character and value of international agreements.

Further elements in support of this position seemed to emerge from the approval first of the 'Basic Principles of the International Socialist Division of Labour' in 1962 and then of the 'Comprehensive Programme for the Further Intensification and Improvement of Cooperation and the Development of Socialist Economic Integration' in 1971.

The special importance, in many particulars, of the Comprehensive Programme has been already illustrated. Furthermore, the solemnity that marked the approval of this document by the Assembly – the 'supreme' organ of CMEA according to the Charter's definition – and the subsequent acceptance by all members after a consideration conducted within each state at the highest levels (Central Party Committee, Council of Ministers and, in some cases, Council of State), while on the one hand it could add nothing to the action from a strictly legal standpoint, on the other has provided significant evidence of the basic importance attributed to the Comprehensive Programme.

According to some distinguished socialist scholars, the Comprehensive Programme constitutes an international agreement of a wholly special kind.[11] In their view, one of the peculiarities of the agreement consists in the fact that it was not the product of direct negotiations among interested countries, but came into being through the action of an intergovernmental organization, without an international instrument having been formally signed.

The thesis of the conversion of an 'accepted' recommendation into an international agreement, even though it has more than one authoritative advocate, does raise serious perplexities. This delicate controversy can be elucidated, at least in part, by considering again the characteristics of CMEA recommendations.

In the first place, it should be stressed again that the concept of recommendation reflects a very broad and general category of actions, which may differ substantially from one another as regards both the legal result intended to be achieved and the effectiveness of such actions.

Within this context, it seems that special attention should be paid to two major kinds of recommendations which, besides providing adequate bases for the improvement of cooperation and the development of integration, are capable of making a significant contribution to the gradual formation of a CMEA legal system.[12]

In this connection, one should consider in the first place the recommendations containing the 'General Conditions' applicable to various fields, as cited above. These instruments have given undeniable impetus to the unification and harmonization of law within CMEA. Even though the concrete results so far achieved have been relatively minor, the process now under way appears to be bound to gather increasing momentum and significance.

Other recommendations whose importance and significance for the progress of socialist integration do not need to be stressed are those in the form of general action programmes, such as the above-mentioned 'Basic Principles of the International Socialist Division of Labour' of 1962 and, above all, the Comprehensive Programme of 1971. These are, in practice, solemn declarations concerning the principles that are to regulate the mutual relations among members in certain sectors, as well as the objectives, general and specific, which are to be attained in this context.

In many cases the provisions contained in the recommendations require the conclusion of international agreements, for they constitute only the initial stage in a process of law creation which takes shape through subsequent conventions concluded between member-countries in order to comply with the provisions of those recommendations.

Among the major functions attributed to the CMEA Secretariat is that of working out, or helping work out, drafts of multilateral agreements on problems connected with economic, scientific and technical cooperation, in accordance with the recommendations and decisions of the organs of the Council (Article X(2) (*d*) of the Charter). In practice, however, it is not always easy to draw a sharp line between agreements actually worked out by the Secretariat and agreements directly negotiated between the interested countries on the basis of the indications contained in the appropriate recommendations.

The recommendations, which are addressed only to member-countries, substantially constitute an indirect rule-making instrument towards the creation of that CMEA community law which, although not as far developed as the law of the European Communities, is not thereby less autonomous with respect to the internal laws of the individual countries; the priority of the community law over state laws has never been questioned by socialist doctrine.[13]

In conclusion, the particular characteristics of some kinds of recommendations do not seem to be such as to justify the thesis of their conversion into international agreements. A recommendation – as provided for in Article IV of the Charter – still remains a collegial act embodying the decisions of the Council's main organs concerning economic, scientific and technical cooperation. The substance of the recommendation, after its acceptance, becomes binding but not directly enforceable; indeed, it becomes effective in the internal legal systems of the member-countries only through an action taken by the competent state organs.[14] This does not mean, however, that the state has the power to 'regulate' concretely the effectiveness of the recommendation, increasing or decreasing its scope to suit any conditions and limitations dictated by its own legislation.

The undoubted complexity of the procedure outlined above and certain practical shortcomings that may derive from it have led certain authorities to suggest that the classic instrument of the international convention would be more appropriate: in this connection one can cite the important example of the Convention on the arbitration of disputes in the field of economic, scientific and technical cooperation concluded in Moscow on 26 May 1972.

On the other hand, while it may be true that the recourse to international agreements makes it possible to overcome the difficulties arising from Article IV of the Charter, it is just as true that the Council's member-countries intend to keep on using recommendations as a basic instrument to achieve cooperation and integration.

As a matter of fact, the problem seems to be not so much one of preferring the conclusion of international agreements to the adoption of recommendations, as that of improving the form and substance of the latter, by drafting them more precisely, by defining more clearly their legal nature and standing within the systems of the member-countries and, last but not least, by developing more adequate instruments to increase the effectiveness of controls over their implementation. Thus, the function of CMEA will be improved, while a more frequent recourse to international agreements would ultimately weaken the Council, relegating it to a subordinate position, more concerned with the study and discussion of problems than with acting on the economic reality of member-countries on an operational plane.

Recommendations appear certain to maintain their leading position as a collegial act resulting from a process which unifies the declarations of the various 'interested' countries into a decision which, by whatever organ it is adopted, is attributable to CMEA as such. The thesis of the recommendation as international agreement – while resting on undoubtedly sound grounds – does seem to attribute greater importance to the stage of the unilateral declarations of will, with which the 'interested' countries express their 'acceptance', than to the unifying stage which characterizes the formation of the collegial act.

6. THE TREATY-MAKING POWER

The second part of paragraph 2, Article III, completes the list of CMEA powers and concerns, as mentioned above, the Council's capacity to conclude international agreements with member-countries, with other countries and with international organizations. Relations with non-member countries and with international organizations are specifically governed by Articles XI and XII of the Charter, which will be discussed later.

It seems appropriate, for the moment, to stress, from a general viewpoint, CMEA treaty-making capacity.

In principle, the capacity to become a party to an international treaty is but one aspect of the more general international legal capacity of a subject. In the case of international organizations, however, the international legal capacity does not seem to constitute a necessary prerequisite of the contracting capacity.

The agreements entered into by the Council with non-member-countries will be discussed later. As regards those concluded with member-countries, mention should be made in the first place of the agreement between CMEA and the USSR on the settlement of questions concerning the location of the Council's institutions in the Soviet Union; this agreement, signed on 7 December 1961, entered into force on 5 March 1962.[15] A special protocol to this agreement was concluded on 3 October 1968, concerning the grant to CMEA, free of charge and for an unlimited period, of the site for the erection of the complex of buildings that now form the Council's new and imposing headquarters.

Similar headquarters agreements concerning other entities of the Council were concluded by the latter with other member-countries (Bulgaria, Hungary, the GDR, Poland and Czechoslovakia) in the 1962–66 period.

7. CMEA'S LEGAL CAPACITY, PRIVILEGES AND IMMUNITIES

Matters pertaining to CMEA legal capacity, privileges and immunities are regulated in a general way by Article XIV (1) to (3) of the Charter, and more specifically by a special Convention on the Legal Capacity, Privileges and Immunities of the Council; the convention, signed in Sofia on 14 December 1959, came into force on 13 April 1960, and was amended in 1962 and 1974.

Article XIV of the CMEA Charter provides first of all, in paragraph 1, that the Council enjoys, in the territory of each member-country, the legal capacity required for the discharge of its functions and the achievement of its purposes. This stipulation was necessary in order to ensure to the Council and its organs full legal autonomy when they operate in the respective internal legal systems of the member-countries.

Paragraph 2 of Article XIV provides that the Council,

representatives of the member-countries of the Council and Council officials enjoy in the territory of each of these countries the privileges and immunities necessary to discharge their functions and achieve the purposes envisaged in the Charter. Paragraph 3 adds that the legal capacity, privileges and immunities indicated in the article shall be determined 'by a special Convention'.

The above-cited clauses of a general nature are more fully specified in the special Convention.

Article I of the Convention provides that the Council is a juridical person and empowered to conclude agreements, acquire, lease and dispose of property and appear in court. Based on this provision, CMEA possesses the capacity of internal law in each member-country. All members must therefore treat the Council, from the standpoint of their internal law, as a juridical person, with all the consequences of this status.

Articles II and III of the Convention specify the privileges of the Council. Its premises are inviolable; the property, assets and documents of the Council, wherever situated, enjoy immunity from any form of administrative or judicial interference, except of course when the Council itself waives immunity in any particular case.

The Council is exempt from all direct national or local taxes and charges. Moreover, the Council is exempted from payment of customs duties and from any import or export restriction as regards articles intended for official use.

Special privileges are also accorded to the Council as regards postal, telegraph and telephone communications.

8. IMMUNITIES AND PRIVILEGES OF REPRESENTATIVES AND OFFICIALS

In addition to the immunities accorded to the Council, the Convention envisages immunities and privileges both for the representatives of the member-countries to the Council and for Council officials.

Under Article IV, paragraph 1 of the Convention, the representatives of member-countries enjoy on the territory of each Council member-country the following immunities and privileges:

a) immunity from personal arrest or detention, and from the jurisdiction of judicial institutions, in respect of any act performed by them in their capacity as representatives

b) inviolability of all papers and documents

c) the same customs privileges in respect to their personal baggage as are accorded to members of diplomatic missions of corresponding rank

d) exemption from personal service obligations and from payment of direct taxes and charges on the salary paid them by the appointing country.

In addition to the above-mentioned privileges and immunities, the representatives of the member-countries and their deputies enjoy, under paragraph 2, the privileges and immunities granted to diplomatic representatives.

Paragraph 3 emphasises that the privileges and immunities are accorded to the persons mentioned in the Article only for the purpose of ensuring the performance of their functions. It is further provided that each member-country has the right and duty to waive its representative's immunity when it would hamper the administration of justice and provided the waiver of immunity is not detrimental to the purposes for which immunity is granted.

Paragraph 5 states that the term 'representatives' includes the representatives themselves and their deputies, the heads, members and secretaries of delegations, as well as advisers and experts.

As regards the Council's officials, it should be mentioned in the first place, from a general standpoint, that paragraph 3, Article X of the Charter provides that the Secretary, his deputies and the staff of the Secretariat, in performing their duties, act as international officials.

Council officials, under Article V of the above-cited Convention, enjoy privileges and immunities generally similar to those accorded to the officials of the specialized agencies of the United Nations.

According to a customary provision, included in paragraph 1, Article V, it is up to the Council to determine the categories of officials to whom the particular provisions of the Convention apply. The special treatment thereunder, in fact, does not apply to all those who work with the Council – since many of them perform clerical duties pertaining solely to the organization's internal functioning – but only to the officials whose action is directly attributed to the Council. This, however, does not necessarily imply that the latter possess the power of representing the Council, a power which is reserved only to ranking officials. A further condition for the according of the said treatment is the giving of notice, by the CMEA Secretariat to the competent organs of the member-countries, of the surnames of all officials entitled to special treatment, such list to be periodically revised as necessary.

Under paragraph 2 of Article V, in the territory of each member-country these officials enjoy: a) immunity from jurisdiction for the acts done in the performance and within the scope of their official functions; b) exemption from personal service; c) exemption from direct taxes and charges on the salaries and emoluments paid them by the Council; and d) the same customs privileges, as regards personal baggage, accorded to the members of corresponding rank of diplomatic missions accredited to the country concerned.

In addition to the foregoing, the Secretary of the Council and his deputies enjoy the privileges and immunities accorded to diplomatic representatives (paragraph 3, Article V).

Again in accordance with a customary formula, paragraph 4 states that the above-mentioned privileges and immunities are not accorded in the direct interest of the individuals holding official positions, but in the more general interest of the organization to which such individuals belong and in order to ensure full autonomy in the discharge of their functions. For this reason, paragraph 4 provides that it is the duty and right of the Secretary of the Council to waive the immunity of an official when it would interfere with the administration of justice and provided such waiver is not prejudicial to the organization's interests. The right of waiver of immunity in relation to the Secretary and his deputies appertains to the Executive Committee.

Finally, paragraph 5 of Article V provides that the exemptions from personal service and from direct taxation envisaged in paragraph 2 do not extend to the officials who are citizens of the state in which the organ of CMEA to which they belong is situated.

9. CMEA'S INTERNATIONAL JURIDICAL PERSONALITY

In the light of the provisions of the Charter and of the Convention discussed above, it now seems appropriate to deal with the problem of CMEA's international juridical personality.

It should be noted, in the first place, that the said documents make no mention whatever of the Council's international juridical personality, while they recognize the personality with respect to the legal systems of the member-countries.

It is clear that the existence of the Council's international juridical personality could in no way be certainly determined by reference only, on the one hand, to the provisions contained in the CMEA Charter and, on the other, to the intent of the member-countries. Since the latter cannot, by any declaration of their own, make the Council a person with respect to third parties, reference must be made to the concrete exercise by the Council of international capacities and to the co-related conduct of third subjects.

Now, since CMEA has been gradually assuming an autonomous position in the international order by developing – in accordance with the above-mentioned Charter provisions, further specified on the occasion of the 1974 amendments – external relations through the conclusion of agreements with other countries which provide for various forms of participation and cooperation and through the establishment of connections with other international agencies, it may be assumed that all this constitutes a concrete manifestation of the possession of personality. The latter seems to consist, substantially, in the Council's capacity to act, in legal terms, outside of its own system.

The situation that has been developing in recent years within the international community with respect to CMEA seems to favour the thesis admitting the organization's international juridical personality, which obviously can neither be compared nor, *a fortiori*, assimilated with that of a state.

It should be noted, however, that this position, now widely shared by Soviet and East European scholars, is the conclusion of a complex and delicate doctrinal process. Indeed, for a long time the doctrine of the socialist countries had ruled out the possibility of international organizations possessing international legal personality, maintaining that states alone could be considered as subjects of international law. Later, a substantial evolution occurred, which has ultimately led to the recognition of CMEA as a subject of international law.[16]

NOTES TO CHAPTER 3

1. Concerning the principal organs, see, for the Assembly, paragraph 1 of Article VI; for the Executive Committee, paragraph 3 of Article VII; for the Committees, paragraph 3*a* of Article VIII; and for the Standing Commissions, paragraph 3*a* of Article IX.
2. See the comments made by J. Caillot in *Le CAEM*, op. cit., p. 90 ff.
3. In effect, the acceptance of the recommendation may take place at any time from the day of the signing of the corresponding protocol by the 'interested' members.
4. See, for all, H. Bräutigam, 'Die wirtschaftliche Zusammenarbeit der Ostblockstaaten im Rat für gegenseitige Wirtschaftshilfe', in *Zeitschrift für ausländisches öffentliches Recht und Völkerrecht*, 1961, p. 710.
5. On this subject see H. de Fiumel, 'Le caractère juridique des résolutions des organes du Conseil d'Assistance Economique Mutuelle', in *Cahiers de droit européen*, 1967, p. 533 ff.; A. Wasilkowski, *Zalecenia Rady Wzajemnej Pomocy Gospodarczej*, Warsaw, 1969, p. 270 ff. For an up-to-date analysis of the question, see E. Usenko's extensive contribution in the collective work *Sovet ekonomicheskoi vzaimopomoshchi. Osnovnye*, op. cit., p. 220 ff. For a close examination of this question by a Western scholar, see J. Caillot, *Le CAEM*, op. cit., p. 90 ff.
6. See Article 29 of the Rules of Procedure of the Assembly, Article 27 of the Rules of Procedure of the Executive Committee, and Article 38 of the Model Rules of Procedure of the Standing Commissions. Similar provisions are contained in the respective Statutes on the three Committees now in existence.
7. See Article 25 of the Rules of Procedure of the Assembly, Article 23 of the Rules of Procedure of the Executive Committee, and Article 33 of the Model Rules of Procedure of the Standing Commissions. The Statutes on the Committees do not set any time limit for consideration of the recommendations.
8. *Sovet ekonomicheskoi vzaimopomoshchi. Osnovnye*, op. cit., p. 222.
9. See M. Kemper and J. Kirsten, 'Rechtsfragen der neuen Etappe internationaler ökonomischer Beziehungen zwischen den Mitgliedstaaten des Rates für gegenseitige Wirtschaftshilfe', in *Staat und Recht*, 1962, No. 12, p. 2179; M. Kemper and J. Kirsten, 'Fragen des gemeinsamen Leitungsmechanismus der RGW-Mitgliedstaaten', in *Staat und Recht*, 1965, No. 1, p. 10.
10. See the contribution by E. Usenko in *Sovet ekonomicheskoi vzaimopomoshchi. Osnovnye*, op. cit., p. 223 ff. See also J. Caillot, *Le CAEM*, op. cit., p. 94 ff.
11. *Sovet ekonomicheskoi vzaimopomoshchi. Osnovnye*, op. cit., p. 226 ff.
12. See J. Jakubowski, 'Le développement du droit économique communautaire des pays du CAEM et les problèmes posés par son application', in *Journal du droit international*, 1973, p. 676 ff.; J. Rajski, 'Le rapprochement et l'unification du droit dans le cadre du CAEM', in *Revue internationale de droit comparé*, 1976, No. 3, p. 461 ff.
13. J. Jakubowski, op. cit., p. 680.

14. If a comparison were to be made between CMEA recommendations and the various categories of action EEC may take, it might be said that CMEA recommendations fall somewhere in between EEC regulations and directives, being at a level higher with respect to the latter, but clearly lower with respect to the regulations.
15. For an analysis of the agreement, see *Sovet ekonomicheskoi vzaimopomoshchi. Osnovnye*, op. cit., p. 127 ff.
16. See *Sovet ekonomicheskoi vzaimopomoshchi. Osnovnye*, op. cit., p. 128 ff. and the references contained therein.

4 Membership and Relations with Third Parties

1. PREREQUISITES FOR FULL MEMBERSHIP

It is a well-known fact that socialist scholars place a strong emphasis on the 'open' character of CMEA, contrasting it with the cooperation and integration bodies existing in the West. Without going into the merit of rather old and in many ways outdated polemics, an attempt should be made here to specify the character and actual scope of this 'openness'.

In the first place, the principle that only states may be admitted to membership emerges clearly both from the communiqué announcing the Council's creation and from the subsequent provisions of the Charter. Actually, both the communiqué and the Charter use the term 'country', but it is generally admitted that in these and other CMEA documents such term really has the meaning of 'state'.

Furthermore, on the basis of the clauses contained in both the Charter and the Comprehensive Programme, it appears that being a fully independent and sovereign state is another requirement for membership.

A very important requirement for full membership of CMEA stems from the particular political and economic context in which objectively the Council operates: the quality of being a socialist state. It appears, in effect, that the set of basic principles and purposes of the Council can be accepted only by socialist states.[1]

In this connection, it is customary to draw a distinction between the early years of CMEA, when allegedly any (European) state could have become a member, and the following period, when such possibility was narrowed down to socialist states. Such a distinction, in many ways questionable, is directly connected with a particular interpretation of the initial purposes of CMEA, considered as essentially limited to the field of trading.

Consequently, it is claimed that, in the early stage of its activity, membership in the Council was, at least in principle, 'open' to any country of Europe, irrespective of its economic and social system. According to some authorities, full participation in CMEA by non-socialist states would have become impossible only after later developments, characterized by the overriding importance assumed by the coordination of the national economic plans.[2] In this connection, it will suffice to refer to the considerations already made, to the effect that the expansion of trade relations among member-countries was never, even during the earliest stage, the sole objective of the Council, which from its inception was already turned towards more thorough and extensive forms of cooperation. It seems therefore correct to hold that, not only in substantial but also in formal terms, full membership in CMEA was from the very beginning limited to socialist states.

It should be recalled that up to 1962 there existed a particular geographic restriction, since the first part of paragraph 2, Article II of the Charter, as drafted in 1959, provided that 'European' countries alone could be members of the Council. Indeed, as appeared from the January 1949 communiqué announcing the creation of the Council, the latter had been essentially conceived as an organism of cooperation among certain countries of the European region. In the second half of the 1950s, the representatives of socialist countries of Asia began to follow CMEA activities as observers. In June 1962, Mongolia changed its status from that of observer to full membership, and thus the bar on non-European countries was lifted.

Certain observers are of the opinion that, in spite of the presence of non-European observers and the admission of Mongolia, Cuba and Vietnam as full members, CMEA continues to be a cooperation entity substantially limited to the European region. The presence of representatives from outside Europe is said to be of importance more in political than in strictly economic terms.

In effect, it is maintained that CMEA is not 'open' to all socialist states, but only to those that have reached a certain stage of economic development and industrialization; only limited cooperation agreements would be possible with socialist countries which are still taking the initial steps towards industrialization.

The events of the last few years have shown that CMEA is an

organization 'open' to socialist states, regardless of their level of socio-economic development. Moreover, it would not seem that any part of CMEA's principles and basic purposes justify a 'closing' of the organisation to the less-advanced countries; in fact, the gradual elimination of inequalities in development occupies a specially important position among the basic lines to be followed by socialist economic cooperation.

It has already been noted that the 1974 Charter amendments included, among other things, an explicit mention of the 'approximation and gradual equalization of the levels of economic development' of the Council's member-countries.

In effect, this provision of the Charter seems to provide an authoritative confirmation of the thesis accepted here. Of course, this should not lead to an underestimation of the very serious difficulties created in the process of cooperation and, even more, of integration promoted by CMEA by significant differences in levels of development between one and the other member-country.

It should be noted, finally, that membership in CMEA, in conformity with the basic principles of the organization, is fully voluntary, since in no case can membership automatically derive from certain qualifications possessed by an entity.

2. ACQUISITION OF MEMBERSHIP

Membership of CMEA is governed by Article II of the Charter, the provisions of which were affected by the 1962 amendments (with the above-mentioned elimination of the 'European' country requirement) but not by those of 1974.

Under the above-mentioned provisions, there are two categories of members: the 'original' members and the members admitted subsequently (hereinafter referred to in brief as 'admitted members').

The former category includes the countries participating in the 12th Session of the Assembly, held in Sofia in 1959, which signed and then ratified the Charter: Albania, Bulgaria, Hungary, the GDR, Poland, Romania, the USSR and Czechoslovakia. Nothing is said in paragraph 1 of Article II about the procedure for the ratification of the Charter, unlike the case of other international agencies; it seems evident, however, that ratification is to take place in accordance with the respective constitutional provisions of the various states. It would also seem that the signature and ratification of the Charter may not be subjected to any reservation.

While original membership in CMEA depended solely on the conduct of the individual states considered, admission is the result of a complex process. According to paragraph 2 of Article II, membership of the Council is open to other countries which subscribe to its principles and purposes and agree to assume the obligations set forth in the Charter.[3]

Under the above provisions of the Charter, therefore, the procedure for admission to the Council begins with a declaration by the applicant state that it subscribes to the principles and purposes of the Council and accepts the obligations imposed by the Charter, and with the subsequent formal application for admission, which is decided upon by the Assembly of the Council.

Fuller details concerning the admission procedure are contained in Articles 30 to 32 of the Assembly's Rules of Procedure. The state which desires to be admitted must submit to the Secretary of CMEA an official statement to this effect, copies of which are transmitted by the Secretary to all member-countries. The admission application is considered by the Assembly in the first session following the filing of the application, if the latter has reached the Secretariat at least 90 days in advance of the opening of the session. An application received later than the period indicated is considered by the next Session, unless the Assembly decides otherwise.

Thus, the final decision on the application depends on the Assembly finding that the applicant possesses all requirements for admission; this decision, because of its very nature, is likely to be of a largely discretionary nature.

The admission must be decided by the Assembly with the unanimous concurrence of all member-countries. The reason for this condition is that paragraph 3 of Article IV of the Charter provides that decisions – as well as recommendations – must be adopted with the consent of the 'interested' member-countries: in the case of admissions, all countries are to be considered as 'interested'. Indeed, it seems that the case cannot be conceived of a member-country having no interest in the admission of a new member. It has been noted in this connection that, in practice, each member is given a 'right of veto' concerning the admission of other countries.[4]

After the approval of the Assembly, the state concerned proceeds with the ratification of the Charter.

According to the provisions originally contained in paragraph 4 of Article XV of the Charter, the latter entered into force immediately upon the deposit of the ratification instrument with the depositary, i.e. the Government of the Soviet Union. The Charter amendments of 1974 introduced a significant modification to this provision, which now appears, in the new version, in paragraph 4 of Article XVI (the preceding Article XV has been renumbered because of the insertion of a new article.)

Under the provisions adopted in 1974, a distinction is made between *permanent* entry into force of the Charter (on the day of the deposit of the instrument of ratification, as previously provided) and *provisional* entry into force, on the day of the decision of the Assembly concerning the admission. It was thus sought to expedite the inclusion of the new member in the organization, overcoming any difficulties and delays connected with the ratification procedure and with the depositing of the instrument of ratification.

As mentioned previously, at present the category of admitted members includes three countries: Mongolia, Cuba and Vietnam.

It may be appropriate to note that, in legal terms, the status of admitted members does not differ from that of original members, both having the same rights and obligations. In effect, the distinction between the two categories does not concern the membership status, but merely the procedure through which membership is acquired.

3. MEMBERS' OBLIGATIONS

The obligations imposed on the states by their membership of CMEA are spelled out in paragraph 4 of Article II.

Members are required, in the first place, to ensure the implementation of the recommendations of the organs of the Council adopted by them, with the connected obligation to inform the Council about the progress made in such implementation.

Furthermore, member-countries are required to give the

Council and its officials the necessary cooperation in the discharge of their functions under the Charter; they are also required to submit materials and information necessary for carrying out the tasks of the Council.

Article XIII – specifically entitled 'Financial Questions' and amended in several respects in 1974 – imposes specific financial obligations on member-countries. In the first place, under the above-mentioned Charter amendments, the Council has been given a budget of its own. According to paragraph 1 of Article XIII, all revenues and expenditures of the Council are to be specified in this budget; the members cover the costs connected with the maintenance and financing of the Secretariat's activities and – according to the 1974 amendments – the other expenditures of the organization in conformity with the budget.

Again under the said paragraph 1, the Assembly determines the amount of the contributions to be made by each member-country to the Council's budget. The criteria adopted to determine the amount of the contribution of individual members have not been disclosed; it seems likely that such amounts are determined in proportion to the population of each member-country.

In accordance with paragraph 3 – which has been left in its initial wording – the expenditures resulting from participation in the meetings of the Council's organs and in all other meetings held within the framework of the Council are covered by the countries so represented.

Paragraph 4, as amended in 1974, provides that the expenses relating to conference premises and to technical facilities necessary for the conferences and meetings referred to in paragraph 3 are borne by the host country; this does not apply to meetings held at Council headquarters in Moscow.

In conclusion, it can be noted that the financial obligations of members, especially after the 1974 Charter amendment, are regulated in considerable detail, with a view to ensuring the actual participation of all countries in meeting expenditure.

4. LOSS OF MEMBERSHIP AND 'INACTIVE' MEMBERSHIP

Loss of membership of CMEA may derive from a number of causes, but the Charter envisages, in paragraph 3 of Article II, only one way of leaving the organization, i.e. withdrawal.

Among the general causes which may lead to loss of membership is obviously the termination of one or more of the basic prerequisites for membership of CMEA.

The cessation of the international capacity of a member or the creation of a relationship whereby a member-country is no longer fully sovereign but becomes dependent on another automatically and necessarily involve the loss of membership. This loss may also be caused by a change in political regime and consequently of the system of organization of socio-economic structures, involving for the country concerned the loss of the quality of socialist country, which is also an essential requirement for full membership of CMEA.

A different case is that of a member which, while not losing the requirements mentioned above, feels that it can no longer subscribe to the purposes and principles of the organization and therefore does not intend to continue to fulfil the obligations imposed by the Charter. In this case – in conformity with the principle of the fully voluntary nature of membership and cooperation expressed in CMEA basic documents – any member has the right to withdraw from the organization.

Under paragraph 3 of Article II, which has remained unchanged in its original wording, such a state must declare that it no longer wishes to be a member of the Council and so inform the depositary of the Charter, which will give notice of such declaration to the other members. Six months after receipt of such notice, the state is automatically excluded from the organization.

As will be noted, there is no provision for suspension or expulsion from CMEA; removal from the organization can take place only by unilateral decision of the country concerned.

It is important to note that the right of withdrawal is not subject to any limitation, in the letter and in the spirit of the Charter.[5] A country wishing to withdraw from the organization is simply required to give notice of its intent to the depositary of the Charter and is under no obligation whatsoever to disclose to either the depositary or the other members the reasons for taking such grave step. The reasons for a member's withdrawal, therefore, not only cannot be considered and evaluated either by the other members or by the organization as such, but may even not be disclosed at all.

To date, no member has availed itself of the right to withdraw from the organization in conformity with the procedure set forth in paragraph 3 of Article II.

However, as previously noted, Albania since the end of 1961 has not been participating in CMEA activities, while on the other hand there is no evidence of its ever having given to the depositary of the Charter notice of its intent to withdraw from the organization.

Albania's non-participation in the activities of the Council has created delicate problems, not least because of the diverging interpretations offered by the parties concerned. Several scholars appear uncertain as to how to determine the current status of that country with respect to CMEA.

It should be recalled, in the first place, that the Albanian representatives began by deserting the 15th Session of the Council's Assembly held in Warsaw in December 1961. On that occasion the Polish Deputy Prime Minister, who had chaired the meeting, told the press that Albania, although it had not participated in the session, continued to be a member of the Council.[6] It should be stressed that during the 15th Session the USSR announced its break of diplomatic relations with Albania. It was also learned from a Soviet source that the Albanian representatives had refused to participate in the session.

In June 1962 the Albanian Government entered a protest because it had not been invited to send its delegates to the Conference of the representatives of the Communist and workers' parties and to the 16th Session of the Council's Assembly, both held in Moscow; it was also pointed out that the decisions of the organs of the Council adopted in the absence of the Albanian representatives were to be regarded as null and void, and in any case not binding on Albania.[7]

On the occasion of the 17th Session of the Assembly, the Secretary of CMEA stated that he had ceased to invite Albania to participate because that country had failed to pay its financial contribution to the organization, as required by the Charter; such contribution had been overdue since September 1961. Based on the foregoing, it was argued that Albania's failure to pay its contribution had resulted in that country's losing its membership of the Council.[8]

Recently, it was also authoritatively reconfirmed that Albania, at the end of 1961, stopped participating in the activities of the organs of CMEA, recalled its nationals serving with the

Secretariat, stopped paying its contributions and, in pratice, has no longer fulfilled any of the obligations deriving from the Charter and from the decisions adopted by the organization.[9]

All this would suggest, at first sight, that Albania no longer possesses membership of CMEA.

There are, however, two important elements that can be neither overlooked nor underestimated.

On the one hand, Albania, in spite of the polemics, has never expressed its intention of withdrawing from the organization, as would have been and would still be its right. In effect, Albania's conduct, even though showing that country's intention no longer to participate in the organization, cannot be considered as amounting to withdrawal, which must always take place in conformity with the provisions of the Charter.

On the other hand, CMEA has not adopted – and probably not even considered – any measure to expel Albania. Apart from the fact that, for many reasons, the expulsion of a state from an international agency is a very rare occurrence, one might point out that such a measure is not envisaged by the CMEA Charter. It does not seem, however, that one can rule out in principle the right of the competent organs of the Council, and more precisely of the Assembly, to expel a member whose conduct persistently conflicts with the principles and purposes of the organization and with the other obligations imposed by the Charter.

As regards the non-payment of contributions, this, although certainly serious, would seem to involve *per se* not the loss of membership but merely a suspension.

In conclusion, it seems correct to state that, from a legal standpoint, Albania has never ceased to be a member of CMEA, since it has never availed itself of the right of voluntary and unilateral withdrawal, nor has it been expelled. Albania's legal status can then be defined as that of an 'inactive' member, with the resulting suspension of rights and obligations.[10] However, to be fully restored to normal membership, it would be sufficient for Albania to show – through an explicit statement or even simply by concrete actions – its will to resume its active participation in the Council's life.

If this thesis is accepted, then there are no further grounds for the perplexities expressed by some authorities concerning the admission of Mongolia and the 1962 Charter amendment. In effect, Mongolia's admission was made possible by the lifting of the geographic restriction limiting membership of CMEA to European countries. But through what process was this restriction repealed and the other Charter amendments adopted?

Under the provisions of Article XVII of the Charter (Article XVI prior to the 1974 amendments), the amendments to the latter are subject to the approval of the Assembly – which must necessarily be unanimous, it being inadmissible for a member to abstain on the grounds of not being interested in the matter – and enter into force when all member-countries have deposited the ratification instruments.

Since Albania, as mentioned above, was present neither at the Conference of the Communist and workers' parties of CMEA member-countries held in June 1962 nor at the 16th Session of the Assembly which decided the admission of Mongolia and adopted other major Charter amendments, it would have been impossible to comply with the said provisions of Article XVII. A similar situation would have occurred on the occasion of the subsequent Charter amendments introduced in 1974.

If, instead, the thesis, outlined above, that Albania has ceased to be an active member of CMEA since the end of 1961, is accepted, Albania's lack of assent to the Charter amendments of 1962 and 1974 is to be regarded as wholly without significance, both formal and substantial. Indeed, an inactive member is, one might say, by definition 'not interested' in the organization's decisions, to employ the terms contained in Article IV of the Charter.

Furthermore, even though it cannot be known what judgment the inactive member might form concerning the line taken by the organization during its non-participation, it seems reasonable to assume that such judgment would not be totally negative, for otherwise it would be difficult to understand why that member should not end its relationship with the organization, availing itself of the right of withdrawal.

5. RELATIONS WITH NON-MEMBER-COUNTRIES

The 'open' nature of CMEA manifests itself not only as regards the above-mentioned possibilities of full participation in its activities but also with respect to other more limited forms of collaboration.

The concrete forms which this collaboration can assume and the various legal conditions which may derive from it as regards the states concerned were not specified in detail by the framers of the Charter. Indeed, this seems to be in keeping with the basic conceptions of CMEA, intended to regulate only the broad outlines of the various possible cases, leaving considerable room for the resources of practice and of a wise pragmatism.

The rules in this area, however, have required – in connection with the progressive development of CMEA and with the intensification and expansion of its foreign relations – elucidations and adjustments which were introduced on the occasion of the 1974 Charter amendment.

The Charter amendments have concerned both of the main fields in which CMEA external relations can develop: on the one hand relations with non-member-countries and on the other relations with other international organizations.[11]

It seems appropriate to begin with a review of the rules concerning the participation of 'non-member-countries', to use the Charter's term, in the Council's activities, in view of the unquestionable importance which they have been assuming, especially in the last few years. These rules are contained in Article XI.

Under the existing provisions, there are two different possibilities as regards non-member-countries: participation in the activities of the organs of the Council (already envisaged in the original 1959 version of the Charter); and cooperation in other forms with such organs (introduced with the 1974 amendments).

It should be noted that, under these provisions, it is always up to the Council – and, in practice, to the Secretariat – to *invite* non-member countries to attend the meetings of the various organs or to carry out with the latter particular forms of cooperation.

Article XI further specifies that the conditions under which the representatives of non-member-countries may participate in the activities of the organs of the Council, or cooperate with them in other ways, are to be established by the Council in agreement with the countries concerned, 'generally through the conclusion of agreements'.

The specific reference to the conclusion of agreements, introduced in 1974, is connected with and in certain respects reconfirms the provisions of the second part of paragraph 2 of

Article III – also introduced in 1974 – whereby the Council 'may conclude international agreements with its member-countries, with other countries and with international organizations'.

6. THE OBSERVERS

The participation of non-member-countries in the activities of the organs of CMEA was already envisaged, as mentioned above, in the initial version of the Charter which, in this respect, formally sanctioned the practice that had been forming in the years immediately preceding. In 1956, on the occasion of the 7th Session of the Assembly, observers (from the Chinese People's Republic and Yugoslavia) had been admitted for the first time. In the years following observers from other countries began participating, although irregularly. Later, some observers became full members. Yugoslavia, for its part, has concluded with the Council, in the autumn of 1964, an important agreement for participation in the activities of certain organs.

It may be useful to discuss briefly the events that have characterized the participation of observers. Even though the above-mentioned provisions of Article XI do not contain the term 'observers', or any more or less equivalent expressions, practically all non-member-countries – except Yugoslavia – which participated in the activities of the Council have done so as observers and were designated as such, for instance, in the official communiqués issued at the end of the Assembly's sessions. As regards the case of Yugoslavia – which will be discussed later – some authorities have spoken of an 'association', even though the use of this term does create certain perplexities.

Representatives from the following countries have participated as observers in the activities of organs of the Council – particularly the Assembly and Standing Commissions: the Chinese People's Republic, the People's Democratic Republic of Korea, the Democratic Republic of Vietnam (now the Socialist Republic of Vietnam), Mongolia, Yugoslavia, Cuba, Laos, Angola and Ethiopia.

China participated for the first time in the Council's activities in 1956 and continued to do so regularly up to 1961.

At the end of that year the 15th Session of the Assembly was held, but Chinese representatives did not participate; they appeared again in October 1963 at an Executive Committee meeting. It seems that in June 1962 China was invited to join the organization as a full member, but the invitation was rejected. Subsequently China participated, albeit very irregularly, in the activities of some Standing Commissions in which it had a special interest. The Chinese participation finally ended in 1966.

North Korea has held observer status since 1957 and its participation has also been irregular. Mongolia and Vietnam became observers in 1958. Mongolia became a full member as early as 1962, while Vietnam's admission to full membership took place in 1978.

Cuban representatives began participating in the activities of some Standing Commissions in March 1963; Cuban observers were present in 1965 at the 19th Session of the Assembly. As mentioned above, Cuba's full participation began in 1972.

Observers from Laos and Angola were present for the first time at the 30th Session of the Assembly in 1976, at which Korean and Vietnamese representatives were also present. Observers from these four countries also participated in the 31st Session of the Assembly in Warsaw, in June 1977. The 32nd Session of the Assembly – held in Bucharest in June 1978 – was attended by observers from Laos and Angola and, for the first time, by observers from Ethiopia; Vietnam's entry into CMEA was announced during the Session.

The People's Democratic Republic of Yemen was granted observer status in June 1979 by the 33rd Session of the Assembly.

7. THE AGREEMENT ON YUGOSLAVIA'S PARTICIPATION

Yugoslavia's participation in the activities of CMEA has been marked by a series of events. After a first attempt in 1949, which failed for political reasons, Yugoslavia was admitted as an observer in 1956 and retained that status until 1958, participating in two Assembly sessions.

In 1959 Yugoslavia made unsuccessful attempts to resume its participation in the activities of certain organs of the Council; the CMEA Secretariat stopped sending Yugoslavia invitations to participate in these activities.

In its turn, in December 1961 it was Yugoslavia which rejected a proposal to join CMEA as a full member.[12]

The matter of Yugoslavia's participation in the Council came up again in 1963 and was considered by the parties concerned.

Finally, on 17 September 1964, an agreement was signed in Moscow to govern Yugoslavia's participation in certain CMEA activities; this agreement was later ratified by both parties and entered into force on 24 April 1965.[13]

After a short Preamble, in which the contracting parties refer to the principles of full equality, national interest and mutual advantage, Article 1 indicates the areas chosen for cooperation: foreign trade, monetary and financial affairs, ferrous and non-ferrous metals, engineering, chemicals, and scientific and technical research.

Article 1 further specifies that other areas may be added to those specifically envisaged, as the need arises. In effect, the economic cooperation between CMEA and Yugoslavia now also extends to fields such as agriculture, electric power, petroleum and gas, transportation, the construction industry, radio and electronics, water management, geology, statistics and legal problems.

To put into concrete effect the cooperation envisaged in Article 1, Article 2 of the Agreement provides for the participation of Yugoslav representatives in the activities of the appropriate Standing Commissions and other organs of the Council. When problems concerning Yugoslavia are discussed by the Assembly or by the Executive Committee, Yugoslav representatives are to be invited to participate therein.

Under Article 3, the decisions and recommendations of the competent organs of the Council concerning Yugoslavia are to be adopted with the concurrence of the representatives of that country, which in effect is to be regarded – pursuant to paragraph 3, Article IV of the CMEA Charter, as an 'interested country'. For its part, Yugoslavia is to implement the decisions of the Council's organs, complying with the same rules applicable to member-countries (Article 4).

Article 5 of the Agreement provides that Yugoslavia may adhere subsequently to recommendations and decisions previously adopted by the organs of CMEA, but only with the consent of the interested countries.

Provision is made, on a basis of reciprocity, for the exchange of documentation and information on matters of common interest between CMEA and Yugoslavia, with the explicit undertaking (Article 9) to keep secret materials and information not intended to be disclosed publicly.

Under Article 11, the Agreement may be denounced by either contracting party by notice to be given at least six months in advance. However, any cooperation between Yugoslavia and Council members already in progress on concrete matters under duly accepted recommendations may continue regularly beyond the end of the said notice period, provided no country interested in it objects and demands that such cooperation be limited or ended.

During the life of the CMEA-Yugoslavia Agreement, cooperation has been expanding considerably and has concerned and concerns projects and programmes of no little importance in many sectors.

Also to be noted is the interest shown by Yugoslavia in a number of projects which have been under way in the last few years within the framework of the Comprehensive Programme. The latter explicitly provides – in paragraphs 6 and 7, Section 17, Chapter IV – for the participation of non-member-countries that share its principles and purposes and intend to cooperate, wholly or in part, in the implementation of the various measures.

8. THE COOPERATION AGREEMENT WITH FINLAND

The formula for Yugoslavia's participation in the activities of CMEA organs, while in many respects affording significant advantages to the parties concerned, was not and could not be easily extended to other non-member-countries interested in some form of cooperation with the Council. In effect, it appears that direct participation in the activities of the Council's organs, although limited to the study and discussion of specific matters, is to be considered as essentially limited – for a number of reasons – to other socialist countries.

Since the Yugoslav case appeared in many respects bound to remain unique, it became necessary for CMEA to explore new ways to establish fruitful relations with non-member-countries. In this respect, the agreement concluded with Finland constitutes a noteworthy example.

In the first place, this is the first agreement concluded by CMEA with a non-socialist country, and as such capable of providing a useful term of reference for agreements with other non-socialist countries.

On the other hand, if one considers the particular position of Finland and its close ties with the Soviet Union in various sectors of the economy, science and technology, this agreement can be considered as hardly capable of being applied to other situations.

The CMEA-Finland Cooperation Agreement, signed in Moscow on 16 May 1973, ratified by the parties in the following month and entered into force on 14 July, consists of nine short articles and one Annex.

The Preamble to the Agreement refers to peaceful coexistence which constitutes, according to the Soviet view, the governing principle of the relations between countries having different socio-economic systems. Reference is also made to the readiness of CMEA countries to develop economic relations with other countries on the basis of equality, mutual advantage and non-interference in internal affairs.

The purpose of the Agreement, according to Article 1, is to develop multilateral economic, scientific and technical cooperation between Finland and the CMEA countries; this cooperation is to extend to all sectors of economic life that are of mutual interest, including industry, science and technology.

In order to determine the opportunities for the development of this cooperation and to put it concretely into effect, a special Joint Commission is created, formed by representatives of Finland and member-countries of CMEA (Article 2).

Like the organs of the Council, the Joint Commission, under Article 3, may make recommendations on matters concerning economic, scientific and technical cooperation and adopt decisions on organizational and procedural matters, such actions to be taken with the consent of all interested countries.

Again according to Article 3, the recommendations accepted by Finland and by the interested CMEA members are to be implemented through agreements, either multilateral or bilateral as required.

The Commission is to carry out its activities in conformity with the rules set forth in the Terms of Reference annexed to the Agreement, which constitute an integral part thereof (Article 5).

Any disputes arising with respect to the implementation of the

Agreement are to be settled by way of negotiations among the contracting parties (Article 7).

It is important to note that, according to Article 8, the Agreement had first to be approved by the Council's members and then be ratified by CMEA and Finland; it entered into force 30 days after the exchange of the instruments of ratification. The Agreement may be amended or supplemented by the same procedure.

The Agreement, of unlimited duration, may be denounced (according to Article 9) at six months' notice; this, however, is not to affect the cooperation already in progress under duly accepted recommendations, unless the parties explicitly decide otherwise.

The Terms of Reference included in the Annex to the Agreement regulate in detail the operations of the Joint Commission, which is required to meet at least once a year and may create temporary or standing working groups, as needed.

To date, the Joint Commission has held some meetings and created sectoral working groups for the study of the areas of cooperation. The latter, which now concerns foreign trade, engineering, chemicals, paper, transport, standardization and statistics, is developing on both bilateral and multilateral levels. Some agreements and protocols on specific problems have already been signed, and others are at an advanced stage of drafting. Efforts are also being made to ensure the uniformity of the period covered by the long-term agreements between Finland and the member-countries of CMEA.

9. THE COOPERATION AGREEMENT WITH IRAQ

Some developing countries have also shown, in recent years, an increasing interest in the activities of CMEA and a wish to establish ties with it. For their part, the Council's member-countries have been growing increasingly aware of the desirability of a less-fragmentary relationship with the developing world.

These requirements found their first concrete expression, in 1975, in the conclusion of cooperation agreements between the Council and, respectively, Iraq and Mexico.

The Agreement with Iraq, concluded in Moscow on 4 July 1975, was a landmark, since it was the first time that CMEA had established a stable cooperative relationship with a nation of the Third World.

The choice of Iraq certainly was not and could not be the product of a simple set of coincidences. Back in 1969 some CMEA members had signed agreements with Iraq for the purpose of assisting that country in the development of its rich petroleum resources; several other important agreements for economic, scientific and technical cooperation were signed in the years immediately following. In a certain sense, therefore, the CMEA-Iraq Agreement reflected the parties' will to intensify and place on a tendentially multilateral plane cooperation which had already been forming on a bilateral level.

As a first approximation, it may be stated that the CMEA-Iraq Agreement duplicates, in its general outlines, the provisions of the Agreement with Finland discussed above. This is fairly readily understandable if it is considered that these international instruments are limited, in substance, to providing a framework within which cooperation can then develop in conformity with prevailing interests and requirements.

The Preamble to the Agreement with Iraq duplicates the formulations contained in the Agreement with Finland but omits references to the principle of 'peaceful coexistence'.

According to Article 1, the purpose of the Agreement is the development of multilateral economic, scientific and technical cooperation in all fields of mutual interest for the parties. As in the case of the Finland Agreement, Article 2 provides for the establishment of a Joint Commission. The latter, indeed, appears to be the most effective instrument for carrying out a systematic review of opportunities for cooperation and for putting them into effect.

The Commission adopts, depending on subject-matter, decisions or recommendations; the duly accepted recommendations are to be implemented by means of multilateral or bilateral agreements (Article 3).

Special mention should be made – for they are not to be found in either the previous Agreement with Finland or in the subsequent one with Mexico – of the provisions of Article 7, which explicitly allow the Council members on the one hand and Iraq on the other to maintain direct relations and enter into bilateral agreements in sectors of the economy, science and technology not covered by the Agreement.

Article 8 – like Article 7 of the Agreement with Finland – provides that any disputes on the implementation of the Agreement are to be settled by way of negotiations among the contracting parties.

Article 9 contains an innovation from the Agreement with Finland, since it provides that, in connection with the progressive expansion and intensification of multilateral cooperation, the parties are to adopt appropriate measures for the further improvement and development of the organizational forms, conditions and methods of that cooperation.

As in the case of the Finland Agreement, the Agreement was to be ratified by CMEA and Iraq after approval by the Council's member-countries; it entered into force on the day of the exchange of the ratification instruments (Article 10).

The Agreement, concluded for an indefinite time, may be denounced at a minimum of six months' notice; denunciation is not to affect the rights and obligations deriving from the agreements concluded between Council members and Iraq (Article 11).

10. THE COOPERATION AGREEMENT WITH MEXICO

The Agreement concluded by CMEA with Mexico on 13 August, 1975, slightly more than one month after that with Iraq discussed above, follows what, in a certain sense, may be defined as a tested model, based essentially on the creation of a Joint Commission, charged with determining the possible sectors of cooperation and with organizing them in practice.

At the same time, the Agreement with Mexico, although based on criteria which are already known and have been discussed above, does present certain noteworthy aspects, especially in view of possible future developments.

As regards the Preamble to this Agreement, mention should first of all be made to the references on the one hand to the principle of peaceful coexistence (already included in the Finland Agreement) and on the other to the Charter of Economic Rights and Duties of States, whose provisions are said to have inspired the cooperation promoted by this Agreement. Again in accordance with the Preamble, the Council members pay great attention to the development of trade and of economic, scientific and technological cooperation with the developing countries.

Also to be noted in Article 1 – which sets out as the basic purpose of the Agreement the establishment and promotion of multilateral economic, scientific and technical cooperation – is the explicit definition of Mexico as a 'developing country'.

The latter statement, as well as the previous references to the strengthening of economic relations between socialist countries and developing countries, is probably designed to preconstitute, through the Agreement with Mexico, a model agreement which might readily be extended, with any required changes and additions, to other countries of the Third World desirous of establishing ties with CMEA.

For the rest, as indicated above, the CMEA-Mexico Agreement is largely patterned after the other two Agreements discussed in the preceding sections. Provision is made for the establishment of the Joint Commission (Article 2), which shall adopt decisions and recommendations; the latter, if duly accepted by the parties concerned, shall be implemented through bilateral or multilateral agreements (Article 3). Here again, any problems concerning the implementation of the Agreement are to be settled by way of negotiations among the parties (Article 7). The Agreement shall be ratified by Mexico and, after approval by the member-countries, by CMEA; it shall enter into force 30 days after the exchange of the instruments of ratification (Article 8). Each party may denounce the Agreement at six months' notice; this, however, shall not necessarily affect the cooperation already began on the basis of Joint Commission recommendations accepted by the interested parties (Article 9).

11. RELATIONS WITH INTERNATIONAL ORGANIZATIONS

After having discussed, with reference to general principles and practice, CMEA relations with non-member-countries, it seems appropriate to review briefly the relations maintained by the Council with other international entities. In this field CMEA activity has shown significant developments in the last few years. Indeed, the striving for contacts and ties with other international organizations has long been a marked feature of the Council's activities.

Article XII of the Charter is entirely devoted to relations with international organizations, and the provisions contained therein were supplemented in various respects on the last amendment to the Charter. This Article states that the Council may establish and maintain relations with the organs of the United Nations, with *specialized international organizations* and with other international organizations. The character and form of these relations are to be established by the Council in agreement with the *competent organs of the United Nations* and with the international organizations, *especially by concluding agreements.*

As will be recalled, the Council's power to conclude agreements with international organizations is explicitly provided for in the second part of paragraph 2, Article III.

The purpose of the Charter amendments of 1974, quoted above in italics, was to better define the pattern and conditions of CMEA external relations.

In concrete terms, CMEA interest in relations with other international organizations dates back to the mid-1950s; this interest was naturally first of all directed towards the 'economic organizations of the United Nations', according to the terminology used in the original 1959 version of the Charter.

In this context, particular importance was attached to the UN Economic Commission for Europe, which the Council had, in fact, first contacted in 1955. In 1959 these contacts also received recognition from a legal standpoint and have subsequently developed systematically since the early 1960s. At last, in 1975, the Council obtained advisory status with the Commission.

At present the sectors in which cooperation between CMEA and the ECE is most active are those of statistics, the construction industry, coal mining, steelmaking and waters.

The exchange of documents and information, the presence of representatives at the meetings of certain specialized agencies, as well as participation in seminars of various kinds, have given the two organizations a better and more detailed knowledge of each other's activities and spheres of interest.

This experience, although on a more limited scale, has been repeated with other regional Economic Commissions of the UN, especially those for Asia and Africa.

CMEA representatives regularly attend the meetings of the UN Economic and Social Council (ECOSOC), to which information is supplied about various activities, in particular concerning the efforts for the coordination of the national economic plans of member-countries.

In 1974 the 29th Session of the UN General Assembly accorded to CMEA (as it did to the EEC) observer status.

The United Nations Conference on Trade and Development (UNCTAD) also maintains contacts with CMEA, whose representatives were present at the first session of the Conference (Geneva, 1964); and at subsequent sessions, and also attended various meetings within the framework of UNCTAD.

Among the other organizations connected with the UN and with which CMEA has established relations, mention should be made of the Industrial Development Organization (UNIDO), the Educational, Scientific and Cultural Organization (UNESCO), the Food and Agriculture Organization (FAO) and the International Atomic Energy Agency (IAEA); CMEA signed an agreement with the last-named on 26 September 1975. Also to be noted is the cooperation agreement concluded in Budapest on 23 June 1975 between CMEA and the Danube Commission.

Finally, mention should be made of the relations which CMEA has established, in different forms, with socialist 'international economic organizations'. As is known, the general term 'international economic organization' covers a diversified and complex reality, embracing many organizations often quite different from one another and whose legal status and activities are not always easily definable. It will suffice to say that at present CMEA maintains relations with about 30 of these organizations, with a view to promoting the exchange of documentation and information and the coordination of activities in sectors of common interest. Representatives of international economic organizations to which CMEA member-countries belong are usually invited to attend the meetings of the Assembly and, particularly, of the Standing Commissions and Committees.

Among the most significant agreements concluded in this area mention may be made of: the Protocol on the nature and forms of cooperation between CMEA and the International Bank for Economic Cooperation (IBEC), signed in Moscow on 20 July 1970; the Protocol on cooperation between CMEA and the International Investment Bank (IIB), signed in Moscow on 6 May 1972; the Protocol for cooperation between CMEA and the International Centre for Scientific and Technical Cooperation

(Moscow, 6 May 1972); the Protocol on the nature and forms of cooperation between CMEA and *Interkhim* (Moscow, 17 May 1972); the Protocol on the nature and forms of cooperation between CMEA and *Intermetall* (Moscow, 9 July 1970).

12. PROBLEMS AND PERSPECTIVES OF THE DIALOGUE WITH THE EEC

As regards Western Europe, apart from contacts with the Nordic Council since 1965, CMEA has encountered and still encounters quite a few difficulties in its efforts at establishing relations with the region's economic organizations, and in particular with the European Economic Community (EEC). In many respects and for many reasons, the latter is CMEA's natural interlocutor.

In spite of this, a number of obstacles – some of which are of an essentially political nature – are still hampering the effective development of a dialogue between the EEC and CMEA, a dialogue which appears to be both possible and necessary.[14]

Western observers have usually stressed an essential difference between the EEC and CMEA: the international legal personality of the former which is not possessed by the latter. In this connection, it has already been stressed in the preceding pages that it cannot be denied that CMEA does possess certain attributes of international personality, among which is the capacity to conclude international agreements with other international organizations and with non-member-countries. The Charter amendments of 1974 were significant from this standpoint, undoubtedly strengthening the Council's position.

Much more substantial on concrete grounds than the problem of international legal personality appears to be the objection concerning the respective competences of the two organizations in the area of trade policy: while there appears to be no doubt about the EEC 'external' competence in this field, the scope of CMEA is said to be strictly limited to trade among member-countries. In this respect, too, it is helpful to refer to the statements contained in the Charter and in the Comprehensive Programme.

As mentioned before, Article III, paragraph 1(*d*) of the Charter states that the Council shall assist the member-countries 'in elaborating, coordinating and carrying out joint measures for: . . . the development of trade and exchange of services between member-countries and between them and other countries'. Furthermore, under paragraph 1(*e*) of the same Article, the Council may take such other actions as may be necessary for the achievement of its purposes under the Charter.

Even more significant are the statements contained in the Comprehensive Programme – Chapter I, Section 1, paragraph 3 – to the effect that, with a view to abolishing 'discrimination' exercised against the socialist states by international economic, scientific and technical organizations, CMEA member-countries 'will coordinate their *foreign economic policy* in the interests of normalizing international commercial and economic relations, especially with a view to abolishing discrimination in this sphere' (italics added). The importance of provisions of this kind appears evident if one considers the fact that negotiations between the Community and CMEA would probably deal, *inter alia*, with the measures still applied in the EEC countries on the goods originating from the Council's member-countries.[15] On the other hand, it must be stressed that EEC has no authority whatsoever in industrial cooperation issues, its activity being confined to trade matters only.

From a chronological standpoint, it should be recalled that the dialogue between the EEC and CMEA has now been in progress for some years. In August 1973, the Secretary of CMEA unofficially suggested to the then President of the Council of the European Communities that contacts between the two organizations would be desirable. The Council of the Communities expressed a favourable opinion on this initiative and reconfirmed its positive attitude in May 1974. In September of that year the President of the Community Commission was invited to Moscow for the purpose of establishing contacts with CMEA. In the following month of November the Community, while accepting the invitation, stressed the desirability of having the planned high-level contacts preceded by adequate preparatory work to be carried out by officials of the two organizations, with a view to clearly defining the sectors and conditions of mutual cooperation.

Between 4 and 6 February 1975, a delegation of the Community Commission, headed by the Director-General of External Relations, met in Moscow with a delegation of the CMEA Secretariat, to start an initial exchange of information and possibly create the bases for regular contacts.

On 16 February 1976, in Luxemburg, the Chairman of CMEA's Executive Committee delivered to the President of the Community's Council of Ministers a message proposing the conclusion of an agreement on the basic principles of mutual relations. Enclosed with the message was a draft agreement to be concluded between CMEA and its members on the one side and the EEC and its members on the other.

The draft agreement proposed by CMEA listed certain areas in which EEC–CMEA relations could fruitfully develop, such as trade and economic cooperation, standardization, environmental protection, statistics and long-term demand and consumption forecasts (Article 3).

Regarding the forms which EEC–CMEA relations might assume, the draft agreement referred to the common study of problems, the exchange of information, systematic contacts between representatives and officials of the two organizations, and the organization of conferences, seminars and symposia (Article 4). The draft agreement then referred, among other things, to the principles of the most-favoured-nation (Article 6) and of non-discrimination in the application of prohibitions and restrictions on imports and exports (Article 7).

References followed to the trade in agricultural products (Article 9) and to the joint study of monetary, financial and credit matters (Article 10). The EEC was to extend the concession of generalized preferences to the developing countries of CMEA (Article 12).

Finally, a specially established Joint Commission was to supervise the implementation of the Agreement (Article 14).

In November 1976, the EEC transmitted its reply to the proposals outlined above. According to the Community, simple working relations could be established between the two organizations, with exchanges of information and contacts in the areas of statistics, economic planning and the environment. Trade relations, on the other hand, should be regulated by agreements between the EEC on the one side and individual CMEA members on the other, according to the November 1974 Community proposal; industrial and financial cooperation was to be regulated by agreements to be concluded by individual members of CMEA and individual members of the EEC.

In April 1977, CMEA – after considering and discussing the Community's letter and the draft agreement enclosed thereto and taking note of the substantial divergences existing between the two organizations concerning the forms and conditions of future mutual relations – suggested an exchange of ideas towards a preliminary clarification of lines and criteria to be followed in further negotiations. The proposed exchange of opinions was to take place between the Chairman of the CMEA Executive Committee and the President of the Community's Council of Ministers, thus excluding the EEC Commission from the contacts.

The idea of the meeting was accepted by the Community in July 1977, with the condition that the President of the Council of Ministers would confine himself to introducing to the Chairman of CMEA's Executive Committee the Vice-President of the European Commission, the latter being responsible for conducting all stages of the negotiations on behalf of the EEC. The talks took place in Brussels on 21 September 1977, following the procedure proposed by the Community.

The real beginning of the negotiations, however, was in Moscow from 29–30 May 1978. A meeting of experts of the EEC and CMEA took place in Brussels in July 1978 to define more precisely the nature and forms of the cooperation agreement. Another meeting between the Secretary of CMEA and the Vice-President of the EEC Commission took place in Brussels from 22 to 25 November 1978. Detailed counter-proposals concerning trade relations between the two organizations were put forward by the CMEA Secretary in June 1979. In response to this move, the EEC presented another draft agreement—modifying to some extent the one transmitted in November 1976—on the occasion of a meeting in Moscow from 26 to 28 November 1979.

In order to overcome persistent divergences other meetings will follow on both political and technical levels; as of now, their outcome appears rather difficult to predict.

NOTES TO CHAPTER 4

1. The term 'socialist states' is applied here to countries which adhere to Marxist ideology and whose economic system is based on the collective ownership of the basic means of production. Until the complete achievement of Communism, the final goal of socialism, the people's collective ownership in practice assumes two mediated institutional forms, i.e. *state* ownership (comprising, in general, mines, industries, transport, trade, banks and part of agriculture), and *cooperative* ownership (mainly agriculture and handicrafts).
2. See J. Caillot, *Le CAEM*, op. cit, p. 31 ff.
3. As noted previously, it seems that socialist states alone can be regarded as eligible for admission.
4. J. Caillot, *Le CAEM*, op. cit., p. 35. It is hardly necessary to point out that

the 'veto' referred to here is essentially of a political rather than legal character, since no real veto is involved. The member voting against the admission of a given state uses exactly the *same* right exercised by the members voting in favour and not a distinct and supplementary power.

5. The right of unilateral withdrawal is said to be founded on the clause *rebus sic stantibus*. For an analysis from the viewpoint of Soviet doctrine, see A. Talalajew, *Das Recht der internationalen Verträge*, Berlin, 1977, p. 176 ff.
6. M. Kaser, *Comecon*, op. cit., p. 96.
7. See the Albanian Government's communiqué in *Zëri i popullit*, 6 June 1962.
8. M. Kaser, *Comecon*, op. cit., p. 96.
9. N. Faddeev, *Sovet*, op. cit., p. 52.
10. N. Faddeev (op. cit., loc. cit.) states that 'at present [1974] nine member-countries *actively* cooperate with the Council' (italics added).
11. See W. Seiffert, *Rechtsfragen der Aussenbeziehungen des Rates für gegenseitige Wirtschaftshilfe*, Göttingen, 1975; J. Rajski, 'Rozwój miedzynarodowych stosunków umownych RWPG z państwami trzecimi', in *Państwo i prawo*, 1976, No. 7, pp. 40–51; H. de Fiumel, 'The CMEA in International Relations', in *Studies on International Relations*, 1976, No. 7, pp. 60–78.
12. It appears that, on this occasion, Yugoslavia was offered the alternative of either participating as a full member or of being totally excluded from CMEA.
13. It should be noted that on 24 April 1965, the agreement came into force *permanently*, having been implemented *provisionally* from the day it was signed.
14. See G. Schiavone, 'The EEC-COMECON Dialogue: Towards a Recognition of Realities in Europe?', in *Comunità internazionale*, 1976, No. 2, pp. 311–20; E. Hewett, 'Recent Developments in East–West European Economic Relations', op. cit., pp. 174–98; A. Lebahn, 'RGW und EG. Faktoren des Ost-West-Handels', in *Aussenpolitik*, 1978, No. 2, p. 123 ff.; E. Kirschen, 'Effects of the European Economic Communities and the CMEA on East–West Economic Relations', in N. G. Watts (ed.), *Economic Relations Between East and West*, Proceedings of a Conference held in Dresden by the International Economic Association, London, 1978, pp. 106–19; M. Senin, 'The Role of the European Communities and the CMEA in Promoting Economic Relations between East and West", in N. G. Watts (ed.), op. cit., pp. 120–31.
15. It should be noted that – in connection with the transfer to the Commission of the national competences in the area of external trade relations – the EEC transmitted in November 1974 to the individual state-trading countries a draft bilateral trade agreement containing the basic lines of future long-term agreements. No CMEA country accepted the agreement proposed by EEC. However, negotiations started on textiles and fishing. On 10 November 1976, Romania signed with the Community an agreement on textile products; this agreement is the first concluded by the EEC with a CMEA country. On 3 April 1978, the Community signed a non-preferential trade agreement with the People's Republic of China; the agreement came into force on 1 June 1978. In early 1980, a special Joint Commission, formed by representatives of Romania and the EEC member-countries, has been set up.

5 The Institutional Structure

1. HISTORICAL EVOLUTION

In the course of three decades of life, CMEA institutional structure, rather complex in many respects, has undergone major changes. Certain organs have had their powers gradually reduced – or, as will be seen in the case of the Conference of Representatives, have been phased out altogether – while other organs have been created and, in certain instances, have grown increasingly important.

The present organs of the Council are in effect the product of a process of adjustment of the institutional structure to the changing requirements that have emerged during the life of the organization. This adjustment process also reveals a gradual transition from extremely simplified structures that allowed only embryonic forms of cooperation, to increasingly complex structures, as CMEA's activities turned increasingly towards goals of integration.

It will be useful, before analysing each of the present major organs of the Council, to review briefly the main steps in this institutional evolution, made possible – or at least easier – by the flexibility and pragmatism which, from the start, have characterized the process of development of economic cooperation among socialist countries.

As has already been noted, during the first period of CMEA's life, between 1949 and early 1954, the activities of the organization were comparatively limited and developed on largely bilateral bases.

Under these circumstances, it is easy to understand how the need to develop a strong institutional framework was little felt. The first three meetings of the Assembly, or 'Session of the Council', enabled CMEA to deal, although to a limited extent, with some basic issues pertaining to trade and to scientific and technical cooperation among member-countries.

From the end of 1950 to the early months of 1954, the Council's activity appeared to grow even more limited, to the extent that during this period the Assembly held no meetings. The limited organizational duties connected with the practical work of CMEA were performed by a special office, located in Moscow, formed by representatives of all member-countries and assisted by a secretariat with a very small staff.

The 4th Session of the Assembly, held in the spring of 1954, marked the beginning of CMEA's second period of existence, characterized by the intensification and development of many aspects of the organization's work. The new impetus given to the Council's activities could not fail to have direct repercussions on the still embryonic institutional structure. An organ was created, in the first place, to ensure the continuity of CMEA action during the intervals between Assembly sessions: the Conference of Representatives, made up of one representative of each member-country, which was to meet, whenever necessary, to follow up the practical implementation of the Assembly's decisions, to consider proposals and to deal with lesser matters in the field of cooperation.

Each representative was required to have a deputy, assisted by experts, at the headquarters of CMEA Secretariat. In effect, again during the 4th Session, there was established, in order to ensure effectively the practical functioning of the Council, an actual Secretariat, a largely technical organ composed of the Secretary, a number of assistant secretaries and the necessary staff.

The intensification of relations between member-countries and the resulting development of cooperation in various branches of industry and of the economy in general led progressively to the formation, within the Conference of Representatives, of special working groups and *ad hoc* committees, responsible for considering, at the level of experts and leading figures in specific areas, questions of a largely technical nature. These working groups and committees were transformed and institutionalized in the course of the 7th Session of the Assembly, held in Berlin in the spring of 1956. Increasing requirements, in effect, called for further changes in the Council's structure, in the sense of a greater articulation and of a more adequate and definite division of tasks among the various organs.[1]

To this end, twelve Standing Commissions were established, eleven of which were responsible respectively for the following sectors: agriculture, coal, electric power, oil and gas, chemistry, steel, nonferrous metals, engineering, timber and cellulose, geology and forestry;[2] the twelfth Commission was given general tasks in the area of foreign trade coordination.

While the groups and temporary committees usually met in Moscow, the Standing Commissions were located each in a capital city of a member-country, thus initiating an interesting experiment in decentralization. Thus, each member-country, excluding Albania, found itself acting as host to at least one Commission, whose competence usually covered the sector or sectors of greatest importance for the country's economic life.

The spring of 1958 saw the start of a new period (the third) for CMEA, characterized by an effort to apply more consistently the principles of the international socialist division of labour, mainly by bringing about a higher degree of industrial specialization in individual areas of production.

From the standpoint of institutional evolution, 1958 may be seen as of considerable importance for two reasons: the adoption of decisions directly pertaining to the Council's activities by the 'summit' of Communist parties and the change in the number and competence of the Standing Commissions.

Mention should be made in the first place of the meeting, held in the spring of 1958, by the Conference of the First Secretaries of the Communist and workers' parties of the member-countries of CMEA. The Conference, which preceded by one month the 9th Session of the Council's Assembly, considered the major problems of cooperation within CMEA and stressed the desirability of intensifying and extending the organization's activities.

The decisions that emerged from the summit of the Communist parties were fully reflected in the measures adopted, a few weeks later, by the 9th Session of the Assembly. In this way, the top-ranking representatives of the Communist parties of the CMEA member-countries substantially intervened – by laying down both basic policies and concrete directives – in the process of development of economic cooperation. The nature of the functions performed, on the more properly institutional level, by the Conference of 1958 and by other meetings that followed it, will be considered later. For the moment it will suffice to stress the participation in CMEA management, at a particularly delicate stage,[3] by an organ completely foreign to it.

Again in 1958, during the 9th and 10th Sessions, new Standing

Commissions were created, while some of the existing ones were closed down.

The institutional framework which had been progressively forming during the 1950s found its formal consecration in the CMEA Charter, adopted by the 12th Session of the Assembly in December 1959 and which came into force in April 1960.

According to Article V, paragraph 1 of the Charter, in its original version, the principal organs of the Council were: the Assembly, the Conference of Representatives, the Standing Commissions and the Secretariat. In addition, paragraph 2 of the same Article provided that 'such other organs as may prove to be necessary' could be established.

In the years immediately following, substantial changes occurred in CMEA, which, during 1962, led to the introduction of several amendments to the Charter. The importance of these changes was such as to constitute another turning point in the life of CMEA, opening a new period of activity: the fourth.

From the middle of 1962, the Soviet Union, with help mainly from Poland, developed a programme intended to encourage more advanced forms of cooperation, through a relaunching of the activities of CMEA and the strengthening of its structure, functions and tasks.

In the institutional area, one highly significant development in this respect was the replacement in June 1962 of the Conference of Representatives – created in 1954 and explicitly recognized by the Charter in 1959 – with the Executive Committee, a new organ endowed with broader competence and powers, as well as with greater prestige because of the higher rank of its members.

As it will emerge later when the various organs of CMEA are discussed, the creation of the Executive Committee was largely due to the need to strengthen the Council and to attempt to invest it with a 'supranational' character, even of a somewhat vague kind.[4] Besides the Executive Committee, and under it, a Bureau for integrated planning problems was created. The number of Standing Commissions was also increased.

Of outstanding importance, in the context of the events outlined above, was the role played by the Conference of the representatives of the Communist and workers' parties of the member-countries of the Council. As mentioned before, it was the Conference that decided, at the meeting held on 6–7 June 1962, the changes to be introduced in the Council's Charter; the

Assembly of CMEA, meeting in a very brief special session on June 7, adopted the measures required to implement the Conference's decisions.

Following those of 1958 and 1962, other meetings of the Communist parties' summit specifically devoted to CMEA problems were held in 1963, 1969 and 1973.[5]

More specifically, in July 1963 the Conference of the First Secretaries of the Communist and workers' parties and of the heads of government of the Council's member-countries discussed the latest developments in cooperation.

While the Conference was in session, a meeting was held in Moscow by the 18th Session of the Assembly, which decided to create the International Bank for Economic Cooperation and to set up other Standing Commissions.

During the remainder of the 1960s, there were no particularly significant institutional developments in CMEA.

The dramatic events which characterized the year 1968 in some East European countries, especially Czechoslovakia, brought the first twenty years of CMEA life to an end on a note of conflict and deep uncertainty.

A new period for CMEA – the fifth, according to the subdivision adopted here – began with the 23rd Session of the Assembly in April 1969. At that Session the foundations were laid for a relaunching of the organization, stressing the need for closer cooperation among member-countries in an 'integrationist' prospect. It should be noted that in the spring of 1969 the Communist parties' summit did not precede the meeting of the Assembly, but constituted an actual special meeting of the latter (the 23rd 'Special' Session). Once the Session's work was done and the economic issues covered, the Party representatives turned to the consideration of strictly political problems.

Special mention should be made of the establishment by the Executive Committee, at the end of 1969, of an important subsidiary organ specifically responsible for dealing with the legal issues raised by the development of cooperation, i.e. the Conference of representatives of CMEA member-countries for legal problems.

The 24th Session of the Assembly, held in Warsaw in May 1970, created the International Investment Bank; it also decided to set up an important international institute to study the economic problems of the world socialist system.

The 25th Session, held in Bucharest in July 1971, approved the Comprehensive Programme, the importance of which has already been repeatedly stressed. As previously noted, in paragraph 2, Section 1, Chapter I of the Comprehensive Programme, it is explicitly stated that socialist economic integration is carried out on a fully voluntary basis and that it 'is not accompanied by the creation of any supranational organs'.

From the standpoint of institutional evolution, it should be recalled that, again during the 25th Session, for the purpose of intensifying and improving the coordination of planning activities and promoting the effective participation of the central planning bodies in such activities, there was established a special Committee for cooperation in the field of planning. The existing Bureau of the Executive Committee for integrated planning problems was converted into the Bureau of the Committee for cooperation in the field of planning, with the rank of 'permanent working organ' of the latter.[6]

In addition, to strengthen cooperation in the field of research, the CMEA Standing Commission for the coordination of scientific and technical research was restructured and converted into a Committee for scientific and technical cooperation. A new Standing Commission was also created, with specific competence in the field of post and telecommunications.

In July 1973, in the Crimea, the summit of the Communist and workers' parties of the member-countries intervened once again authoritatively to indicate to CMEA, at a time of uncertainty and crisis, the lines to be followed.

The 28th Session of the Assembly – held in Sofia in June 1974 – made explicit reference to the decisions on cooperation and integration adopted by the Crimea Conference of the leaders of the Communist and workers' parties.

The 28th Session marked a significant turning point for CMEA activities and prospects and it may be said to have opened a new period, the sixth, in the organization's life, a period which is still in progress.

To the two Committees already existing and operating, respectively, in the fields of planning and coordination of research, there was added by the Assembly a new Committee for cooperation in the field of material and technical supply, charged with dealing, in particular, with matters connected with raw-material supplies and utilization of energy sources.

As previously noticed, one of the most important results of this Session was the adoption of several amendments to the CMEA Charter, of major importance also from the institutional standpoint. In particular, the three Committees already mentioned moved up from the rank of *subsidiary* organs to the much more important one of *principal* organs of CMEA.

The 29th Session, held in June 1975 in Budapest, further broadened the institutional framework, creating two new Standing Commissions concerned respectively with civil aviation and with health.

In the second half of the 1970s, the necessity of strengthening the institutional mechanism of CMEA and possibly changing voting procedures has been strongly advocated by the USSR. Since the 30th Session of the Assembly in the summer of 1976, the Executive Committee has been given the task of studying adequate measures. The 32nd Session, in June 1978, adopted a set of measures further to improve the mechanism, functions and tasks of CMEA, but no major innovations or Charter amendments were introduced.

Finally, the 33rd Session (Moscow, June 1979) unanimously agreed to insert in the Charter 'more precise definitions in order to further improve the activities of CMEA and to increase the operational efficiency of its work'. The amendments have not been published so far, but it seems doubtful that they may involve a significant move towards enhanced supranational authority for CMEA organs.

2. ROLE OF THE CONFERENCE OF THE FIRST SECRETARIES OF THE COMMUNIST AND WORKERS' PARTIES

The peculiar effectiveness of the meetings of the Conference of the First Secretaries of the Communist and workers' parties in directing cooperation within CMEA has created some perplexity about how the Conference fits into the Council's institutional framework.

It appears clearly from what has been said before that the meetings of the First Secretaries of the Communist parties and of the heads of governments of the Council's member-countries are a factor of substantial weight, nor should it be forgotten that, apart from the cases in which the same person is at the same time leader of the party and head of the Government, the heads of government are always members of the Politbureau of a Party Central Committee and, as such, subordinates of the First Secretary.

The Communist parties of the member-countries, and especially the CPSU, have always played a leading role within CMEA. Apart from a series of pressures indirectly brought to bear on the Council in the first half of the 1950s, about which there is no reliable information, the weight of the 'summit' of Communist parties began to make itself felt in 1958.

As previously mentioned, the communiqué of the May 1958 Conference of party representatives indicated that the Conference had adopted certain decisions, which had been transmitted to the Assembly. For its part, the communiqué following the 9th Session of the Assembly stated that, in conformity with the resolutions of the Conference, adequate practical measures had been taken. In 1978 – twenty years later – in both the communiqué issued after the 32nd Session of the Assembly and the declaration of the heads of the national delegations it was clearly stated that the long-range cooperation programmes adopted had been 'elaborated in conformity with the resolutions of the Communist and workers' parties of the member-countries'. The communiqué also contained a clear reference to 'the agreements reached by the leaders of the fraternal parties in 1977 in the Crimea and during other meetings'. In consequence, some Western observers believe that the Conference has assumed *de facto* the role of principal organ of the Council, with a resulting diminution of the importance of the Assembly; the Conference decisions would in practice be binding on the competent organs of the Council. It is therefore believed that, while not mentioned formally in the Charter, the Conference fits into the Council's institutional structure.

This contention is indeed backed by certain evidence which, however, does not appear such as to make it fully acceptable. In fact, it appears that the Conference's resolutions concerning the major problems of cooperation which have arisen from time to time within CMEA, are to be regarded as authoritative political guidelines laid down for the organs of the Council, and not as decisions legally binding on such organs.[7]

As a matter of fact, the experience of these last few years – and not only in the socialist camp – has shown that certain periods of stagnation or even crisis in the activity of an intergovernmental organization cannot always be overcome by resort to ordinary procedures and instruments, but require extraordinary actions reconfirming, at the highest level, a political will to cooperate. The Conference has intervened in CMEA's affairs only in special circumstances, when cooperation had to be relaunched politically and new guidelines for the Council's activity issued, but it has never concerned itself regularly and continuously with the running of the Council.

3. PRESENT INSTITUTIONAL STRUCTURE

According to Article V of the Charter, as amended in 1962 and 1974, the principal organs of CMEA responsible for performing the functions and exercising the powers envisaged by Article III of the Charter are the Assembly, the Executive Committee, the Committees, the Standing Commissions and the Secretariat. It seems therefore appropriate to consider the individual organs, in order to highlight their essential features and specific competence, as they have changed in the course of the years and as indicated from time to time in the Charter's provisions.

Brief mention will also be made of the subsidiary organs which, in many respects, round off the Council's institutional machinery and enable it to meet operational requirements.

3.1. The Assembly

The whole of Article VI, which was substantially amended in the Charter revision of 1962, is devoted to the Assembly; the provisions concerning the Assembly were not amended in 1974.[8]

It should be noted here that the importance of the Assembly – which paragraph 1 of Article VI still defines as CMEA's 'supreme organ' – has been progressively decreasing, due both to the creation of the Executive Committee in 1962 and to the predominant role played, in crucial moments of the organization's life, by the Conference of the First Secretaries of the Communist and workers' parties of the member-countries.

The Assembly consists of the delegations of all Council member-countries; each delegation casts one vote.

Under paragraph 2 of Article VI, each government is free to determine as it sees fit the composition of its national delegation. The delegations of the various countries were usually headed by the respective permanent representatives to CMEA, on a deputy prime minister level; it must be stressed that in the 1970s the meetings of the Assembly have been attended by the prime ministers themselves.

Paragraph 3 of Article VI provides that regular sessions of the Assembly shall be convened once a year in the capital of each of the member-countries of the Council, under the chairmanship in turn of the head of the delegation of the host country.[9] Paragraph 4 explicitly provides for the convening of extraordinary sessions of the Assembly, at the request or with the consent of at least one-third of the members.

Under paragraph 1 of Article VI, the Assembly may discuss all questions within the competence of CMEA and adopt recommendations and decisions according to the Charter. More specifically – under paragraph 5, substantially revised in 1962 – the Assembly shall consider fundamental problems connected with economic, scientific and technical cooperation, determine major policies of the Council and consider the Executive Committee's reports on the activities of the Council.[10]

These are broad attributions, but on the whole far less significant than those vested in the Assembly prior to the 1962 Charter revision.

According to Article 3 of the Rules of Procedure, the draft preliminary agenda for each session of the Assembly is prepared by the Secretariat and, after prior approval by the Executive Committee, is sent to the member-countries at least 30 days before the opening of the ordinary session of the Assembly. The agenda includes: a) the Executive Committee's report on the activities of the Council; b) the issues whose inclusion had already been decided in previous sessions; and c) the issues proposed by any member-country, by the Executive Committee and by other organs of the Council.

3.2. The Executive Committee

The Executive Committee, created in June 1962 to replace the

Conference of Representatives and regulated by Article VII, amended in 1974, appears to be the most important organ of the Council.[11]

The Executive Committee is composed of the deputy prime ministers of the member-countries and is chaired, in turn, by one of them.[12]

In the earlier version of Article VII of the Charter, no provisions were made concerning the rank of the members of the Conference of Representatives; moreover, the representative of each country could choose to be replaced by a deputy – who had to be at all times available at Secretariat headquarters – with consequent negative repercussions on the organ's prestige and political importance.

Unlike the Conference of Representatives, for whose meetings no particular frequency was fixed, the Executive Committee, under paragraph 2 of Article VII, as amended in 1974, must meet at least once every three months.[13]

The Executive Committee, defined in paragraph 1 of Article VII as the 'principal executive organ' of the Council, is given powers much broader than those originally vested in the Conference of Representatives.

In the first place, according to paragraph 4, which contains an extensive listing of its functions, the Executive Committee 'systematically' supervises the fulfilment by member-countries of their obligations arising from the adoption of the recommendations made by the organs of the Council.

The careful and continuing supervision over the concrete implementation of the decisions of CMEA organs constitutes a factor of basic importance in the process of development of economic cooperation. Indeed, the promoters of the Charter revision of 1962 were concerned with eliminating the far-from-infrequent cases in which measures adopted by the Council, especially in the area of the division of labour and production specialization, were actually disregarded by the competent national authorities, reluctant to cease production of certain goods and begin that of others, or to cancel projects which sometimes had already been set in motion.

The task of carrying out a systematic supervision assigned to the Executive Committee is far more significant than the mere 'consideration of the proposals by member-countries, by the Standing Commissions and by the Secretariat concerning the implementation of the Assembly's decisions and recommendations' which the original version of paragraph 4 of Article VII assigned to the Conference of Representatives. The very high rank of the members of the Executive Committee may afford a political guarantee that the decisions adopted will be put into effect.

Furthermore, paragraph 4 continues, the Executive Committee shall direct work on the coordination of the national economic development plans and organize the elaboration of basic trends of a rational division of labour in key industries of the member-countries. It is unnecessary to stress the special importance of the task assigned in this area to the Executive Committee.

In addition to promoting specialization in production and industrial cooperation in the CMEA area, the Executive Committee, again according to paragraph 4, shall work out basic trends and measures for the development of trade and exchange of services, as well as scientific and technical cooperation, between member-countries.

The Executive Committee's functions also include directing the work of the Committees, of the Standing Commissions and of the Secretariat, *as well as* – according to the 1974 amendment – *of the other competent organs of the Council.*

Substantially, the Executive Committee – while limited in its operation by the unanimity rule, which does not allow it to adopt majority decisions – wields broad powers, in any event such as to enable it to take significant initiatives towards the acceleration and intensification of the cooperation and integration process.

One further aspect of the significant functions performed by the Executive Committee lies in the fact that it is now the duty of the Committee – and no longer of the Secretariat – to submit to the periodic sessions of the Assembly the report on the activities of the Council.

3.3. The Committees

The Committees, covered by Article VIII introduced with the 1974 Charter revision, constitute a major innovation in the structure of the Council, of which they have become a new principal organ.

The Committees, under paragraph 1 of the said Article VIII, are established by the Assembly to ensure a comprehensive examination and a multilateral settlement of major problems of cooperation among member-countries in the fields of the economy, science and technology. The Committees perform the functions laid down in the provisions applicable to them, as well as such other functions as may derive from the recommendations and decisions of the Assembly and of the Executive Committee.

Paragraph 2 provides that the Committees comprise the leaders of the relevant bodies of the member-countries – one representative for each country, reconfirming the principle of equality. There also emerges in this provision, with the reference to the rank of the Committee members, the familiar concern with involving in the activities and especially in the decisions of the Council's organs the top-ranking leaders of the member-countries, with a view to ensuring the political will needed to bring about the practical implementation of the said decisions.

The competence of the Committees is set forth in paragraph 3, which provides that they are empowered to: a) adopt recommendations and make decisions; b) submit proposals to the Assembly and to the Executive Committee; c) create working groups and convene scientific and technical conferences; and d) request the Standing Commissions and other relevant organs of the Council to furnish information and suggestions on matters connected with their activity. Under paragraph 4, the Committees are required to submit to the Executive Committee annual reports on their activities.

The Committees – of which there are now three – seem bound to carry out functions of major importance in promoting the attainment of CMEA objectives.

The Committee for cooperation in planning activities – set up in July 1971 under an Assembly decision – is responsible for ensuring the effective participation of member-countries in the difficult and delicate stage of implementation of the guidelines of the Comprehensive Programme. The Statute on this Committee[14] specifically indicates as its principal function that of identifying and seeking solutions for the main problems requiring a multilateral approach to cooperation in the fundamental economic sectors. It is to be stressed that the Statute mentions among the Committee's purposes the promotion of a faster growth of the less-industrialized member-countries. As mentioned before, this very important Committee is assisted in its activities by a special Bureau, as its permanent working organ.

The Committee systematically observes the fulfilment by member-countries of the obligations arising out of its own recommendations and of the recommendations of the Assembly and of the Executive Committee adopted at its instance.

The Committee for scientific and technical cooperation – also set up in July 1971 – is responsible for facilitating and encouraging, in the area of its competence, the attainment of the goals set forth in the Comprehensive Programme; the development of scientific and technical cooperation is pursued by the Committee on both bilateral and multilateral levels.[15] The Committee has an important permanent working organ, the Council on matters related to the conservation and improvement of the environment.

The Committee for cooperation in material and technical supply, since its establishment in 1974, has found itself dealing with difficult major problems on a multilateral level;[16] this Committee will play an important role in ensuring for all member-countries of CMEA adequate and timely supplies, especially in the field of energy sources.

3.4. The Standing (Permanent) Commissions

The Standing Commissions – governed by Article IX of the Charter, as amended in 1962 and 1974 – are organs established by the Assembly for the purpose of promoting the development of economic relations among member-countries and the organization of multilateral economic, scientific and technical cooperation in individual sectors of the economy of such countries.[17]

The number of Commissions is not predetermined, and therefore they can be established or abolished in accordance with the needs of the moment. Moreover, their scope of activity may be changed, expanded or restricted to conform with the interests of the Council.

Not all member-countries cooperate in the activities of each Standing Commission, since certain fields are of little or no interest to certain countries, which therefore do not take part in the respective Commissions. For instance, Mongolia does not participate in the Standing Commissions on oil and gas, the peaceful uses of atomic energy, and chemicals; Cuba is absent from the Commission on coal.

The Commissions are composed of representatives of the member-countries; the rank of such representatives is high, being usually ministers or deputy ministers who, in their respective countries, are directly responsible for the economic sectors or branches of industry with which the individual Commissions are concerned. As noted with respect to the Executive Committee, the rank of the officials forming a given organ seems to afford reasonable guarantees concerning the existence of the political will actually to implement the resolutions adopted by that organ.

Representatives of non-member-countries or of international organizations may participate in the activities of the Commissions. In special cases, and with a view to ensuring a more articulated approach to certain matters, members of other Commissions are allowed to participate in the activities of a Commission.

According to the Charter provisions repealed in 1974, the Assembly decided the location of each Commission, bearing in mind appropriate criteria and seeking to strike a balance between technical, geographical and other considerations. As a result of this, the Commissions have been located in the capitals of the various member-countries of the Council.

It should be noted, however, that the Commissions – while required in principle to meet at the place where they are permanently located[18] – have not infrequently chosen to carry out their activities either in other cities of the country in which they are located or other capital cities, especially Moscow.

In recent years, the decentralization that was intended to be achieved by dividing the Commissions' locations among the various members has been proving less efficient for a number of practical reasons. In any case, since 1962, there exists for each Commission, at and under the CMEA Secretariat in Moscow, a special section – composed of a certain number of officials – acting as secretariat to that Commission, assisting it in the performance of its functions.[19]

The national delegations to the Commissions are usually fairly large and avail themselves of the services of advisers and experts.

Under paragraph 3 of Article IX, the Standing Commissions, in order to carry out their functions and within the limits of their authority, may set up working groups charged with looking into certain matters that fall within the competence of the Commissions. Moreover, as from time to time required, the Commissions may convene scientific and technical conferences and other such meetings.

The Commissions have, in fact, created a number of working groups and often convene scientific and technical conferences.

Under paragraph 4 of Article IX, the Commissions are required to submit yearly reports to the Executive Committee on their work and on their future activities.

Paragraph 3 of Article IX provides that the Standing Commissions, within the limits of their competence, may adopt recommendations and make decisions. They may also submit proposals to the Assembly and to the Executive Committee, and submit – according to the amendment introduced in 1974 – *by request or on their own initiative, information and proposals to other relevant organs of the Council.*

As regards more recent practice, it should be noted that not infrequently the Commissions prefer to submit proposals to the Executive Committee rather than making decisions on their own. The Executive Committee, for its part, may accept the proposals and adopt related recommendations, or it may confine itself to approving the proposals in general and leave it for the competent Commission to issue the relevant recommendations.

It has already been noted that the number of Standing Commissions is not strictly laid down, for they are organs which may be created or suppressed as needed. With the intensification of cooperation within CMEA a tendency has emerged progressively to increase the number of Commissions, in order to articulate more effectively that cooperation.

The existing Standing Commissions may be divided into two major categories, depending on whether they deal with strictly sectoral problems or with matters of a more general nature.

The general economic commissions include those concerned with foreign trade, statistics, currency and financial problems, and standardization.

The sectoral commissions include those concerned with the chemical industry, ferrous metallurgy, nonferrous metallurgy, oil and gas, coal, electric power, engineering, the radio-technical and electronic industry, light industry, the food industry, agriculture, the peaceful uses of atomic energy, geology, etc.

Some of the Commissions listed above, both general and sectoral, have been and are playing a major role not only in promoting and carrying out cooperation as provided for in the Charter, but also in harmonizing the activities of the international economic organizations formally extraneous to the Council with the policies and fundamental purposes of the latter. One example is provided by the important role played by the Standing Commission for currency and financial problems in connection with the establishment of the International Bank for Economic Cooperation and of the International Investment Bank.

3.5. The Secretariat

The CMEA Secretariat, whose seat is located in Moscow by explicit provision of paragraph 4 of Article X, has become increasingly important in recent years, even though remaining in substance a largely technical-administrative organ which takes care of the practical working of the organization and ensures its continuity of action.[20]

As mentioned before, in the first five years of its life, the Council lacked an actual Secretariat; it was only in 1954 that the Assembly created this organ, headed by a Secretary assisted by two deputy secretaries.

Under paragraph 1 of Article X, the Secretariat consists of the Secretary, his deputies and such staff as may be required for the performance of the Secretariat's functions.[21] The text, as amended in 1962, of the said paragraph 1, states that the Secretary shall be appointed by the Assembly and his deputies by the Executive Committee. This latter organ is responsible for supervising the work done by the Secretariat.

Again under paragraph 1 of Article X, the Secretary is the chief official of the Council and represents it in its relations with member-countries, with other countries and with international organizations. The Secretary and deputy secretaries may take part in all the meetings of the organs of the Council. It should be noted that the Secretariat is the only organ for which the Charter does not prescribe an equal participation of member-countries.

According to paragraph 3, in performing their duties the Secretary, the deputy secretaries and the staff of the Secretariat shall act as international officials. Thus, the member-countries recognize the international nature of the functions performed by the members of the Secretariat, allowing them to operate in full independence of any national influence, considering solely the interests of the Council.

The powers and functions of the Secretariat are listed in paragraph 2 of Article X, a paragraph which was extensively amended in 1962 and again in 1974. In the first place, the Secretariat has been relieved of its previous task of submitting to the ordinary sessions of the Assembly reports on the Council's activities; since 1962 this task has been entrusted to the Executive Committee, evidently regarded as much better-qualified than the Secretariat to draw up a balance sheet, not only economic but also political, of the organization's activities and to lay down its future guidelines.

In spite of this, the position of the Secretariat has on the whole been strengthened by the Charter revisions of 1962 and 1974. In effect, while in the past the Secretariat had to confine itself to *collaborating* in the preparation and conduct of the meetings of the various organs, under the new version of paragraph 2 it is responsible for *organizing* such meetings.

In addition, the abolition in 1962 of the Secretariats of each Standing Commission and the establishment in their place of special Secretariat Sections, responsible for each Commission, contributed largely to increasing the importance of the Secretariat as regards the organization and coordination of the Council's activities. On the occasion of the Charter revision of 1974, an amendment was introduced in paragraph 2 of Article X, whereby it is now a function of the Secretariat to *ensure the implementation of the secretariat responsibilities of the other organs of the Council.*

Another function of the Secretariat concerns the preparation of economic studies, using the material supplied by member-countries, and the publication of bulletins and documents of various kinds on matters of economic, scientific and technical cooperation. It should be noted that, according to the original wording of paragraph 2, such studies were to be conducted by the Secretariat only at the explicit request of the Assembly or of the Conference of Representatives.

The Secretariat is also responsible for preparing proposals on specific matters concerning the Council's activities, for submission to the competent organs of the Council.

The Secretariat also works out or *contributes to working out* draft multilateral agreements in the field of economic, scientific and technical cooperation in accordance with the recommendations and decisions adopted by organs of the Council.

Of major significance appears to be the function assigned to the Secretariat – since the Charter revision of 1962 – concerning the delicate matter of the implementation of the recommendations and decisions adopted by the Council's organs. More specifically, the Secretariat is required to organize and record the implementation of such recommendations and decisions and to make proposals in this respect.

In addition to its administrative, executive, technical and coordination functions, one should finally consider the financial functions vested in the Secretariat, which – under paragraph 2 of Article XIII, also amended in 1974 – is required to submit to the Executive Committee the *draft budget of the Council* for each calendar year and a report on the implementation of the previous budget. Again under paragraph 2, *the financial activities of the Secretariat are audited annually*.

It seems reasonable to expect in the near future an increase in the Secretariat's responsibilities in relation to the important tasks and goals assigned to the Council by the Comprehensive Programme and to the negotiations with the EEC.

Even though the Secretariat's power of initiative is limited by the Charter to the submission of 'proposals' to the other organs of the Council, one should not underestimate the extent of the powers which in practice it wields, by ensuring and promoting coordination between various organs, closely participating, through its Sections, in the activities of the Standing Commissions, centralizing the handling of numerous questions, as well as by gathering, analysing and eventually disseminating information and data about cooperation within CMEA and on the cyclic and structural conditions of the economies of the member-countries.

Also, as mentioned above, a broad field for the Secretariat's initiatives should open up with the implementation – based on the guidelines contained in the Comprehensive Programme – of the indispensable coordination between the activities of CMEA and those of the various specialized intergovernmental institutions connected with it in various ways. The Secretariat should thus find itself best placed for a full understanding of the progress of development of cooperation and integration, with the resulting possibility of exercising an appreciable influence on the activities and policies of the Council.

It is possible, too, that the strengthening of the Secretariat's position, besides affecting the 'internal' balance of power between CMEA principal organs and the connected institutions, may also influence the Council's 'external relations', through the taking of initiatives of an essentially political significance.[22]

4. THE SUBSIDIARY ORGANS: CONFERENCES AND INSTITUTES

In addition to the principal organs, CMEA, as is the case of most international organizations, possesses other lesser organs, which round up its structure and make it more responsive to various requirements arising from time to time.

In line with the progressive broadening of the general purposes and with the diversification of the goals and functions assigned to the Council, extensive use was made of the power to establish subsidiary organs, as explicitly provided for in paragraph 2 of Article V, under which 'such other organs as may prove to be necessary' shall be established.

The subsidiary organs operating within the Council are numerous and designed to meet a broad range of requirements, which have gradually arisen during CMEA's existence. Even though it can seldom be precisely evaluated the significance of the role played by the subsidiary organs should be considered far from negligible.

While it is true that the creation of subsidiary organs can in no way involve a broadening of the organization's functions nor take away from the principal organs their essential competence, it is equally true that, through subsidiary organs, the Council may carry out functions, sometimes of major importance, which previously had been not exercised, or ignored or neglected.

Among the most important subsidiary organs of CMEA one can mention the Conferences (now numbering seven) and the Institutes (two).

The Conferences are those of:

(a) the representatives of the shipping and freight organizations of member-countries, created by the Assembly in February 1952

(b) the heads of the national water administration agencies, active since 1962 and connected with CMEA since 1965

(c) the ministers for the interior market of member-countries, created in 1968 by the Executive Committee, which approved its charter in 1972

(d) the representatives of the price agencies of member-countries, created by the Executive Committee in September 1973

(e) the representatives of member-countries for legal problems, created by the Executive Committee in December 1969

(f) the heads of the institutions of the member-countries for the protection of inventions and patents, created by the Assembly in 1971

(g) the heads of the state agencies dealing with labour problems, created by the Executive Committee in 1968.

The Conference of the representatives of member-countries for legal problems deals in particular with the following matters: material responsibilities of the states deriving from economic cooperation agreements; material responsibilities of the enterprises for total or partial defaults on the obligations; functions of arbitration boards on foreign trade; legal and organizational aspects concerning the establishment and operation of international economic organizations; conclusion and implementation of agreements on production specialization and cooperation; patents and licences.

The two Institutes are concerned, respectively, with standardization and with the study of economic problems of the world socialist system.

The Institute of Standardization was established by an Assembly resolution of June 1962, concurrently with the establishment of the Standing Commission on Standardization, under whose supervision the Institute operates.

Under the Statute approved by the Executive Committee in December 1962, the Institute is composed of specialists from CMEA countries, assisted by a highly qualified staff. The Institute is headed by a Director, assisted by deputy directors, all appointed by the Executive Committee. The Institute's Council is a consultative organ which considers its programme and issues opinions on the proposals submitted by the Directorate to the competent organs of CMEA, in particular to the Commission on Standardization.

The Institute is responsible essentially for formulating recommendations and proposals in the field of standardization; its interest is concentrated mainly on the sectors of metallurgy, chemicals and engineering.

The standards proposed by the Institute and adopted by the competent agencies now number several thousands. During the

1970s standardization has been introduced in the drawings, designs, products and parts of products, tolerances, tares and packaging for a wide range of goods.

The International Institute for the economic problems of the world socialist system, created by a resolution of the Assembly in May 1970, carries out – under a Director assisted by experts from CMEA member-countries – in-depth research, in theory, practice and methodology, on the major economic, scientific and technical problems originated by socialist cooperation and integration. The Scientific Council of the Institute determines the main orientations of research.

Finally, it should be noted that the secretariat services of the subsidiary organs briefly described above are performed – under paragraph 2 of Article X – by special Sections of the Secretariat. This arrangement ensures, also with respect to the subsidiary organs, the centralization with the Council Secretariat of technical-administrative, information and documentation functions.

NOTES TO CHAPTER 5

1. For fuller details, see M. Kaser, *Comecon*, op. cit., pp. 73–6.
2. The last three Standing Commissions had a rather short life, for they were abolished in 1958. The Standing Commission on geology, however, was re-established in the summer of 1963.
3. See M. Kaser, *Comecon*, op. cit., p. 84 ff. Apart from the troubled political and economic events of this period in certain East European countries, the repercussions in the socialist camp that followed the signing of the Treaties of Rome in March 1957 should be borne in mind.
4. It should be stressed again, with reference to the latest events within CMEA, that so far calls for the achievement of integration through the creation of supranational organs have not found acceptance. In fact, the Comprehensive Programme explicitly rules out such a possibility.
5. The representatives of the Communist and workers' parties also held meetings in 1960 (2–3 February) and in 1966 (7 July), devoted respectively to the problems of the development of agriculture and to questions of foreign policy.
6. See paragraph 5, Section I of the Statute on the Committee for cooperation in planning. The level of the members of the Bureau has remained unchanged (deputy heads of the central planning agencies of the member-countries).
7. See J. Caillot, *Le CAEM*, op. cit., p. 52.
8. The Assembly adopted its new Rules of Procedure on 26 June 1975.
9. The Assembly has met at varying intervals during the 30 years of life of the

Council. The original version of the Charter, in 1959, called for two ordinary meetings a year, but this frequency was not respected; the Charter amendment in 1962 provided for one meeting a year, but even this rule has not always been observed, for the Assembly did not hold sessions in 1964 and in 1968. As for the rotation of meetings between the capitals, established on the basis of the alphabetical order, in the Russian language, of the member-countries, this rule – already embodied in the January 1949 communiqué announcing the creation of the Council – has been fully applied only since the 11th Session, held in Tirana in May 1959. The two extraordinary sessions so far convened, the 16th in 1962 and 23rd in 1969, were not included in the normal rotation and were held in Moscow.

Article 1 of the existing Rules of Procedure specifies that the ordinary session of the Assembly shall be held, as a rule, in the second quarter of each year.

10. Before the Charter amendment of 1962, the Reports to the Assembly on the Council's activities were drafted and submitted by the Secretariat.
11. The Executive Committee adopted its own Rules of Procedure on 12 July 1962, and subsequently amended them on 20 December 1962, 7 October 1967, 21 April 1973 and 24 April 1975.
12. For fuller details, see Articles 8 to 11 of the Rules of Procedure; note the increasing importance of the functions attributed to the Chairman of the Executive Committee by Article 11 of the Rules. The term to be served as Chairman by each representative has also been changed to one year (Article 10 of the Rules of Procedure).
13. As a rule, the Executive Committee meets in the country where the CMEA Secretariat has its seat, unless explicitly otherwise decided (Article 2 of the Rules of Procedure). The 79th meeting of the Executive Committee, for instance, was held in Havana from 17 to 19 January 1977.
14. The Statute on the Committee was adopted on 20 January 1972 by the Executive Committee, which subsequently amended it on 24 April 1975.
15. The Statute on the Committee on scientific and technical cooperation was also adopted on 20 January 1972 and amended on 24 April 1975.
16. The Statute on the Committee was adopted on 17 October 1974.
17. The Model Rules of Procedure of the Standing Commissions were adopted on 29 July 1960 by the Assembly and amended by the Executive Committee on 20 December 1962, 21 April 1973 and 24 April 1975.
18. This obligation is confirmed by Article 4 of the Model Rules now in effect which, however, explicitly provides that exceptions may be made when warranted by the particular nature of the issues to be considered.
19. Previously, up to end of 1962, each Commission had its own secretariat, independent of the CMEA Secretariat.
20. The Statute on the Secretariat was adopted by the Conference of Representatives (an organ abolished in 1962) on 3 March 1961, and subsequently amended by the Executive Committee on 12 July, 28 September and 20 December 1962, 2 February 1965 and 24 April 1975.
21. Under paragraph 3, Section II of the Secretariat's Statute, the Secretary and his deputies are appointed for a renewable four-year term; for many years now this position has been held by a Soviet citizen, Nikolai V. Faddeev.

    The size of the Secretariat's staff in the early years of the organization was extremely small, before growing apace with the expansion of the Council's activities. The staff is recruited among nationals of the member-countries according to appropriate criteria, seeking to ensure an equitable distribution by countries.

22. It seems that in 1975 Romania refused to agree to a proposed CMEA declaration which would have strengthened the position of the Secretariat in the negotiations with the EEC. See A. J. Smith, 'The Council of Mutual Economic Assistance in 1977', op. cit., p. 170.

6 Monetary and Financial Cooperation

1. THE SOCIALIST COUNTRIES' 'MONETARY SOLIDARITY' AREA

A review of the main features of the monetary and financial cooperation between socialist countries and of the most significant of the institutions through which it is carried out – under the influence of CMEA or as a result of its direct action – presents intricate problems because of the nature of the relations existing in such areas between centrally planned economies. These problems have only arisen in a tangible form in the last few years, when the need for integration within CMEA has become more pressing, demanding an overall coordination of the economic, monetary and financial policies of the member-countries.

The intensification of trade and exchanges of services between CMEA member-countries has required a search for mechanisms that would allow at least a certain degree of transferability of currencies, while tentative suggestions are being made, although on a longer-term basis, for a more or less extensive convertibility.

The solidarity existing also on a monetary plane among the CMEA countries and the forms in which it has been organizing itself, have sometimes caused explicit references to be made to a 'ruble area'. This seems incorrect, for these nations are not using, for mutual payments, a 'currency' in the proper sense of the term; also missing are those special characteristics which belong to the classic monetary areas, such as those of the franc and sterling.[1]

Outside what might be called more simply a socialist 'monetary solidarity' area stand certain countries which nevertheless base their socio-economic organization on the Marxist ideology, such as Albania, Yugoslavia, the People's Republic of China and the Democratic People's Republic of Korea. Links with this area have been recently established by two non-European socialist countries, Cuba and the Socialist Republic of Vietnam, which joined the two banks created among CMEA countries, the IBEC and the IIB. It should be noted, in this connection, that it appears that the USSR never actively exerted itself to bring about the formation of an actual ruble area. Instead, it reconciled, within CMEA, the strict planning of foreign trade by each country and the resulting bilateralism with the increasing need for an international payments mechanism, whereby debit and credit balances among member-countries could be settled.

2. HISTORICAL BACKGROUND

In dealing with the problems of payments within CMEA, it is necessary to stress once again the particular position of the USSR *vis-à-vis* the other member-countries. Self-sufficient in many areas, a producer and exporter of gold in undetermined but substantial amounts,[2] the Soviet economy has always had a very limited degree of dependence on foreign trade. In this it differs from the economies of the other European socialist countries, which generally need to trade extensively to obtain the raw materials or products needed for the expansion of their production systems and for the attainment of the goals set in their respective national economic plans.

From the historical standpoint, it may be mentioned that, on the eve of World War II, the Soviet economy had reached a very high degree of self-sufficiency, its foreign trade being extremely limited and generally of negligible importance.

The countries of Eastern Europe – which in a few years' time were to become people's democracies – were, on the other hand, engaged in a substantial amount of trading, especially with Western Europe.

Several events, in the crucial period following World War II, led the East European countries progressively to develop their mutual trade and, at the same time, substantially to curtail their economic relations with the West.

In the course of the last decade, the increase in trade and exchanges of services promoted by CMEA has had increasing and substantial repercussions in the payments area.

At present, the pressing demands of economic development are leading the planned-economy countries to become increasingly interested in trade. Such interest concerns, in different degrees varying with the requirements of each economic system, trade with the other socialist countries, with the West and with some Third World countries.

The attempt to expand foreign economic relations and the accompanying search for an equilibrium in the balance of payments which characterize the present attitude of CMEA countries assume different features, depending on the particular needs and resources of the individual countries: Hungary, for instance, depends very largely on foreign trade, while in the USSR foreign trade, in the early 1970s, accounted for less than 8 per cent of the net material product.

3. FUNCTIONS OF CURRENCY IN THE CENTRALLY PLANNED COUNTRIES

The payments problems arising among the CMEA countries cannot be adequately understood without bearing in mind the specific functions which the currency performs in centrally planned economies. The monetary system existing in the USSR since the early 1930s, in effect, arises from the adoption of the policy of planning and has been gradually introduced in all countries of Eastern Europe.

The currency plays a limited and largely secondary role in the socialist economies. Generally, prices are fixed by administrative action and monetary values do not reflect the value of goods in terms of real costs and current demand. Within the production system, the currency is essentially an accounting instrument, used to convert into physical magnitudes the real production figures.

In certain socialist countries which, during the last few years, have moved further on the road to economic reforms, granting to enterprises a modicum of autonomy, especially as regards supply and wage policies, currency has gone beyond its traditional role as an instrument of accounting and control by the central authorities, creating inflationary stresses which are not always easily controllable.

In the consumption sector, the currency tends to play a more dynamic role; the individual consumer enjoys a certain freedom of choice, even though the total share of production to be allocated for consumption is rigidly predetermined, as are the prices of the various goods offered. In spite of the planners' efforts, however, consumer purchasing power may exceed the amount of goods available on the market, creating inflationary pressures and causing shortages of goods.[3]

The planners try to redress these imbalances by acting on prices, incomes and the supply of goods and services; for its part, the State Bank operates, through the issue policy, in such a way as to adjust the amount of money in circulation to the actual volume of transactions by consumers. In transactions between enterprises, the currency is not called upon – in principle – to play any specific role, since such transactions are, as a rule, planned 'in kind'. Moreover, the money supplies of enterprises must be used in strict conformity with the directives issued by the planners.

The functions – on the whole of limited significance – performed by the currency within each socialist country, also appear in many respects substantially limited in the area of international monetary relations.

The non-convertibility of the currencies of the CMEA countries and the complete state monopoly on foreign trade make the internal monetary circuit free from any external stress, and the internal circulation entirely independent of the balance-of-payments situation.

The separation existing between internal monetary questions and monetary questions related to international trade is, indeed, one of the features that should always be borne in mind when considering the international payments problems of the socialist economies.

In the Soviet Union, the dissociation between the 'internal' ruble and the 'international' ruble dates back to the late 1920s. In 1926 the Soviet authorities prohibited the export of rubles and in 1928 their import. From the latter date, the separation between the two currencies may be defined as total, and it would therefore be meaningless to compare the internal purchasing power of the ruble and its international course.

4. INSTITUTIONS DEALING WITH FOREIGN–EXCHANGE TRANSACTIONS

The settlement of international accounts in the USSR, as in the other socialist countries, is based on the state monopoly on foreign currency, gold and other exchange transactions.

In the USSR, this monopoly belongs to the State Bank or *Gosbank*,[4] the central and issue bank. More specifically, the *Gosbank* handles foreign financial operations, the determination of exchange rates and the management of gold and currency reserves.

By delegation from the state, foreign currency transactions are also handled by the Foreign Trade Bank or *Vneshtorgbank*,[5] which extends from three to twelve months credit, executes payment orders and performs other banking services connected with imports and exports, buys and sells Soviet and foreign currency; the purchase for rubles of foreign exchange and other instruments denominated in foreign currency is subject to special rules and limitations.[6] In Poland too, foreign currency transactions have been turned over by the Central Bank to the Commercial Bank (*Bank Handlowy*), which also extends export-financing credit.

In effect, the sizeable increase in trade with foreign countries – particularly with the industrialized countries of the West – and the growing complexity of payments operations connected with such trade have induced the central banks of the CMEA countries to give up handling commercial transactions. The banking systems have been progressively evolving and the importance of their functions has been increasing, resulting in a remarkable development of their structures.

Information concerning the present structure of the banking systems of the CMEA countries is contained in the table, which also shows the international financial organizations of which the respective countries are members.

As regards banking cooperation in a strict sense among socialist countries, mention should be made of the conferences which the representatives of the central banks of these countries have been holding periodically since 1958 to discuss questions of common interest.

Practically all the foreign trade banks and most central banks of the socialist countries maintain relations with a considerable number of Western banks; moreover, several of these socialist banks have branches or representative offices in the West.

One phenomenon which has been growing to significant proportions is the establishment, in the world's leading financial centres, of separate banks wholly or partly owned by socialist countries. In this respect significant activity – although as it is

Banking Systems of the CMEA Countries

Country	Central and issue bank	Specialized institutes: For investment	Specialized institutes: For foreign transactions	Participation in international financial organizations
USSR	USSR State Bank (*Gosbank*)	Investment Bank (*Stroibank*)	Foreign Trade Bank (*Vneshtorgbank*)	IBEC, IIB
Bulgaria	Bulgarian National Bank	–	Bulgarian Foreign Trade Bank	IBEC, IIB, BIS
Czechoslovakia	Czechoslovak State Bank	–	Czechoslovak Commercial Bank. Zivnostenská Bank	IBEC, IIB, BIS
Poland	Polish National Bank	–	Warsaw Commercial Bank. Bank Polska Kasa Opieki.	IBEC, IIB, BIS
German Dem. Republic	GDR State Bank	–	German Foreign Trade Bank	IBEC, IIB
Romania	Romanian National Bank	Investment Bank	Romanian Foreign Trade Bank	IBEC, IIB, BIS, IMF IBRD

Hungary	Hungarian National Bank	—	State Development Bank	Hungarian Foreign Trade Bank. Bank for Trust and Trade	IBEC, IIB, BIS
Mongolia	Mongolian State Bank		—	—	IBEC, IIB
Cuba	National Bank of Cuba		—	—	IBEC, IIB
Vietnam	State Bank of the SRV		—	Foreign Trade Bank of the SRV	IBEC, IIB, IMF, IBRD

Note: Savings banks and similar institutions do not appear in this table.

Abbreviations: IBEC: International Bank for Economic Cooperation; IIB: International Investment Bank; BIS: Bank for International Settlements; IBRD: International Bank for Reconstruction and Development (World Bank); IMF: International Monetary Fund.

only partially known its implications are hard to evaluate – is carried out by the Moscow Narodny Bank, with its head office in London and subsidiaries in Beirut and Singapore, and by the Banque Commerciale pour l'Europe du Nord (Eurobank), at present the largest foreign bank in Paris.

Narodny and Eurobank, whose shares are owned by the USSR State Bank and Foreign Trade Bank, have, for decades, been doing a substantial amount of business. Their annual balance sheets – published regularly in compliance with the regulations in force, respectively, in the United Kingdom and France – are drawn up in such a way as to prevent a detailed analysis of the nature and scope of the various operations carried out. It seems unquestionable, however, that these two banks have been for years among the leading operators on the Eurocurrency market,[7] acting also on behalf of the central banks of some East European countries. Some believe the term 'Euro-dollar' to be a direct derivation from Eurobank. Indeed, when in the early 1950s the USSR transferred its substantial dollar assets from the United States to Europe for fear of its funds being frozen in US banks because of the deterioration of the international political situation, Narodny and Eurobank received in deposit a substantial portion of these idle dollars and began offering them on the London and Paris monetary markets, extending short-term loans.

It is unnecessary to stress, on the other hand, the significant role played by these banks in financing East–West trade and the placement of Soviet gold on Western markets.

From a general viewpoint, it should be noted that the socialist countries' banks located abroad do not confine themselves to the various operations mentioned above, but often participate in banking syndicates extending loans to third countries and, on the whole, engage in a very wide range of business.

The two banks mentioned above, which have been in business for a long time, have been followed in recent years by other institutions, such as the Wozchod Handelsbank (with its head office in Zurich), the Ost-West Handelsbank (with its head office in Frankfurt) and the Donau Bank (with its head office in Vienna). The shares of these banks are also owned by the USSR State Bank, Foreign Trade Bank and various Soviet foreign trade organizations.

In addition to these Soviet organizations, institutions created by four other CMEA countries – Poland, Hungary, Romania and Cuba – are operating on the major financial markets.

Finally, it should be noted that the IBEC and the IIB – as will be discussed in detail later – have been carrying out since the early 1970s substantial operations on the Eurocurrency market.

5. THE SOCIALIST COUNTRIES AND THE FINANCIAL AND MONETARY INSTITUTIONS OF THE WESTERN WORLD

At present the Soviet Union and the socialist countries in general do not participate in the international organizations of universal scope operating in the monetary and financial fields. In particular, these countries are not members of the International Monetary Fund and the World Bank, apart from Romania which has been a member of both the Bank and the Fund since 1972, and Vietnam.

From time to time, however, many socialist countries have shown a close interest in international economic organizations, including financial and monetary ones. Romania's entry into the IMF and the World Bank in the early 1970s has been one of the most significant indications of this interest and has attracted widespread attention.

In fact, the advantages which the socialist countries could enjoy from full participation in the international financial organizations are far from negligible. Joining the IMF would give access to the resources needed to cope with balance-of-payments difficulties, and therefore to utilize for the purposes of economic development some of the funds now used to overcome such difficulties.[8] Admission to the World Bank would, in the first place, make it possible to obtain substantial loans for the financing of projects important to the growth of the socialist economies; moreover, the other countries borrowing from the Bank could utilise part of the loans for purchases of machinery, equipment, plant and the like in the socialist countries, for which new export opportunities would thus open up.

In any event, whatever the possible advantages to the socialist countries, the attitude of the latter towards the international economic organizations will necessarily be one – as has been the case with membership of GATT – of great caution, based on participation formulas carefully defined country by country. The possibilities of cooperation between such organizations as the IMF and the IBRD and organizations operating in the socialist countries, in more or less similar fields, such as the IBEC and the IIB, will be of even greater complexity.

Mention should be made, finally, of the participation of the central banks of European socialist countries (excluding the USSR and the German Democratic Republic, but including Albania and Yugoslavia) in the Bank of International Settlements. This participation, however, appears to be essentially formal (except as regards Yugoslavia), since these countries are not playing any appreciable role in the management and carrying-out of the activities of the BIS, which have been expanding considerably, especially in the course of recent years.

The IBEC, whose Charter envisages the possibility of establishing relations with other international institutions, has recently contacted the BIS; moreover, in October 1965, the IBEC Council has authorised this organization to conclude settlement agreements with Western banking institutions.

6. EVOLUTION OF THE SYSTEMS OF PAYMENTS BETWEEN SOCIALIST COUNTRIES

6.1. The Bilateral and 'Triangular' Agreements

In the initial period of activity of CMEA, trade between member-countries was generally based, under bilateral clearing agreements, on a strict balance of the respective trade flows, and it was only in the latter half of the 1950s that various projects were initiated aimed at the creation of a system of multilateral payments.

For many years, starting with the immediate postwar period, trade and payments between CMEA countries were characterized by a strict bilateralism. It is unnecessary to stress that the maintenance of trade on strictly bilateral bases can of itself create serious obstacles to any policy designed to promote economic cooperation.

The bilateral trade agreements between European socialist countries were generally accompanied by clearing agreements. Clearing accounts were opened with the state banks of the contracting parties to enter therein, in non-convertible *clearing rubles*, debits and credits. The two sides of the account had necessarily to balance, since any credit of a country with its partner could not be used to pay a debt with a third country.

To obviate, at least in part, the serious difficulties connected with the maintenance of a series of bilateral balances and the resulting stagnation of trade, some socialist countries signed between them 'triangular' clearing agreements, allowing a credit balance to be used for purchases not only from one but from two countries. It was obvious, however, that even the system of 'triangular' agreements was insufficient to increase trade significantly between the countries concerned.

Bilateralism also resulted in negative consequences as regards early attempts at the division of labour, and therefore specialization of production within CMEA.

One country's specialization in the manufacturing of a given product to be supplied to other Council member-countries required the latter to pay for such product by exporting other goods to the specializing country. The latter, however, in a system of strictly bilateral balances, could already find itself in the condition of structural creditor of another country, to which it had no interest in supplying more goods, increasing its debit balance.

In effect, in cases of this kind, the creditor specializing country finds it desirable to cut down on supplies to its debtor partner, rather than to continue to export and thus swell a credit balance which, for various reasons, it is unable to utilize. Consequently, trade tends to shrink and drop to the level regarded as most appropriate by the creditor country which, having no interest in increasing imports, will cut down on exports. At the same time, the debtor country which is unable to purchase abroad a certain item it needs will be forced to produce it itself, thus jeopardizing attempts to achieve a rational division of labour.

In the monetary field, the Soviet Government carried out, at the beginning of the 1950s, a revaluation of the ruble, which was officially pegged to gold.

On 1 March 1950, the Soviet currency – previously defined against the US dollar at the rate of 1 dollar to 5·30 rubles and with a parity corresponding to 0.167673 gramme of fine gold – had its gold parity raised to 0.222168 gramme; consequently, the official exchange rate went to 4 rubles to the dollar.

In the course of 1950, in connection with the revaluation of the ruble, some socialist countries fixed the gold parity of their respective monetary units to correspond exactly with the ruble (this was done, for instance, in the cases of Mongolia's tughrik and Poland's złoty). It should be noted, however, that this resulted in no direct linkage of these monetary units with the ruble or gold, since neither Mongolia, nor Poland, nor any other people's democracy possessed sufficient ruble and gold reserves to ensure the convertibility of their currencies.

It should be stressed again, in this respect, that the internal purchasing power of the currencies of the socialist countries is determined by the price system fixed by their respective governments and is maintained by establishing a more or less stable balance between the mass of distributed incomes and the amount of consumer goods placed on the market. Prices vary considerably from country to country and have no relation to the parity of the national currencies with the ruble. External purchasing power varies depending on the goods and on the provisions included in the clearing agreements concluded with the foreign countries.

From 1950–1, the ruble became the currency commonly used in trade between CMEA countries, but this function was mostly fictitious since the unit of account called the 'ruble' had nothing to do with the Soviet currency and with its purchasing power.

In the credit area, as it was natural, the Soviet Union was the major lender to the people's democracies. Among the long-term credits, special importance was assumed by those extended in gold and convertible currencies to make purchases in Western countries, and by those made in rubles to buy industrial equipment in the USSR.

6.2. Steps Towards 'Multilateralization'

A first major step towards the 'multilateralization' of payments was taken in 1957; it seems that in this connection some proposals made by Poland and Hungary played an important role.

On 20 June 1957, the CMEA countries concluded in Warsaw an agreement for the introduction of a multilateral clearing system. More specifically, the agreement created a clearing house for the trade balances between the signatory countries.

The USSR State Bank, with which special accounts were

opened, served as clearing house, so that the creation of a special institution was unnecessary. It should be noted that the multilateral clearing arrangement was concerned solely with trade transactions in excess of the annual volume of trade indicated in the bilateral agreements. Each transaction could take place only with the explicit consent of all countries concerned. In practice, to carry out the operation the creditor's consent was required and the debts unpaid within the short time allowed had to be paid by goods specially listed in an annex to the agreement.[9] Throughout the period of its application, the number of settlements made with this clearing arrangement did not exceed 1·5 per cent of the total volume of transactions.

The signatories of the agreement were not required to make any capital subscription, nor was any provision made for credit facilities that would effectively help the debtor countries to redress their balance-of-payments.

The arrangement created by this agreement of June 1957 therefore introduced the multilateral settlement of payments only to a very limited extent and was certainly not such as to promote the desired intensification of trade. These continuous problems were repeatedly discussed in the course of the meetings of the competent organs of CMEA, and thus the awareness gradually emerged of the need to set up an *ad hoc* body, equipped to facilitate wider and easier access to multilateral payments and to aid the debtor countries by the extension of credit from specially established funds.

In 1961 the USSR undertook a monetary reform and carried out a 'heavy ruble' operation by multiplying by ten the unit value of its currency.[10] As a result of the reform, on 1 January 1961, the parity of the ruble was raised to 0·987412 gramme of fine gold, greater – and the Soviets placed much emphasis on this fact – than that of the dollar (0·888671 gramme). The official exchange rate went to 0·90 rubles to the dollar (1 ruble = 1·11 dollars) and stayed at that level till 23 December 1971.

As mentioned before, during the Conference of the Communist and workers' parties of the CMEA member-countries, held in Moscow on 6–7 June 1962, the 'Basic Principles of the International Socialist Division of Labour' were approved. In these Basic Principles, explicit reference was made to the desirability of creating a system of multilateral settlement of payments among the countries of CMEA.

Subsequently, the CMEA Executive Committee, in its third session held in Bucharest from 16 to 20 December 1962, adopted a recommendation relating to the creation of an international bank.

To develop a draft agreement concerning international settlements in transferable rubles, and to define the procedures connected with the establishment and operation of a banking institution, there was specially established – again in December 1962 – within and as an organ of CMEA, a new Standing Commission on currency and financial questions. This Commission has made a notable contribution towards the solution of some of the most delicate problems arising in its area of specific authority, among other things working effectively towards the creation of the IBEC and the IIB.[11]

The above-mentioned recommendation adopted by the Executive Committee in December 1962 was approved by the Conference of the First Secretaries of the Communist and workers' parties and of the heads of government of the CMEA member-countries held in Moscow from 24 to 26 July 1963, concurrently with the 18th Session of the Council Assembly, which also gave its approval. Finally, on 22 October 1963, in the course of a separate meeting held at the end of the 9th Session of the Executive Committee, the representatives of Hungary, Bulgaria, the German Democratic Republic, Mongolia, Poland, Romania, the USSR and Czechoslovakia signed in Moscow an 'Agreement on multilateral payments in transferable rubles and on the organization of the International Bank for Economic Cooperation', which included the Charter of the Bank. As expected, the Albanian representatives did not participate in the conclusion of the Agreement. The latter came officially into force on 18 May 1964, but was provisionally applied from 1 January 1964.

Basically, the IBEC was assigned the following functions: operating a multilateral system of payments in the 'collective currency', the 'transferable ruble', which was fixed at a gold content equal to that of the Soviet ruble; extending loans for the financing of foreign trade and other transactions; financing investments made jointly by member-countries; carrying out transactions in transferable rubles with non-member-countries.

In the last few years, the intensification of trade between CMEA member-countries has created new and even more pressing needs in the field of payments. On the whole, the role assigned to the IBEC was a modest one and fell short even of the expectations created by its establishment. The multilateralization of payments has been very relative and has failed to free a substantial portion of the trade between CMEA countries from the rigid patterns of bilateralism.

Early in 1971, to meet more effectively investment financing requirements in the CMEA area, the International Investment Bank began its operations. Created with an agreement signed in Moscow on 10 July 1970, the IIB has the basic task of extending to member-countries medium- and long-term credits for the implementation of projects of common interest, supplementing to a certain degree the work done by the IBEC.

For its part, the Comprehensive Programme of 1971 appears mainly to have improved the mechanisms and procedures that now characterize foreign trade, without promoting any substantial progress towards at least a relative liberalization of trade and payments.

As regards specifically currency and financial relations, the Comprehensive Programme mentions their 'improvement' and includes fairly detailed information on this matter. In particular, conditions and procedures should be developed for the convertibility of the collective currency, i.e. the transferable ruble, into the currencies of CMEA countries and for the interconvertibility of such currencies. Between 1976 and 1979 a study had to be made of the possibilities and the premises had to be created for the introduction of a single exchange rate of the monetary unit of each country, while by 1980 a decision should be made concerning the introduction of the said exchange rate and the actual date of its entry into effect. However, the actual fulfilment of these goals now appears further away and certainly more difficult than it was reasonable to expect at the time of the launching of the Comprehensive Programme.

The Comprehensive Programme makes no mention of the dates by which convertibility should be introduced *vis-à-vis* the countries outside CMEA, but it does stress the desirability of promoting through adequate measures the participation of non-member-countries – in the first place the other socialist countries and the developing countries – in the multilateral payments system based on the transferable ruble.

Among recent landmarks of the economic evolution, mention

should be made of the changes in the official exchange rate of the ruble with the dollar, the gold content of the ruble remaining unchanged. As a result of this action, on 24 December 1971, the official rate was changed from 0·90 to 0·829 rubles to the dollar. In March 1980 the official rate was 0·6475 rubles = US$1.

It should be noted that no socialist country (with the exception of Yugoslavia) has changed the gold parity of its currency following the devaluation of the dollar and the differentiated realignments of the respective monetary units decided upon by the members of the Group of Ten in Washington on 18 December 1971.[12]

The table shows the gold content of the monetary units of the socialist countries, the official parities with the ruble and the official rates (expressed in rubles) for the non-commercial transactions of the Soviet Union with the socialist countries.

Gold Parities and Ruble Exchange Rates of the Socialist Currencies

Country	Monetary unit	Exchange rate in rubles, per 100 monetary units		Gold parity, gramme
		Official parity	Non-commercial transactions	
Albania	Lek	18·00	11·94	0·1777
Bulgaria	Lev	76·92	128·21	0·759548
Czechoslovakia	Koruna	11·81	10·36	0·123426
China	Yuan	42·17	77·52	0·36098
North Korea	Won	74·93	69·44	0·740559
Cuba	Peso	90·00	–	0·888671
GDR	Mark	40·50	31·25	0·399903
Mongolia	Tughrik	22·50	23·92	0·222168
Poland	Złoty	22·50	6·54	0·222168
Romania	Leu	15·00	12·05	0·148112
Hungary	Forint	7·67	7·63	0·075757
Vietnam	Dong	30·60	52·08	0·302
USSR	Ruble	–	–	0·987412

7. THE DIFFICULT GOAL OF CONVERTIBILITY

In spite of the evolution that has taken place in the payments systems within CMEA, many problems are still unsolved, with negative repercussions on trade development.

The strict separation between domestic market prices and foreign trade prices makes it extremely hard to compare the prices and costs of the various goods and services in the CMEA member-countries.

Mention has already been made of the fact that in the CMEA area the domestic price systems may vary even very widely from country to country and are completely independent of one another, besides having no relation to international market prices. In fixing prices, the demand level may be disregarded, and therefore a product which is cheap in one country and expensive in another will not necessarily be in greater supply in the former.[13]

The exchange rates between socialist currencies – not infrequently set at levels that vary in accordance with the particular nature of the transaction – perform a function which is partial and limited in many respects.[14] Generally speaking, the exchange rate is fixed with reference to the relation existing between the average domestic market price level and the level of prices of a given number of goods traded between the two countries.

The introduction of more realistic exchange rates between the currencies of the CMEA area would involve profound changes in the structure and system of determination of domestic prices, with consequences that would be hard to estimate on several levels.

In spite of the many unknown factors, major steps towards a narrowing of the gap between domestic prices and world market prices have been taken in Hungary since 1968 and in Poland and Bulgaria since 1971.

The USSR, for its part, has repeatedly shown an interest in the development of a specifically 'regional' price system, i.e. one applicable to trade throughout the CMEA area, but it seems that Soviet proposals to this effect have been repeatedly rejected by the other socialist countries. In particular, the proposed system would have involved a substantial increase in the prices of raw materials and a reduction – or at least a stabilization – of the prices of finished products, with undoubted advantages to Soviet foreign trade.[15]

The adoption in 1964 of a system of multilateral clearing in transferable rubles, managed by the IBEC, has certainly been an advance. The payments for commercial transactions, made on the basis of suitably modified and 'adjusted' world market prices, are entered into bilateral accounts in transferable rubles and the balances (plus or minus) are transferable between the accounts of member-countries. For non-commercial transactions, payments are entered into bilateral accounts denominated in the various national currencies, which are then converted into transferable rubles on the basis of rates that vary with the nature of the transaction.

This multilateral mechanism, however, operates to a limited extent, for trade agreements continue to be concluded on a bilateral basis, a fact that has led some authorities to believe that the creation of the transferable ruble should be regarded as largely a psychological operation.

It is unnecessary to stress that the adoption of the ruble as the collective currency of the socialist countries does not produce any specific material benefit to the USSR which, like all other partners, can earn transferable rubles only by exporting goods and services in the CMEA area.

The non-convertibility of the collective currency has far-reaching consequences on the relations of CMEA members with one another and with third countries. The 'internal' (within-CMEA) convertibility of the transferable ruble, as previously mentioned, is provided for in the Comprehensive Programme. The Comprehensive Programme calls, among other things, for the creation of the conditions and the organization of appropriate measures aimed at introducing convertibility of the individual currencies with one another and with the transferable ruble.

The impossibility of using the surpluses built up in transferable rubles to make purchases outside the CMEA area discourages the permanent creditor countries from increasing their exports towards the other members – in fact, it induces them to curtail sales to the weaker partners and, in the last analysis, to seek bilateral balances, in spite of the existence of a multilateral mechanism.

The introduction of the 'external' convertibility of the collective currency would make it possible to overcome the existing situation, encouraging the CMEA countries to increase exports, to improve the quality of products and to fit their foreign trade policy into a truly multilateral context.

However, while the Council members which are permanent creditors have an unquestionable interest in the convertibility into Western currencies of the respective surpluses in transferable rubles, the economically weaker and less-developed countries are with some justification afraid of such a situation, which could cause a further deterioration in their balance-of-payments.

The approximation of CMEA price levels to those of world markets that will result from measures designed to reform the price-fixing systems may create, in time, conditions more favourable to the introduction of convertibility, reducing its risks.

On the other hand, the problem of convertibility cannot be tackled regardless of the purposes of CMEA. Does 'external' convertibility, which would bring unquestionable benefits to certain countries of the area, really meet, and to what extent, the requirements of integration?

The arguments of the opponents of convertibility – and primarily those advanced by the USSR[16] – are based on this broader approach. In the first place – it is pointed out – a direct connection with the world monetary system at this stage would do more harm than good to the socialist countries. Moreover, and above all, the ultimate purpose of the integration process is actually that of strengthening the economic and commercial ties between the countries concerned, which should continue to develop trade among themselves thus reducing their dependence on the rest of the world. The introduction of convertibility would hardly help increase the multilateralization of trade within the area.

In spite of these negative arguments, tending to stress the many unfavourable implications of convertibility, the debate on this matter in the Soviet Union and in the other CMEA countries is far from over. In fact, a number of interesting proposals are slowly emerging, designed to achieve the 'internal' convertibility of the transferable ruble on relatively broad bases and gradually to achieve a limited 'external' convertibility for specified kinds of transactions. Some hold that this latter convertibility should be in some ways tied to the intensification of the integration process. Thus, a country could convert into Western currencies a certain percentage of its surpluses in transferable rubles, provided it had reached certain targets in trading with the other CMEA countries. It has also been proposed to arrive by degrees at convertibility for settlements concerning transactions in given sectors, in particular that of consumer goods, while excluding certain others, notably that of capital goods.

NOTES TO CHAPTER 6

1. See in this respect J. Marczewski, 'La zone rouble et les problèmes d'unification monétaire des pays du COMECON', in *Revue d'économie politique*, 1970, p. 608 ff.; M. Kaser, 'Le mécanisme des paiements internationaux dans l'Europe de l'Est', in *Economie appliquée*, 1970, p. 123 ff.; J. M. Brabant, *Eastern European Cooperation: The Role of Money and Finance*, New York, 1976; F. D. Holzman, 'CMEA's Hard Currency Deficits and Rouble Convertibility', in N. G. Watts (ed.), *Economic Relations Between East and West*, op. cit., pp. 144–63.
2. The USSR is the world's second largest gold producer; Soviet gold exports for 1976 were estimated at between $1,000 and 1,500 million.
3. Soviet scholars, after many hesitations, have begun admitting, since the 1960s, the presence of inflationary processes in the USSR. Indeed, it appears that in virtually all CMEA countries – to a degree obviously varying in time and from country to country – there is a permanent gap between monetary flows and real flows, with an excess of distributed incomes over the mass of goods and services placed on the market.
4. More precisely, this institution is called *Gosudarstvennyi Bank SSSR* (USSR State Bank).
5. The USSR Foreign Trade Bank (*Bank dlia Vneshnei Torgovli SSSR*) carries out most of its transactions through the State Bank.
6. For a detailed discussion both of the characteristics, functions and activities of the said Soviet banking institutions and the evolution of the banking systems in the other East European countries, see W. Jaworski, *Banki i kredyt w europejskich krajach socjalisticznych*, Warsaw, 1971.
7. In this connection, the statement is made by M. Kaser ('Le mécanisme', op. cit., p. 132) that, initially, both banks were forced to charge 'des taux d'intérêt calculés très justes pour vaincre une certaine réserve de la part des banques déjà établies, mais – en particulier, à la suite des ventes d'or soviétique, et une fois acquise une réputation d'honnêteté commerciale – elles purent bientôt opérer à la marge à des taux commerciaux intermédiaires des taux américains et européens.'
8. On this delicate matter, see M. Baumer and H.-D. Jacobsen, 'CMEA and the World Economy: Institutional Concepts', in US Congress, Joint Economic Committee, *East European Economies Post-Helsinki*, op. cit., pp. 1012–15.
9. Fourteen commodities were involved, namely: coal, synthetic rubber, tyres, sawn timber, fuel oil, motor oil, rolled steel, aluminium, zinc, potassium salts, wheat, sugar, meat and tobacco.
10. That is: 1 new ruble = 10 old rubles, with the same conversion rate for all debit and credit items – unlike the monetary reform of December 1947, which had fixed different conversion rates to penalize high incomes deriving from speculative activities.
11. The Commission on currency and financial questions – J. Caillot points out (*Le CAEM*, op. cit., p. 257) – 'est parvenue à des résultats non négligeables dans plusieurs domaines, notamment en ce qui concerne les modes de règlement des dépenses effectuées d'après les prix intérieurs et les tarifs applicables par des pays membres du CAEM lors de la construction

d'usines, pour le règlement de travaux de recherche ou en ce qui concerne les conditions de transferts pour un certain nombre d'opérations.'

12. On the occasion of the meeting held at the Smithsonian Institution, a 7·89 per cent devaluation of the dollar was decided upon.
13. In effect, in a case such as that now considered – as noted by J. Marczewski ('La zone rouble', op. cit., p. 623) – the application of domestic prices in international trade would result in 'vider les pays de produits rares à prix bas et à rendre impossible l'exportation des produits abondants moins chers.'
14. With reference to the statements previously made concerning monetary reforms, and in particular the changes introduced in the gold parity of the ruble in 1950 and 1961, one may speculate about the real meaning of the devaluation or re-evaluation of a currency which is not used in international transactions (see M. Lavigne, *The Socialist Economies*, op. cit., p. 264 f.). Generally speaking, Soviet scholars answer this question by stressing the disadvantages deriving, in the area of foreign trade, from a continuing overvaluation – or undervaluation – of the national currency.

    When the currency is overvalued, the State foreign trade agencies export at a loss, for they purchase the products to be exported, paying to the enterprises, in national currency, prices higher than those which can be obtained from the sale of such products on foreign markets; the opposite happens as regards imports, for the foreign trade agencies sell the foreign products to the national enterprises at higher prices than those paid to purchase them.

    Even though export losses and import gains can to some degree offset each other, the fact remains that imports are artificially cheap while exports are uneconomical; this can lead the state monopolies in charge of foreign trade into difficulties and errors of judgment when considering the desirability of carrying out certain buying and selling operations on foreign markets.

    In the USSR, the 1961 reform is said to have actually produced the effect, *inter alia*, of correcting the situation of a considerable overvaluation of the ruble created by the preceding monetary reform of 1950.
15. For further details, see J. Marczewski, 'La zone rouble', op. cit., p. 624 ff.
16. The Soviet attitude, however, does not seem to be such as to rule out completely the possibility that the USSR may find it advantageous, in the fairly near future, to create a ruble convertible on the financial plane *only*, maintaining its present non-convertibility in goods. As regards this interesting hypothesis, see the comments by P. Wiles, 'On Purely Financial Convertibility', in *Banking, Money and Credit in Eastern Europe* (Main Findings of Colloquium held from 24 to 26 January 1973 in Brussels), NATO Information Service, Brussels, 1973, pp. 119–25.

7 The Institutions for Multilateral Payments and for Investments

1. THE INTERNATIONAL BANK FOR ECONOMIC COOPERATION

The International Bank for Economic Cooperation (IBEC) constitutes an important milestone in the development of the cooperation that is carried out under the influence, more or less direct, of CMEA. It therefore appears useful to examine the purpose, the structure and the other features of the IBEC's operation and activities, and the results it has achieved in its fifteen years of life.

The Bank – created by the 'Agreement on multilateral payments in transferable rubles and on the organization of the International Bank for Economic Cooperation' concluded by the CMEA member-countries on 22 October 1963 – began operations on 1 January 1964.

The IBEC's Charter is an integral part of the Agreement; several changes – designed to intensify the Bank's activities, to expand the system of multilateral settlements and to increase the role of short-term credit towards the development of reciprocal trade – are contained in subsequent protocols.

In determining the basic policies and the activities of IBEC, a significant role is performed by the Standing Commission on currency and financial questions that has been operating within CMEA since December 1962. Thus, the governing body of the IBEC has adopted certain measures in conformity with recommendations issued by that Commission.

The relations between CMEA and the IBEC form the object of a special Protocol, signed on 20 July 1970, intended to regulate the nature and forms of cooperation between the two organizations and, more specifically, between the appropriate Standing Commissions and the Secretariat of CMEA on the one hand and the Council and Board of the IBEC on the other.

Cuba was admitted to the IBEC – as well as the IIB – on 22 January 1974; the Socialist Republic of Vietnam also became a member in the first half of 1977.

1.1 Principles, General Purposes and Functions

In the Preamble to the Agreement of 1963, the signatory governments express the intention of developing and extending the international socialist division of labour, of expanding and strengthening trading and economic links, and, in particular, of improving the system of multilateral payments and expanding the financing in currencies for the fulfilment of mutual obligations.

The Bank for Economic Cooperation was created for the purpose of facilitating the achievement of these goals, both general and particular. The tasks to be performed by the Bank constitute, in a certain sense, a practical implementation of the guidelines set forth in the Basic Principles relating to the international socialist division of labour.

The IBEC does not have a specifically regional character, even though most of its members are from the socialist countries of Eastern Europe; any country, in fact, may become a member, provided it subscribes to the Bank's principles and purposes.

The general purposes of the Bank, as laid down in Article II of the Agreement and the Preamble to the Charter, are to further economic cooperation and the development of the national economies of the member-countries, as well as the development of economic and trade relations with third countries. However, as will be seen shortly, in spite of these general statements, the IBEC's functions largely fall within the scope of monetary cooperation, while economic development and the financing problems connected with it are considered partially and in a wholly subordinate way.

It can be readily seen that the purposes of the IBEC significantly differ from those of other intergovernmental banks: while the latter are essentially development banks, the IBEC's functions are basically of a monetary character.[1]

The basic principle underlying and regulating the Bank's

activity is the full equality of rights and the respect for the sovereignty of the member-countries, in accordance with Article IV of the Agreement, which adds that members enjoy equal rights as regards the study of the various problems and the decisions concerning the Bank's activity.

Each member-country has the same rights as the others, regardless of the size of its contribution to the Bank's capital; there is therefore no system of weighted voting, such as that in effect in the Board of Governors of the International Bank for Reconstruction and Development.

Furthermore, under Article 27 of the Charter, the decisions of the Council – the Bank's highest organ of administration – must be adopted unanimously.[2]

Any member-country may propose amendments to the provisions of the Charter; such amendments, however, may be introduced only with the consent of all members. Unanimity, however, is not required for the termination of the Bank's activity; to this end a decision made by not less than two-thirds of the member-countries shall be sufficient, to determine the terms of the winding-up. Also the Agreement provides, in Article XV, that it shall cease to have effect if denounced by not less than two-thirds of the contracting parties.

The functions of the IBEC are listed in Article II of the Agreement and, in fuller detail, in Articles 9 to 24 of the Charter. These functions include:

a) carrying out the multilateral payments in transferable rubles envisaged by bilateral and multilateral agreements, by contracts for mutual deliveries of goods and by agreements relating to other payments between member-countries

b) extending credit for foreign trade and other transactions by member-countries

c) creating and holding in deposit funds in transferable rubles

d) receiving in account or deposit, from member- and other countries, gold, freely convertible, and other currencies, and carrying out transactions with such funds, within the limit of the sums received

e) performing other banking operations in accordance with the purposes and tasks set forth in the Charter.

In addition to the functions listed above, the Bank was also to carry out, on the application of the countries concerned, the financing and extension of credit for the construction, reconstruction and joint utilization of industrial enterprises and other properties, using the resources allocated by the member-countries for such purposes. In the early 1970s, however, a special institution was established, the IIB, charged with extending medium- and long-term loans for the financing of investment projects, thus taking over such functions from the IBEC.

1.2. Membership: Admission and Withdrawal

The admission and withdrawal of IBEC members are governed by Article 43 of the Charter, which refers to the relevant articles of the Agreement. As indicated above, participation in the Bank is open to any country subscribing to the Bank's purposes and principles. The latter, however, are of such a nature that they can be accepted only by socialist countries. It thus appears that being a socialist country is to be regarded as a tacit requirement for admission.[3]

More precisely, under Article XIII of the Agreement, a country desiring to be admitted shall submit to the Bank's Council an official statement expressing its intention of subscribing to the Bank's purposes and principles and its willingness to assume the obligations deriving from the Agreement and the Charter.

The application for admission shall then be submitted by the Bank's Council to the consideration of the member-countries, whose unanimous consent is required.

Any member-country, under Article XV of the Agreement, may withdraw from the IBEC upon giving six months' notice to the Council. During this period the relations between the Bank and the withdrawing country shall be settled, taking into account the reciprocal obligations. Under Article 5 of the Charter, the withdrawing country has the right to be refunded for any payments made into the Bank, minus its indebtedness to the latter.

1.3. Financial Resources

The Bank's financial resources are of various kinds. In the first place, the Bank possesses its own resources, which include: (a) the charter capital, (b) the reserve fund and (c) the special funds. Moreover, as mentioned above, the Bank may receive in account or deposit, from both member- and non-member-countries, sums in transferable rubles, gold or convertible currencies. Unlike the other international banks, the IBEC is not allowed to raise funds through the issuing and placement of securities.[4]

At present, the Bank's charter capital amounts to 305·3 million transferable rubles (TR).

The share of contribution of each country to the capital is determined in proportion to the specific weight of the volume of its exports in the mutual trade of the Bank's members.

The largest subscription shares are, in decreasing order, those of the Soviet Union, the German Democratic Republic, Czechoslovakia and Poland.

In addition to the charter capital, the IBEC has available a reserve fund and special funds. It is for the Council to fix the amount, destination and terms for the creation of the reserve fund. The special funds may be created only under an agreement among member-countries.

In order to allow the various countries to settle their participation in transferable rubles from the excesses of exports over imports, the payment required for the Bank's first fiscal year, 1964, was limited to 20 per cent of each quota; payments could also be made in gold or freely convertible currencies.[5] The payment of the balance of the participation shares is to be made at the times fixed by the Bank's Council.

At present, the actually paid-in capital amounts to 40 per cent of the charter capital, i.e. 121·6 million TR, of which half in gold or convertible currencies. The reserve capital, in transferable rubles and convertible currencies, which amounted in 1978 to 115·3 million TR was raised to 133·4 million TR in March 1979.

1.4. The Organs and their Competences

According to Article 25 of the Charter, the organs responsible for the administration of the IBEC are the Council and the Board. However, from the standpoint of management, the Chairman of the Board and the Audit Commission are particularly important, so that it seems appropriate to include here some information about their functions, as laid down in the Charter.

The Council, defined by Article 26 as the 'highest organ of administration', is responsible for the general direction of all IBEC activities;[6] it is formed by the representatives of all member-countries, each of which may appoint not more than three persons (usually a Deputy Minister of Finance, a Deputy Minister of Foreign Trade and the Governor of the Central Bank).

Each country, however, may cast one vote, regardless of the amount of its contribution to the capital and of the number of its representatives on the Council; decisions, as mentioned above, are adopted by a unanimous vote. The Council meets whenever necessary, but not less than twice a year; the meetings are held, in turn, under the chairmanship of the representative of each member-country.

In accordance with the provisions of Article 28 of the Charter, the Council:

a) determines the general policies of the Bank as regards relations and cooperation with other banks and organizations

b) approves, on the proposal of the Board, credit and other plans, the annual report, the balance sheet, as well as the directions concerning lending and financing operations, international settlements and currency transactions

c) sets interest rates and decides, after agreement with the member-countries, the establishment of special funds

d) appoints the Chairman and members of the Board, as well as the members of the Audit Commission, which reports to it

e) lays down internal regulations and the status of Bank personnel and authorises the opening and closing of departments, agencies and missions

f) as mentioned above, submits for the consideration of member-countries applications for the admission of new members

g) performs any other function which proves to be necessary for the achievement of the Bank's purposes.

The Board, under Article 29 of the Charter, is the executive organ directly responsible for all activities of the IBEC, within the limits imposed by the Charter and by the Council's decisions. The Board consists of a Chairman and members – chosen, for a term not to exceed five years, from nationals of the member-countries – whose number is fixed by the Council. The Chairman and members of the Board are international officials and, as such, are not responsible to persons or agencies of the respective countries of origin.

It is the Board's duty, under Article 31, to pass on all the principal matters connected with the carrying-out of the Bank's operations. In particular, the Board considers questions on which a decision lies with the Council and to this end it draws up and submits to the Council documents and proposals. The Board prescribes the form of financial and accounting documents and the rules concerning their signature, supervises the activity of administration and sections of the Bank, its departments, agencies and missions. The Board's decisions, under Article 31, are cast in the form of protocols.

The Chairman, under Article 32, directs the Board's activities and takes the necessary action to ensure the attainment of the purposes laid down in the IBEC Charter. In particular, he represents the Bank, manages its assets and resources in accordance with the provisions of the Charter and the decisions of the Council, signs – jointly with another member of the Board – the commitments made by the Bank, and appoints and dismisses employees, except the directors who are members of the Board.

The Audit Commission, as laid down in Articles 34 and 35, consists of a chairman and four members appointed by the Council for two-year terms. It controls the cash assets, accounts, records, assets and inventory of the Bank and audits the annual report of the Board, which is required to make available all necessary documents. The Commission's reports are submitted to the Council.

To carry out the functions attributed to the IBEC, the Council has set up three departments. The Economic and Monetary Department is responsible for studying economic conditions in the various countries and the existing credit systems, following the activity of the international economic organizations operating in the sectors of principal interest to the IBEC, and analysing the evolution of gold prices and of the major currencies on the principal world markets. The Planning and Credit Department is responsible for dealing with the various stages of credit operations in transferable rubles. The General Affairs Department is responsible for more strictly operational matters.

1.5. Personality, Privileges and Immunities

The legal capacity, privileges and immunities of the IBEC are regulated in the first place by Article XI of the Agreement and further detailed in some articles of the Charter. Article XI provides that the Bank should command, in the territory of each member-country, the juridical capacity required for the performance of its functions and the attainment of its goals. Moreover, the Bank, its officials and the Council members should enjoy, again in each member's territory, the privileges and immunities required for the performance of their duties and the attainment of the purposes set forth in the Agreement and in the Charter.

More specifically, under Article 2 of the Charter, the IBEC may conclude agreements, purchase, lease and sell property, and stand in court; it may also open departments and agencies, issue instructions and rules concerning all matters within its competence, and carry out any other operation consistent with the purposes laid down in the Charter. The Bank therefore possesses the capacity of internal law in each member-country.

The Bank, again according to Article 2, is liable for the obligations assumed within the limits of its property; it is not liable, however, for the obligations of the member-countries, which in turn are not liable for the Bank's obligations.

The Bank's privileges and immunities include specifically immunity from any administrative or jurisdictional action, exemption from all direct taxes and charges, inviolability of its premises and records, and exemption from seizure of its property and assets (Article 38 of the Charter).

The Council members enjoy a number of immunities and privileges, such as immunity from arrest, exemption from personal services, customs exemptions, etc. (Article 39). The Bank officials at certain levels enjoy similar immunities and privileges (Article 40).

The IBEC, as mentioned above, may contact and maintain relations with other international institutions operating in fields of its specific interest. Particular mention should be made in this respect of the cooperation agreement concluded by the IBEC with the IIB in Moscow on 26 July 1971, for the coordination of their respective activities in sectors of common interest; in addition permanent relations have been established with banking institutions of both member- and non-member-countries. After the relations established with the Moscow Narodny Bank and the Banque Commerciale pour l'Europe du Nord, the IBEC has concluded agreements with various banks in the USA, Switzerland, Great Britain, Sweden, France, Italy, etc. By the end of the 1970s, the IBEC had operated in convertible currencies, maintained current and deposit accounts, and concluded credit transactions with more than 300 banks in the West.

As regards the relations of the IBEC with member-countries, mention may be made of the agreement entered into with the Soviet Union.

The Bank, under Article IX of the Agreement and Article 14 of the Charter, may effect payments in transferable rubles with non-member-countries, on the terms and conditions agreed upon by the Council with the country concerned. In the 1970s, efforts were made to encourage non-member-countries and their banks to operate in transferable rubles; in October 1976 the IBEC adopted new provisions concerning the use of transferable rubles by Western commercial banks and traders.[7]

1.6. The IBEC's Operations and Results to the Present

The IBEC's operations, besides being specified in certain articles of the Agreement, are regulated in detail by the Charter.

Roughly speaking, operations may be divided into two major categories: multilateral settlements in transferable rubles; and the extension of credit.

Since 1 January, 1964, all settlements, both commercial or otherwise, between IBEC member-countries have been made in a special unit of account – the transferable ruble – with a gold content equal to that of the Soviet ruble, which, as mentioned above, is fixed at 0·987412 gramme. Each member-country disposes freely of its funds in transferable rubles, held in the Bank for the settlement of debts with the other members. Upon the conclusion of trade agreements, each country ensures the balancing of the credit and debit items with all other members. Since 1971, this balance has been based on a pluriennal period, not, as previously, on the calendar year.

The principal form of settlement is collection against documents, which involves immediate payment. The payment documents, accompanied by the invoices for the shipment of goods, are transmitted directly by the bank of the exporting country to a duly authorized bank of the importing country. Each exporting country submits daily to the Bank a request for payment, the amount of which is charged by the Bank against the accounts of the banks of the corresponding importing countries and, at the same time, credited to the accounts of the banks of the exporting countries.

According to the original version of the Charter, the IBEC could extend to the member-countries a series of credits under various arrangements.[8] By the Protocol of 18 December 1970, substantial changes were introduced, with a view to simplifying and expanding IBEC's activity.

In connection with the further expansion of the functions and activities of the Bank at the end of 1977 a number of amendments were introduced in the Agreement on multilateral payments in transferable rubles and the organization of IBEC and in the Charter.

The facilities include short-term credits to meet current requirements connected with ordinary trade transactions and credits for 1 to 3 years, intended to correct conditions of disequilibrium in the balance-of-payments, allow the increase in trade between two or more countries, and so forth. Interest rates have been set between 2 and 5 per cent, depending on the length of the period for which the credit has been granted. It is to be noted that very low interest rates are charged to favour seasonal exports.

In 1978 credits extended by the Bank amounted to 5·7 billion TR (46·2 billion TR from 1964 to 1978).

The IBEC pays interest on the funds deposited with it; at present, the rates are between 1·5 and 4 per cent.

In spite of the creation of the IBEC and the subsequent measures designed to increase its efficiency and further to promote transactions, the member-countries of CMEA seem to continue to plan their foreign trade on mainly bilateral bases; at present only part of the total foreign trade is settled through the Bank. At the end of 1978, the CMEA countries' mutual settlements through the IBEC had reached 106 billion TR, i.e. 4·6 times the amount of 1964, the first year of activity. IBEC's future prospects, on the other hand, appear to be strictly connected with the attainment of the monetary and financial goals indicated in the Comprehensive Programme; at present it appears that a good many of these goals have been set aside.[9]

The table summarizes the most significant data concerning the Bank's activity since the beginning of its operations to 1978.

As regards in particular the transactions carried out by the Bank in convertible currencies, it should be noted that these operations occupy an increasingly important place in the overall picture of IBEC's activities. The total sum of these operations amounted to 82·4 billion TR in 1978. One may wonder, however,

Balance Sheet of the International Bank for Economic Cooperation
(million TR as of 31 December)

	1964	*1965*	*1966*	*1967*	*1968*	*1969*	*1970*	*1971*	*1972*	*1973*	*1974*	*1975*	*1976*	*1977*	*1978*
Assets															
1. Liquid assets:															
(a) Current account and cash	0·6	3·1	5·3	11·1	11·7	15·1	11·6	11·1	9·5	15·2	22·7	32·0	35·2	42·4	44·2
(b) Time deposits	42·8	68·7	123·2	220·3	303·6	406·6	614·0	512·7	1150·0	1144·0	1342·1	1744·9	2017·7	2099·9	2018·4
	43·4	71·8	128·5	231·4	315·3	421·7	625·6	523·8	1159·5	1159·2	1364·8	1776·9	2052·9	2142·3	2062·6
2. Credits outstanding	125·8	203·5	248·8	313·6	351·4	380·3	519·5	741·8	1079·0	1630·0	1722·0	1482·0	1494·3	1992·9	1920·6
3. Inventory property	0·1	0·1	0·1	0·1	0·1	0·1	0·1	0·2	0·2	0·4	0·5	0·5	0·6	0·6	0·6
4. Other assets	–	0·5	6·1	4·3	3·0	4·5	15·8	1·7	6·4	7·5	0·3	47·0	49·3	40·7	36·3
Total assets	169·3	275·9	383·5	549·4	669·8	806·6	1161·0	1267·5	2245·1	2797·1	3087·6	3306·4	3597·1	4176·5	4020·1
Liabilities															
1. Capital:															
(a) Paid up	59·7	59·7	89·7	89·7	89·7	89·7	89·7	104·7	119·7	119·7	119·7	120·1	121·0	121·5	121·6
(b) Reserve	–	0·6	0·9	1·4	1·6	3·2	5·5	9·2	16·8	25·4	36·3	55·3	73·4	93·2	115·3
	59·7	60·3	90·6	91·1	91·3	92·9	95·2	113·9	136·5	145·1	156·0	175·4	194·4	214·7	236·9
2. Deposits received:															
(a) Current	43·9	46·1	112·0	164·3	121·1	134·9	111·0	92·0	226·0	462·0	271·0	426·7	716·9	250·6	401·7
(b) Time	65·1	168·7	173·4	288·9	452·6	562.0	904·0	958·0	1659·0	1942·0	2293·0	2175·6	2244·5	3227·5	2887·2
	109·0	214·8	285·4	453·2	573·7	696·9	1015·0	1050·0	1885·0	2404·0	2564·0	2602·3	2961·4	3478·1	3288·9
3. Credits received and other liabilities	–	0·6	6·3	3·8	3·2	12·7	43·8	91·6	210·6	230·5	345·8	504·0	414·8	454·9	463·5
4. Net profit	0·6	0·2	1·2	1·3	1·6	4·1	7·0	12·0	13·0	17·5	21·8	24·7	26·5	28·8	30·8
Total liabilities	169·3	275·9	383·5	549·4	669·8	806·6	1161·0	1267·5	2245·1	2797·1	3087·6	3306·4	3597·1	4176·5	4020·1

to what extent the increase in convertible currency transactions can be reconciled with the objectives of the Comprehensive Programme and with the intended functions of the transferable ruble.

In conclusion, it may be said that the IBEC is probably going to play an increasingly important role in promoting cooperation both among its member-countries and between the latter and the major countries of the West. The Bank may constitute an important link between the socialist and the 'capitalist' sectors of the world economy in the financial field. The financing of trade between CMEA members and Western countries could become one of the major functions of the IBEC which, in addition, is engaged in considerable activity on the international monetary markets, with substantial operations in gold and in Western currencies.

It should be noted, finally, that since 1962 Western banks have extended to the IBEC several loans, amounting in all to several hundreds of millions of dollars.

2. THE INTERNATIONAL INVESTMENT BANK

The problems connected with the financing of the common investments made by the member-countries and of the extension of medium- and long-term credit, even though falling within the competence assigned to the IBEC, were generally dealt with, during the latter half of the 1960s, within CMEA and outside the IBEC.

The action carried out to this end by the appropriate organs of CMEA proved largely inadequate to meet the growing demands of the development, especially industrial, of the various countries, and therefore several proposals were made for an intensification of the IBEC's activities in the sector of common-investment financing and for the establishment of a special fund for these purposes, provided with substantial resources.

The debates on this matter developed fairly actively through the year 1968. At last, the First Secretaries of the Communist and workers' parties and the heads of government of the CMEA countries met in Moscow in the spring of 1969 and, after a thorough study of the question, decided to create a special banking institution charged with the financing of investment projects and completely independent of the IBEC.

As in the case of the IBEC, the CMEA Standing Commission on currency and financial questions played a leading role in establishing the main lines of activity of the new banking institution and in defining its structure.

The International Investment Bank (IIB) was created by an Agreement concluded in Moscow on 10 July 1970 between the CMEA member-countries, with the exception of Romania which joined six months later, on 12 January 1971. The Agreement creating the IIB came into force provisionally on 1 January 1971 and permanently on 5 February of the same year.

Like the IBEC, the IIB is not a closed institution and any country subscribing to its principles and purposes may participate in it. Cuba joined the IIB in 1974, followed in 1977 by the Socialist Republic of Vietnam. On 26 April 1974, an agreement was signed in Moscow on the basic principles of cooperation between the IIB and Yugoslavia.

The IIB has concluded with CMEA an agreement aimed at coordinating the respective activities in the important sector of investment financing. On 9 January 1973, the IIB concluded an agreement with *Interkhim*, an organization for the coordination of production in the sector of light chemicals among the European members of CMEA.

The main function of the IIB, designed to operate specifically in the investment field, is to extend loans – medium-term (up to 5 years) and long-term (up to 15 years) – for the implementation of projects of common interest to member-countries, connected with the international socialist division of labour and with specialization and cooperation in the field of production. Loans are also extended for projects aimed at the development of the individual national economies of the member-countries. Initially, the IIB charged interest at the rate of 4–4$\frac{1}{4}$ per cent on medium-term loans and of 4$\frac{1}{2}$–6 per cent on long-term loans; such rates were later lowered and now apparently range from 3 to 5 per cent.

In the loan agreements, specific economic criteria are laid down which make it possible to evaluate the project to be financed, as well as the terms and conditions of the loan: disbursement, use and repayment (Article 15 of the IIB Charter). The Bank may extend loans to banking institutions, business organizations and enterprises of the member-countries, to international organizations and enterprises formed by member-countries, and to organizations of non-member-countries (Article VII of the Agreement).

In addition to the activities mentioned above, the IIB may carry out normal banking operations, create its own special funds and manage funds for third parties. The Bank's Charter (Article 11) makes explicit provision for a fund to be used to provide credit for the joint construction of installations in member-countries, and a fund for the financing of economic and technical aid to developing countries. The latter fund, amounting to 1,000 million TR, was created by an agreement signed in Moscow on 11 April 1973.

Under Article 21 of the Charter, the highest management organ of the Bank is the Council, on which all member-countries are represented, each with one vote. Its decisions are adopted unanimously on 'basic' questions and by a three-quarter majority in other cases (Article 22). The executive organ of the Bank is the Board, formed by the Chairman and his three deputies (Article 23).

The charter capital of the IIB was set initially at 1,000 million TR and later, and when Romania joined, at 1,052·6 million TR.

At present, the charter capital of the Bank has reached 1,071·3 million TR. The largest subscription shares are, in decreasing order, those of the Soviet Union, the German Democratic Republic, Czechoslovakia and Poland.

Seventy per cent of the charter capital is required to be in transferable rubles and thirty per cent in gold or convertible currencies.

For the year 1971, the calls on capital subscription amounted to 184·2 million TR, of which 55 million TR was in convertible currencies; an additional payment, to the same amount, was made in 1972. By the end of 1978, 374 million TR, slightly over one third of the capital required by the Charter, had been paid in.

As in the case of IBEC, convertible currencies have been taking up an increasing importance in the transactions of IIB. Since 1973, the Bank has obtained from Western banks substantial amounts of credit on the Eurocurrencies market.

2.1. The IIB Financing Activities

IIB credits have been granted to finance specific projects envisaged by the five-year 'Coordinated Plan', the agreements on production specialization and the national economic plans.

Balance Sheet of the International Investment Bank
(million TR as of 1 January)

	1972	*1973*	*1974*	*1975*	*1976*	*1977*	*1978*	*1979*
Assets								
1. Liquid assets	188·3	366·3	344·1	338·9	372·6	340·4	153·4	284·7
2. Credits outstanding	0·5	24·6	82·8	186·3	554·5	1157·4	1857·4	2025·5
3. Inventory equipment	0·2	0·3	0·3	0·3	0·4	0·4	0·5	0·5
4. Other assets	0·4	–	6·1	6·6	15·1	41·9	63·3	119·0
Total assets	189·4	391·2	433·3	532·1	942·6	1540·1	2074·7	2429·7
Liabilities								
1. Capital:								
(a) Paid up	184·2	368·4	368·4	368·4	369·2	372·0	373·9	374·0
(b) Reserve	–	4·8	11·3	18·0	25·5	41·5	53·7	64·1
	184·2	373·2	379·7	386·4	394·7	413·5	427·6	438·1
2. Special fund for credits	–	–	–	25·0	25·2	25·8	26·4	26·9
3. Deposit and credits received	–	–	37·3	102·7	495·5	1061·1	1572·9	1870·7
4. Other liabilities	–	7·7	4·6	4·3	10·2	22·5	30·3	76·1
5. Profit	5·2	10·3	11·7	13·7	17·0	17·3	17·5	17·9
Total liabilities	189·4	391·2	433·3	532·1	942·6	1540·1	2074·7	2429·7

Some indications concerning the evolution of the IIB balance sheet in the first eight years of its activity appear in the table.

The total sum of credits granted by the Bank to finance projects in its member-countries in the period 1971 to 1978 amounts to over 3 billion TR, covering more than 35 per cent of the global estimated cost of the said projects. Credits granted included: 625·5 million TR to Poland; 518·9 to Hungary; 516·7 to the German Democratic Republic; 500 to Bulgaria; 445 to Czechoslovakia; 294·6 to Romania; 158 to USSR; 5·5 to Mongolia.

Since the Bank began its activities in 1971, 38 projects financed by it have been put into operation.

With regard to the distribution by branches of credits granted by IIB in the period 1971 to 1978, the leading position is occupied by energy and fuel (78·4 per cent of the total), followed by engineering (10·2 per cent), metallurgy (6·2 per cent), chemical industry (2·0 per cent), other industries (1·7 per cent) and transport (1·5 per cent).

The Bank has agreed to grant its first credit to a non-member-country, Yugoslavia, in keeping with the Agreement on the main principles of cooperation signed with that country.

NOTES TO CHAPTER 7

1. In Western literature on the IBEC, comparisons are often made with the European Payments Union and with the European Monetary Agreement and, in certain respects, with the Bank of International Settlements.
2. In this connection J. Caillot (*Le CAEM*, op. cit., p. 275) points out the convenience of 'rapprocher la BICE de l'Union européenne des paiements et de son successeur, l'Accord monétaire européen, administré par le Conseil de l'OCDE où les décisions sont également prises à l'unanimité'. Caillot goes on to note that 'la similitude entre le CAEM e l'OCDE est très grande', so that it is logical 'qu'il en soit de même pour deux organisations bancaires poursuivant des buts similaires et qui ont été créées sous l'égide du CAEM d'une part et de l'OCDE puis de l'OECD d'autre part.' There is no need to stress, on the other hand, the difficulties that can arise for the efficient performance of the work of an agency from the strict application of the unanimity principle.
3. A different opinion is held by J. Caillot (*Le CAEM*, op. cit., p. 265), to the effect that the condition of a socialist state, unquestionable as regards membership of CMEA, would not be mandatory for membership of the IBEC. Caillot, however, does admit that 'l'absence du règlement en devises convertibles des soldes enlève tout intérêt pour les pays europeéns, même

pour ceux qui sont encore en régime de clearing avec les pays de l'Est.' Only the developing countries, according to Caillot, might possibly have a concrete interest in joining the IBEC.

4. This fits, on the other hand, into the framework of the Bank's own aims which do not include, as is usually the case with the other international banks, the possibility of granting long-term loans. In this latter connection, however, it seems that similarities can be found between the provisions of the Agreement cited and the Charter of the Bank, and some provisions of the European Monetary Agreement.
5. Under Article 41 of the Charter, the Bank's fiscal year begins on 1 January and ends on 31 December.
6. The Council's functions are largely similar to those carried out in other international banks by the Board of Governors.
7. See the *Financial Times*, 17 December 1976.
8. More precisely, the following types of credit could be extended:

   (a) clearing credits, for the purpose of ensuring the settlement of the items temporarily not covered in the clearing between payments and receipts relating to the imports and exports of goods and services; such credits were paid back at the time when freely useable funds were credited to the account of the debtor bank;

   (b) seasonal credits, intended to cover deficits caused by seasonal fluctuations or other factors that had affected production or export earnings; the duration of such credits could not extend beyond the end of the calendar year in which they had been granted;

   (c) credits intended to cover a temporary excess of payments due to delays in the deliveries of goods; such credits were to be repaid before the end of the calendar year and carried a higher interest rate;

   (d) credits to finance an increase in trade due to the exceeding of the quotas of goods laid down in the trade agreements between countries; such credits could not be extended beyond the end of the calendar year following that for which they had been granted;

   (e) credits to finance balance-of-payments deficits caused by temporary and exceptional trade difficulties; the duration of such credits could extend beyond the term of the calendar year following that in which they had been granted.
9. In this connection see, finally, the comments made by H.-D. Jacobsen, 'Operation and importance of the COMECON Banks and the Quest for Credits', in *COMECON: Progress and Prospects*, op. cit., pp. 177–86.

Appendix A

1. SESSIONS OF THE CMEA ASSEMBLY

1st Session – Moscow, 26–30 April 1949
Organizational measures and definition of general objectives in the fields of trade and technical assistance.

2nd Session – Sofia, 25–27 August 1949
Adoption of the standard draft of agreements on technical and scientific cooperation.

3rd Session – Moscow, 24–25 November 1950
Measures on trade.

4th Session – Moscow, 26–27 March 1954
General coordination of plans for the period 1956–60.

5th Session – Moscow, 24–25 June 1954
Coordination of plans for the period 1956–60 and consideration of the measures to promote production specialization in certain sectors.

6th Session – Budapest, 7–11 December 1955
Preparation of bilateral trade agreements for 1956–60. Proposals for coordination in the engineering construction sector.

7th Session – Berlin, 18–25 May 1956
Measures to facilitate trade. Proposals for the coordination of transport and of production and development in various sectors, especially steel, engineering, chemicals, oil and natural gas, coal. Considerations of the problems of agriculture. Conversion of the temporary 'working groups' into 'Standing Commissions' charged with developing practical measures designed to facilitate the work of coordination.

8th Session – Warsaw, 18–22 June 1957
Measures for the elaboration and coordination of economic plans for a period of 10–15 years. Establishment of new Standing Commissions. Coordination problems in the sector of energy. Conclusion of an agreement on the introduction of a multilateral clearing system, with the USSR *Gosbank* acting as the clearing house.

9th Session – Bucharest, 26–30 June 1958
Changes in the number and competence of the Standing Commissions. Recommendations for the coordination of plans for the period 1961–5.

10th Session – Prague, 11–13 December 1958
Recommendations in the field of production specialization (chemicals and steel). Decision to build the Friendship Pipeline (*Druzhba*).

11th Session – Tirana, 13–16 May 1959
Proposals for coordination in the engineering, steel and mining sectors. Recommendation for the unification of the electric power networks of various member-countries. Celebration of the 10th anniversary of the Council.

12th Session – Sofia, 10–14 December 1959
Approval of the Charter of the Council and of the Convention on the Legal Capacity, Privileges and Immunities. Proposals for the coordination of plans for the period up to 1965 and the following period.

13th Session – Budapest, 26–29 July 1960
Problems of specialization in agricultural production and in the construction of farm machinery. Coordination of plans to 1980.

14th Session – Berlin, 28 February – 3 March 1961
Consideration of the coordination of plans for the period 1961–5.

15th Session – Warsaw, 12–15 December 1961
Adoption of the 'Basic Principles of the International Socialist Division of Labour'.

16th Session (Extraordinary) – Moscow, 7 June 1962
Approval of Charter amendments and establishment of the Executive Committee. Admission of Mongolia to full membership. Establishment of new Standing Commissions and of the Standardization Institute.

17th Session – Bucharest, 14–20 December 1962
Coordination of investment plans. Problems of energy sources and of specialization in agriculture. Consideration of the possibility of establishing an international bank among socialist countries and creation of a new Standing Commission.

18th Session – Moscow, 25–26 July 1963
Agreement on the Draft Charter of the International Bank for Economic Cooperation (IBEC). Establishment of new Standing Commissions. Coordination of plans for the period 1966–70.

19th Session – Prague, 28 January – 2 February 1965
Coordination of plans for the period 1966–70. Consideration of problems in the field of scientific and technical cooperation. Ratification of the agreement between the Council and Yugoslavia for Yugoslav participation in the activities of some organs of the Council.

20th Session – Sofia, 8–10 December 1966
Consideration of preliminary questions concerning the coordination of plans for the period 1971–5. Problems connected with joint investments in the sector of nonferrous metals.

21st Session – Budapest, 12–14 December 1967
Proposals for the coordination of the 1971–5 plans.

22nd Session – Berlin, 21–23 January 1969
Celebration of the 20th anniversary of the Council and proposals for closer cooperation.

23rd Session (Special) – Moscow, 23–26 April 1969
Consideration of monetary and financial problems. Proposals for the elaboration of a long-term programme for the intensification of cooperation.

24th Session – Warsaw, 12–14 May 1970
Agreement (without Romania's participation) on the creation of the International Investment Bank (IIB).

25th Session – Bucharest, 27–29 July 1971
Approval of the 'Comprehensive Programme for the Further Intensification and Improvement of Cooperation and for the Development of Socialist Economic Integration among Member-Countries of CMEA', which sets forth the basic criteria and the progressive stages of cooperation and integration in the medium- and long-term (1971–80 and beyond).

26th Session – Moscow, 10–12 July 1972
Consideration of the initial stage of the Comprehensive Programme. Admission of Cuba to full membership.

27th Session – Prague, 5–8 June 1973
Review of the results of the implementation of the Comprehensive Programme. Measures concerning supplies of fuels and energy sources and the coordination of plans for 1976–80. Ratification of the cooperation agreement with Finland.

28th Session – Sofia, 18–21 June 1974
Approval of amendments to the Charter. Celebration of the 25th anniversary of the Council. Review of the results of the implementation of the Comprehensive Programme. Coordination of the 1976–80 plans and framing of a common five-year plan, calling for specific integration measures and represented as a 'more advanced and qualitatively new' form of cooperation. Measures for energy supply. Establishment, with the participation of Yugoslavia, of a joint organization for the production of synthetic fibres.

29th Session – Budapest, 24–26 June 1975
Approval of multilateral integration measures to be included in the 1976–80 five-year plans of 'interested' countries. Decision to build new joint production complexes in the sectors of energy and raw materials. Thorough study of the problems connected with the utilization of nuclear energy. Problems of coordination of the 1976–80 plans. Conclusion of a general agreement for financial cooperation and joint action by CMEA members

(excluding Mongolia) for the development of nickel and cobalt products in Cuba. Establishment of new Standing Commissions.

30th Session – Berlin, 7–9 July 1976
Review of the progress made in the first five years of implementation of the Comprehensive Programme. Determination of the forms and methods for the further intensification of the international socialist division of labour. Need for coordinating the national economic plans beyond the usual five-year period. Agreement for the creation of common systems in the sectors of electric power and transport. Problems of the supply and prices of raw materials and energy sources. Aspects of the long-term coordination of common agricultural policies. Aid to the less-developed member-countries.

31st Session – Warsaw, 21–23 June 1977
Discussion of the specialized long-term cooperation programmes in the key sectors of production, following the guidelines laid down in the Comprehensive Programme. Study of the programme for the fullest development of the production of components for the nuclear industry and scheduling for 1978 the conclusion of an agreement for international multilateral specialization in this field. Adoption of measures for the further expansion of scientific and technical cooperation. Approval of the programme for the coordination of national economic plans for the period 1981–5. Measures to accelerate the industrialization of Mongolia and Cuba. Problems of the intensification and strengthening of relations with the other socialist countries, with the Third World and with the industrialized nations of the West.

32nd Session – Bucharest, 27–29 June 1978
Adoption of special programmes for long-term cooperation (up to 1990) in the following sectors: energy, fuels and raw materials; agriculture and the food-processing industry; engineering construction. Plans for the further development of multilateral specialization in the production of equipment for nuclear power plants. Problems of coordination of plans for the period 1981–5. Admission of Vietnam to full membership. Reconfirmation of the 'unanimity rule' in the decision-making process within CMEA. Adoption of organizational measures for the further improve-

ment of the mechanism, the forms and the method of the activities of CMEA. Improvement of relations with non-member-countries and with the EEC.

33rd Session – Moscow, 26–28 June 1979
Adoption of two long-term programmes of cooperation concerning industrial consumer goods and the development of transport facilities. Agreements covering international specialization in production for several branches, including the production of equipment for nuclear power stations. Coordination of plans for 1981–5. Introduction in the Charter of amendments designed to improve the activities of CMEA and to increase its efficiency. Extension to Vietnam, after Mongolia and Cuba, of the Comprehensive Programme special provisions concerning the faster development of the national economy. Observer status granted to People's Democratic Republic of Yemen. Declaration on the 30th anniversary of CMEA adopted by the heads of the national delegations. Restated readiness to conclude an agreement on mutual relations with the EEC and its member-countries.

2. ORGANIZATION CHART OF CMEA

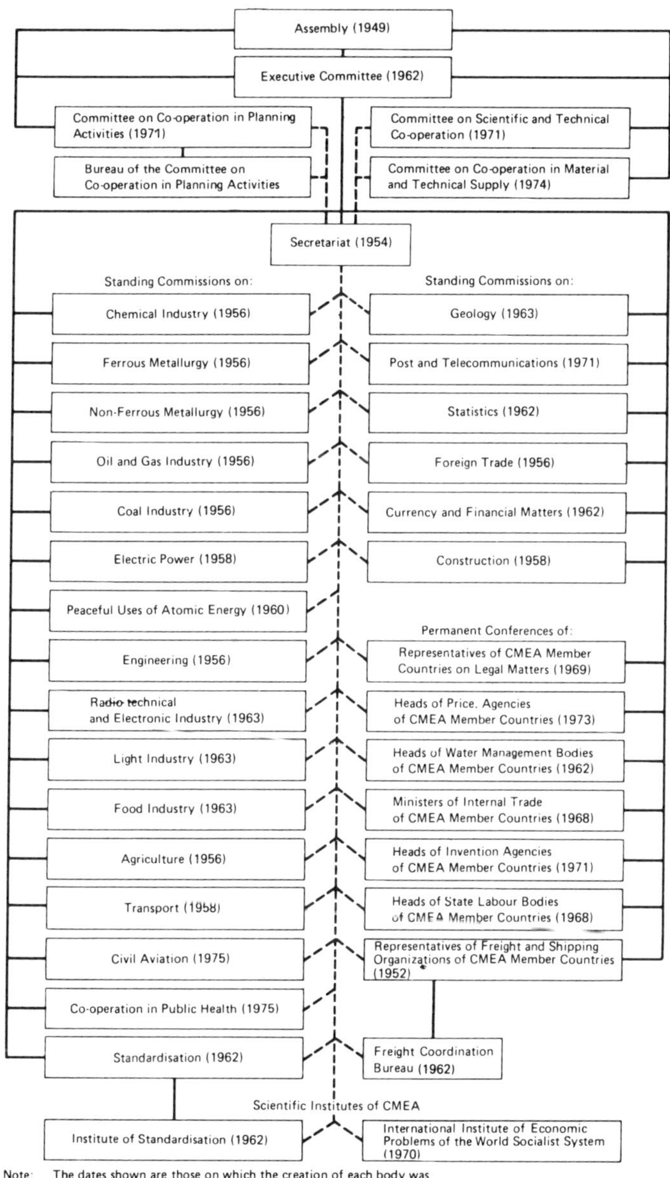

Note: The dates shown are those on which the creation of each body was decided and therefore they do not necessarily coincide with the dates on which the bodies actually began operating.

Appendix B

THE CHARTER OF CMEA*

The Governments of the People's Republic of Albania, the People's Republic of Bulgaria, the Hungarian People's Republic, the German Democratic Republic, the Polish People's Republic, the Romanian People's Republic, the Union of Soviet Socialist Republics and the Republic of Czechoslovakia,

Considering that the economic cooperation successfully carried out between their countries contributes to the most rational development of the national economy, to raising the living standards of the population and to strengthening the unity and solidarity of these countries;

Fully resolved to develop in the future all-round economic cooperation, on the basis of the consistent implementation of the international socialist division of labour to the end of building socialism and communism in their countries and of ensuring a lasting peace throughout the world;

Convinced that the development of economic cooperation among their countries contributes to the achievement of the purposes defined in the Charter of the United Nations;

Confirming their readiness to develop economic relations with all countries, irrespective of their social and political systems, on the basis of equality, mutual advantage and non-interference in domestic affairs;

Recognizing the ever-growing role of the Council for Mutual Economic Assistance in organizing economic cooperation among their countries;

Have agreed for these purposes to adopt the present Charter.

* The Charter – signed in Sofia in 1959 and amended in 1962 and in 1974 – was translated from the original Russian text by Giuseppe Schiavone.

ARTICLE I: PURPOSES AND PRINCIPLES

1. The aim of the Council for Mutual Economic Assistance is to contribute, by uniting and coordinating the efforts of the member-countries, to the further intensification and improvement of cooperation and the development of socialist economic integration, the planned development of the national economies, the acceleration of economic and technical progress, the raising of the level of industrialization in the less-industrialized countries, the steady increase in the productivity of labour, the approximation and gradual equalization of levels of economic development and the constant improvement in the welfare of the peoples of the member-countries.

2. The Council is based on the principle of the sovereign equality of all member-countries.

Economic, scientific and technical cooperation among member-countries is carried out in accordance with the principle of socialist internationalism, with respect for state sovereignty, independence and national interests, non-interference in internal affairs, full equality of rights, mutual advantage and mutual fraternal assistance.

ARTICLE II: MEMBERSHIP

1. The original members of the Council are the countries which signed and ratified the present Charter.

2. Membership in the Council is open to other countries which subscribe to its purposes and principles and agree to assume the obligations set forth in the present Charter.

The admission of new members shall be effected by decision of the Assembly, on the basis of official applications by countries for membership.

3. Each member-country may withdraw from the Council by giving notice to that effect to the depositary of the present Charter. Such notice shall come into force six months after its receipt by the depositary. Upon receipt of such notice the depositary shall inform the member-countries.

4. The member-countries of the Council agree:

a. to ensure the implementation of the recommendations of the organs of the Council adopted by them;

b. to give the Council and its officials the necessary cooperation in the discharge of their functions under the present Charter;

c. to submit to the Council materials and information necessary for carrying out the tasks assigned to it;

d. to inform the Council about the progress made in the implementation of the recommendations adopted in the Council.

ARTICLE III: FUNCTIONS AND POWERS

1. In conformity with the purposes and principles laid down in Article I of the present Charter, the Council shall:

a. organize all-round economic, scientific and technical cooperation between the member-countries, with a view to making the most rational use of their natural resources and accelerating the development of their production capacities; contribute to the development of socialist economic integration;

b. foster the improvement of the international socialist division of labour through the coordination of the national economic development plans and the specialization and cooperation relating to production in the member-countries;

c. take the necessary measures to study economic, scientific and technical problems which are of interest to the member-countries;

d. assist the member-countries in elaborating, coordinating and carrying out joint measures for:

- the development of industry and agriculture in the member-countries;
- the development of transport, with a view to ensuring priority for increasing export, import and transit shipments of goods in the member-countries;
- the most efficient use of investment funds allocated by the member-countries for the development of mining and manufacturing industries and for the construction of major projects which are of interest to two or more countries;

– the development of trade and exchange of services between member-countries, and between them and other countries;
– the exchange of scientific and technical expertise and advanced production experience;

e. take such other action as may be necessary for the achievement of its purposes.

2. In conformity with the present Charter, the Council:
   a. may adopt recommendations and decisions through the agency of its organs acting within the limits of their competence;
   b. may conclude international agreements with its member-countries, with other countries and with international organizations.

ARTICLE IV: RECOMMENDATIONS AND DECISIONS

1. Recommendations are adopted on questions of economic, scientific and technical cooperation. Recommendations are to be submitted for consideration to member-countries.

Recommendations adopted by member-countries are implemented by decision of the governments or other competent organs of such countries, in conformity with their respective national legislatures.

2. Decisions are adopted on organizational and procedural questions. Decisions enter into force on the day of signing of the minutes of the meeting of the competent organ of the Council, unless otherwise provided therein or because of the nature of the subject-matter.

3. Recommendations and decisions are adopted only with the consent of the interested member-countries, each country having the right to declare its interest in any question considered by the Council.

Recommendations and decisions do not apply to the countries which declared they had no interest in the question. Each such country, however, may subsequently join in recommendations and decisions adopted by other member-countries.

ARTICLE V: ORGANS

1. The Council, in order to exercise the functions and powers referred to in Article III of the present Charter, has the following principal organs:

Assembly,
Executive Committee,
Committees,
Standing Commissions,
Secretariat.

2. Such other organs as may prove to be necessary shall be established in conformity with the present Charter.

ARTICLE VI: ASSEMBLY

1. The Assembly is the supreme organ of the Council. It may discuss all questions within the competence of the Council and adopt recommendations and decisions in conformity with the present Charter.

2. The Assembly consists of delegations from all the member-countries of the Council. The government of each member-country determines the composition of its delegation.

3. The Assembly meets for its regular session once a year in turn in the capital of each member-country, under the chairmanship of the head of the delegation of the host-country.

4. The Assembly may meet for an extraordinary session, at the request or with the consent of at least one-third of its member-countries.

5. The Assembly shall:

a. consider:

- fundamental questions of economic, scientific and technical cooperation and determine major policies of the Council;
- the report of the Executive Committee on the activities of the Council;

b. exercise such other functions as may be necessary for the achievement of the purposes of the Council.

6. The Assembly may establish such organs as it deems necessary for the exercise of the functions conferred on the Council.

7. The Assembly adopts its own rules of procedure.

ARTICLE VII: EXECUTIVE COMMITTEE

1. The Executive Committee consists of representatives of all the member-countries, at the level of the deputy head of the government, on the basis of one from each country.

The Executive Committee is the principal executive organ of the Council.

2. The Executive Committee meets, as a rule, once every three months.

3. The Executive Committee, within the limits of its competence, is entitled to adopt recommendations and decisions in conformity with the present Charter. The Executive Committee may submit proposals for consideration by the Assembly.

4. The Executive Committee shall:

a. direct all activities relating to the fulfilment of the tasks facing the Council, in conformity with the decisions of the Assembly, and systematically supervise the fulfilment by member-countries of the obligations arising from the adoption of the recommendations of the organs of the Council;

b. direct work on the coordination of the national economic development plans and on the specialization and cooperation relating to production in member-countries, and organize the elaboration of basic approaches towards a rational division of labour in key industries of these countries;

c. examine proposals of the member-countries and the relevant organs of the Council concerning questions of economic, scientific and technical cooperation, and analyse such cooperation and elaborate measures to promote its further development;

d. elaborate basic approaches and measures for the development of:

– trade and the exchange of services between member-countries;

– scientific and technical cooperation between member-countries;

e. direct the work of the Committees, of the Standing Commissions and of the Secretariat as well as of the other competent organs of the Council, and determine the fundamental direction and policies;

f. approve:
- the staff of the Secretariat, the budget of the Council and the report of the Secretariat on the use of the budget;
- the rules of procedure of the Committees, of the Standing Commissions and of the Secretariat as well as of the other organs of the Council;

g. establish control bodies for auditing the expenses of the Secretariat;

h. exercise other functions under the present Charter as well as on the recommendations and decisions of the Assembly.

5. The Executive Committee may establish such organs as it deems necessary for the exercise of its functions.

6. The Executive Committee adopts its own rules of procedure.

ARTICLE VIII: COMMITTEES

1. The Committees are established by the Assembly to ensure a comprehensive examination and a multilateral settlement of the major problems of cooperation among member-countries in the fields of the economy, science and technology.

The Committees perform the functions laid down in the provisions applicable to them as well as such other functions as may derive from the recommendations and decisions of the Assembly and of the Executive Committee.

2. The Committees consist of the leaders of the relevant bodies of the member-countries, one representative for each country.

3. The Committees, within the limits of their competence, are entitled to:

a. adopt recommendations and decisions in conformity with the present Charter;

b. submit proposals to the Assembly and to the Executive Committee;

c. establish working groups to study problems within the competence of the Committees, to be examined and agreed upon by the Committees, and convene scientific and technical conferences and other meetings;

d. request the Standing Commissions and other relevant organs of the Council to furnish information and suggestions on questions connected with their activity.

4. The Committees submit annual reports on their activities to the Executive Committee.

5. The Committees adopt their own rules of procedure.

ARTICLE IX: STANDING COMMISSIONS

1. The Standing Commissions are established by the Assembly for the purpose of promoting the further development of economic relations among the member-countries and the organization of multilateral economic, scientific and technical cooperation in individual sectors of the national economy of such countries.

The Standing Commissions work out measures and prepare proposals for the implementation of the above-mentioned cooperation, including preparation of the relevant multilateral agreements. They exercise, in addition, other functions under the present Charter as well as on the recommendations and decisions of the Assembly, the Executive Committee and the Committees.

2. The Standing Commissions consist of the delegations appointed by member-countries.

3. The Standing Commissions, within the limits of their competence, are entitled to:

a. adopt recommendations and decisions in conformity with the present Charter;

b. submit proposals to the Assembly and to the Executive Committee and, by request or on their own initiative, submit information and proposals to other relevant organs of the Council;

c. establish working groups to study problems within the competence of the Commissions, to be examined and agreed upon by the Commissions, and convene scientific and technical conferences and other meetings.

4. The Standing Commissions submit annual reports on their work and on their future activities to the Executive Committee.

5. The Standing Commissions adopt their own rules of procedure.

ARTICLE X: SECRETARIAT

1. The Secretariat consists of the Secretary, his deputies and such staff as may be necessary for the performance of the functions assigned to the Secretariat.

The Secretary is appointed by the Assembly and his deputies by the Executive Committee.

The Secretary and his deputies direct the work of the Secretariat. The staff of the Secretariat is recruited from nationals of the member-countries, in conformity with the rules governing the Secretariat.

The Secretary is the chief official of the Council. He represents the Council in relations with officials and organizations of the member-countries, of other countries and of international organizations. The Secretary may empower his deputies as well as the officials of the Secretariat to act on his behalf.

The Secretary and his deputies may take part in all the meetings of the organs of the Council.

2. The Secretariat shall:

a. make arrangements for and assist in holding meetings of the organs of the Council and of the conferences convened within the framework of the Council and prepare or assist in preparing documents for the meetings of the organs of the Council, in conformity with the working plans of these organs; ensure the implementation of the secretariat responsibilities of the other organs of the Council;

b. prepare economic surveys and carry out economic studies on the basis of the material supplied by member-countries, prepare and publish information, reference and other documents on questions of economic, scientific and technical cooperation of the member-countries, and prepare other surveys and studies;

c. prepare proposals on specific questions concerning the activities of the Council for consideration by the relevant organs of the Council;

d. work out or contribute to working out drafts of multilateral agreements in the fields of economic, scientific and technical cooperation, in conformity with the recommendations and decisions of the organs of the Council;

e. organize and record the implementation of the recommendations and decisions of the organs of the Council and prepare the relevant proposals for consideration by these organs;

f. take other actions under the present Charter, or on the recommendations and decisions of the Council, as well as under the rules governing the Secretariat.

3. The Secretary, his deputies and the staff of the Secretariat, in performing their duties, shall act as international officials.

4. The seat of the Secretariat is in Moscow.

ARTICLE XI: PARTICIPATION OF OTHER COUNTRIES IN THE ACTIVITIES OF THE COUNCIL

The Council may invite non-member-countries to participate in the activities of its organs or to cooperate with the latter in other ways.

The conditions under which the representatives of non-member-countries may participate in the activities of the organs of the Council or cooperate with the Council in other ways are established by the Council in agreement with the countries concerned, generally through the conclusion of agreements.

ARTICLE XII: RELATIONS WITH INTERNATIONAL ORGANIZATIONS

The Council may establish and maintain relations with the organs of the United Nations, with specialized international organizations and with other international organizations.

The character and form of these relations are established by the Council in agreement with the competent organs of the United Nations and with the international organizations concerned, especially by concluding agreements.

ARTICLE XIII: FINANCIAL QUESTIONS

1. All the revenues and expenditures of the Council are specified in its budget. Member-countries bear the costs of maintaining the Secretariat and financing its activity as well as the other expenditures of the Council in conformity with its budget. The amount of the contributions to be paid by each member-country to the Council's budget is determined by the Assembly.

2. The Secretariat submits to the Executive Committee the draft budget of the Council for each calendar year and a report on the implementation of the previous budget. The financial activities of the Secretariat are audited annually.

3. The expenditures resulting from participation in the meetings of the Council's organs as well as in the conferences held within the framework of the Council are covered by the countries so represented.

4. The expenditures relating to conference premises and to technical facilities necessary for the meetings and conferences referred to in paragraph 3 of the present Article are born by the host-country, except when such meetings and conferences are held at Council headquarters.

ARTICLE XIV: MISCELLANEOUS PROVISIONS

1. The Council enjoys, in the territory of each member-country, the legal capacity required for the discharge of its functions and the achievement of its purposes.

2. The Council, representatives of the member-countries and Council officials enjoy, in the territory of each of these countries, the privileges and immunities necessary to discharge their functions and achieve the purposes envisaged in the present Charter.

3. The legal capacity, privileges and immunities indicated in the present Article are determined by a special Convention.

4. The provisions of the present Charter do not affect the rights and obligations of member-countries arising from their membership of other international organizations and from the international treaties concluded by them.

5. The representatives of the member-countries on the Executive Committee are concurrently the permanent representatives of their countries on the Council. The permanent

representative of a country on the Council has a deputy, advisers and such other staff as may be necessary in the seat of the Secretariat.

ARTICLE XV: LANGUAGES

The languages of all the member-countries are the official languages of the Council. Russian is the working language of the Council.

ARTICLE XVI: RATIFICATION AND ENTRY INTO FORCE OF THE CHARTER

1. The present Charter is subject to ratification by the signatory countries in conformity with their respective constitutional procedures.

2. The instruments of ratification shall be deposited with the depositary of the present Charter.

3. The Charter shall enter into force immediately upon the deposit of the instruments of ratification by all signatory countries; the depositary shall inform the countries concerned.

4. With regard to each country which, in conformity with paragraph 2, Article II, of the present Charter, is admitted to the Council and ratifies the present Charter, the latter shall enter into force provisionally on the day on which the Assembly decides to admit the country in question as a member of the Council and permanently on the day of the deposit by that country of the instrument of ratification; the depositary shall inform the other member-countries.

ARTICLE XVII: PROCEDURE FOR AMENDING THE CHARTER

Each member-country of the Council may submit proposals for the amendment of the present Charter.

The amendments approved by the Assembly shall enter into force as soon as all the member-countries have deposited with the depositary their instruments of ratification of the amendments.

ARTICLE XVIII: FINAL PROVISIONS

The present Charter is executed in a single copy in the Russian language. The Charter shall be deposited with the Government of the Union of Soviet Socialist Republics which shall send certified copies to the Governments of all the other member-countries and shall inform these Governments and the Secretary of the Council of the deposit of the instruments of ratification.

In witness whereof the representatives of the Governments of the member-countries of the Council have signed the present Charter.

Done in the city of Sofia on 14th December 1959.

Appendix C

A SELECTIVE BIBLIOGRAPHY

Linda Ervin

The major portion of this bibliography (entries up to October 1975) was originally published as Bibliography Series 2 of the Norman Paterson School of International Affairs, in cooperation with the Institute of Soviet and East European Studies, Carleton University, Ottawa, Canada. The present bibliography revises and updates the earlier one, with works up to November 1978 being included.

The Bibliography is a selective listing of published materials on the Council for Mutual Economic Assistance (Comecon/CMEA) which have appeared in English, French or Russian during the time period delineated above. Studies previous to 1965 which were considered substantial and important to the area have also been included. News stories and other topical articles have generally been excluded. Material published by translation services (i.e. US Joint Publications Research Services, Radio Free Europe Research) have not been indexed systematically.

In most cases, the actual item has been examined, not only for correct bibliographical citation, but also for quality and relevance to the subject.

The Bibliography has been divided into three major sections. The first section lists books, monographs and other major works on the subject. The second section lists articles and other shorter studies, dividing them according to their predominant content. The third section lists texts of agreements among Comecon member-nations, and Comecon publications. In each section, materials are listed alphabetically by author, or in the absence of an individual author, by title.

Linda Ervin is a graduate of the Institute of Soviet and East European Studies, Carleton University, Ottawa, Canada.

Russian language entries have been transliterated according to the Library of Congress scheme.

The preface to the original bibliography, by Carl H. McMillan, Director, Institute of Soviet and East European Studies, Carleton University, has been included.

Ottawa, Canada
January 1979

Linda Ervin

TABLE OF CONTENTS

PREFACE TO BIBLIOGRAPHY

The compilation of this bibliography was undertaken within the framework of the East-West project of the Institute of Soviet and East European Studies and financed in part through a grant by the Donner Canadian Foundation. It was felt that a bibliography of intra-regional economic relations would complement the Institute's other bibliographic work under its special programme on East–West relations.[1] We also hope that the bibliography will contribute to teaching and research in the Norman Paterson School of International Affairs, and in particular to the School's seminar on 'Integration in Eastern Europe'.

Founded in 1949, the Council for Mutual Economic Assistance (CMEA or Comecon) has served increasingly as the vehicle through which common goals and coordinated policies are pursued in Eastern Europe. It has therefore seemed appropriate to make it the focus of this second bibliography in the Carleton series on international integration.[2]

It is possible to distinguish three periods in this evolution. In an initial phase, covering approximately the first five years of the organization's history, its activities and membership were limited, and it served primarily as a forum for inter-state consultation. In a second period, from the mid-1950s to the late 60s, the organization's objectives were broadened (the 1962 Basic Principles of the International Socialist Division of Labour), its institutional framework strengthened (the 1959 Charter of the Council for Mutual Economic Assistance) and its activities and membership enlarged. In a third period, attempts were made to give new impetus both to the concept and mechanism of integration and to establish guidelines for integration in the 1970s (the 1971 Comprehensive Programme for the Further Extension and Improvement of Cooperation and the Development of

[1] See L. Ervin and C. H. McMillan, 'A Selective Bibliography of East–West Commercial Relations', *Law and Contemporary Problems*, Vol. 37, No. 4 (East–West Trade, Part II), pp. 682–97. (Reprinted in K. Grzybowski, ed., *East–West Trade*, Dobbs Ferry, N.Y.: Oceana Publications, and Leiden, Netherlands:, A. W. Sijthoff, 1973, pp. 292–307).

[2] The first bibliography covered the more general theoretical literature on integration. (A. Abonyi and B. Campbell, *International Integration: a Select Bibliography*, Bibliography Series 1, The Norman Paterson School of International Affairs, Carleton University, December 1975).

Socialist Economic Integration by the CMEA Member-countries).

While this bibliography concentrates on materials published during the most recent period, many of the works cited document and assess developments in the earlier periods as well. The bibliography is divided into substantive sections which deal with the concepts and goals of the organization, and with major areas of its activity, such as plan coordination, production specialization, scientific and technical cooperation, trade and financial relations. A special section lists works on the relations with the organization of individual member- and associated states. Another is devoted to the growing relations between the CMEA and the European Economic Community. The expanding activities of the organization are reflected in the increased number of documents and publications issued by the CMEA Secretariat in Moscow, listed in a final section.

It is hoped that by listing the principal English, French and Russian language sources under useful substantive headings, this bibliography will both generate and facilitate further scholarship in this field. Much of the work on integration in the West has been focused on the Western European experience, and the concepts and methods thereby developed have limited relevance to CMEA. It is for this reason that an attempt has been made to include as much as possible the Eastern literature, either in the Russian language, or in English or French translation.

The bibliography was compiled by Mrs Linda Ervin of the National Library of Canada, a graduate of the Institute. Mr Arpad Abonyi, a graduate of the School of International Affairs and presently a doctoral candidate in the Department of Political Science at Carleton made many valuable contributions. We are grateful to the School for making possible the publication of this bibliography, and in particular to Mrs Jane Beaumont, the general editor of this series, for handling the arrangements.

Carl H. McMillan
Director

Institute of Soviet and East European Studies
Carleton University
Ottawa
December 1975

I. MAJOR STUDIES (BOOKS, MONOGRAPHS, COLLECTIONS OF PAPERS, CONFERENCE PROCEEDINGS, SPECIAL JOURNAL ISSUES)

1. Agoston, Istvan. *Le marché commun communiste; principes et pratiques du Comecon.* Geneva: Librairie Droz, 1965.
2. Akademiia Nauk SSSR. Institut gosudarstva i prava. *Pravovye voprosy deiatel'nosti SEV.* Moscow: Mezhdunarodnye otnosheniia, 1977.
3. Alampiev, Petr Martynovich, and Bogomolov, O. T. *Ekonomicheskaia integratsiia–ob'ektivnaia potrebnost' razvitiia mirovogo sotsializma.* Moscow: Izdatel'stvo Mysl', 1971.
4. Amacher, Ryan C. *Yugoslavia's foreign trade – a study of state trade discrimination.* New York: Praeger, 1972.
5. Apro, A. *Mezhdunarodnye organizatsii – chlenov SEV v usloviiakh sotsialisticheskoi integratsii.* Moscow: Izdatel'stvo Ekonomika, 1972.
6. Atlas, M. S. *Razvitie bankovskikh sistem stran sotsializma.* Moscow: Izdatel'stvo Finansy, 1967.
7. Ausch, Sandor. *Bilateralism and multilateralism in CMEA.* Budapest: Akademiai Kiado, 1969.
8. Ausch, Sandor. *Theory and practice of CMEA cooperation.* Revised edn. Budapest: Akademiai Kiado, 1972.
9. Baikov, V. S. *Razvitie ekonomiki stran uchastnitsy SEV v 1963–1964 gg.* Moscow: Znanie, 1965.
10. Bautina, Ninel. *CMEA today: from economic cooperation to economic integration.* Moscow: Progress Publishers, 1975.
11. Bautina, Ninel. *Ekonomicheskie problemy razvitiia mirovoi sistemy sotsializma.* Moscow: Izdatel'stvo Moskovskogo Universiteta, 1967.
12. Bautina, Ninel. *Sovershenstvovanie ekonomicheskikh vzaimootnoshenii stran-chlenov SEV: voprosy teorii.* Moscow: Izdatel'stvo Ekonomika, 1972.
13. Bekarevich, Anatolii Danilovich. *Kuba: vneshnezkon. otnosheniia.* Moscow: Nauka, 1970.
14. Beliaev, Iurii Nikolaevich. *CMEA and competition between two systems.* Moscow: Novosti Press Agency Publishing House, 1965.

15. Beliaev, Iurii Nikolaevich. *Sblizhenie urovnei ekonomicheskogo razvitiia sotsialisticheskikh stran – ocherk teorii.* Moscow: Izdatel'stvo Mysl', 1967.
16. Beliaev, Iurii Nikolaevich. *Strany SEV v mirovoi ekonomiki.* Moscow: Mezhdunarodnye Otnosheniia, 1967.
17. Beliaev, Iurii Nikolaevich and Semenova, L. S. *Sotsialisticheskaia integratsiia i mirovoe khoziaistvo.* Moscow: Izdatel'stvo Mezhdunarodnye Otnosheniia, 1972.
18. Bogomolov, O. T. *Ekonomicheskaia effektivnost' mezhdunarodnogo sotsialisticheskogo razdeleniia truda; voprosy metodologii.* Moscow: Izdatel'stvo Ekonomika, 1965.
19. Bogomolov, O. T. *Teoriia i metodologiia mezhdunarodnogo sotsialisticheskogo razdeleniia truda.* Moscow: Izdatel'stvo Mysl', 1967.
20. Boltho, A. *Foreign trade criteria in socialist economies.* Cambridge: Cambridge University Press, 1971.
21. Bondarenko, E. L. *Sotsialisticheskaia mezhgosudarstvennaia spetsializatsiia i kooperirovanie proizvodstva* (*na primere stran-chlenov SEV*). Moscow: Izdatel'stvo Moskovskogo Universiteta, 1968.
22. Brabant, Jozef M. P. van. *Bilateralism and structural bilateralism in intra-CMEA trade.* Groningen, Netherlands: Academic Book Services Holland for Rotterdam University Press, 1973.
23. Brabant, Jozef M. P. van. *East European cooperation: the role of money and finance.* New York: Praeger, 1977.
24. Brabant, Jozef M. P. van. *Essays on planning, trade and integration in Eastern Europe.* Groningen, Netherlands: Rotterdam University Press, 1974.
25. Bracewell-Milnes, Barry. *Economic integration in East and West.* London: Croom Helm, 1976.
26. Broner, Adam. *Economic integration in Eastern Europe.* Ann Arbor, Michigan: University Microfilms, 1976.
27. Brown, Alan A., and Neuberger, Egon (eds). *International trade and central planning: an analysis of economic interactions.* Berkeley: University of California Press, 1968.
28. Caillot, Jean. *Le CAEM: Aspects juridiques et formes de coopération économique entre les pays socialistes.* Paris: Librairie Générale de Droit et de Jurisprudence, 1971.
29. Colloque sur la Problématique Comparée de l'Intégration, 2ème, Louvain, 1975. *L'intégration en Europe: la CEE et le*

Comecon. Actes du deuxième Colloque sur la Problématique Comparée de l'Intégration, organisé par E. Cerexhe et M. Léonard. Louvain, 8 et 9 octobre 1975. Brussels: Bruylant, 1976.

30. "Comecon survey". *Banker*, CXXVIII (May 1978). Special issue on CMEA.
31. Degtyar', L. S. *Trudovye resursy i ikh ispol'zovanie v zarubezhnykh sotsialisticheskikh stranakh – chlenakh SEV.* Moscow: Izdatel'stvo Nauka, 1969.
32. Domes, Alfred and Hauptmann, Jerzy (eds). *United Europe faces the West.* Kansas City: Governmental Research Bureau, 1972. (East Europe Monographs, No. 3.)
33. Dracheva, N. E., and Popov, N. N. *Germanskaia Demokraticheskaia Respublika v sisteme mezhdunarodnogo sotsialisticheskogo razdeleniia truda.* Moscow: Izdatel'stvo IMO, 1963.
34. Dudinskii, I. V. (ed.). *Faktory povysheniia effektivnosti proizvodstva v mirovoi sotsialisticheskoi sisteme, na primere stran chlenov SEV.* Moscow: Izdatel'stvo Mysl', 1965.
35. Dutoit, Bernard. *L'Union Soviétique face à l'intégration européenne.* Lausanne: Centre de recherches européennes, Ecole des H.E.C., Université de Lausanne, 1964.
36. *Ekonomicheskii mekhanizm sotrudnichestva stran sotsializma; voprosy teorii i metodologii.* Moscow: Izdatel'stvo Mysl', 1970.
37. Emmanuel, A. *La division internationale du travail et le marché socialiste.* Paris: Ecole Pratique des Hautes Etudes, 1966.
38. Evstigneev, R. N. *Novye tendenstii v upravlenii ekonomikoi (iz opyta evropeiskikh stran SEV).* Moscow: Izdatel'stvo Mysl', 1972.
39. Evstigneev, R. N. *Stimulirovanie razvitiia novoi tekhniki v stranakh SEV.* Moscow: Izdatel'stvo Ekonomika, 1969.
40. Eygout, F. *La Banque internationale de coopération économique.* Mémoire D.E.S. Paris: Université de Paris, 1971.
41. Faddeev, Nikolai Vasil'evich. *Sovet Ekonomicheskoi Vzaimopomoshchi, 1949–1974.* Moscow: Ekonomika, 1974.
42. Fainshtein, Anatolii Aleksandrovich. *Dogovornaia otvetstvennost' sotsialisticheskikh organizatsii.* Moscow: Izdatel'stvo Mezhdunarodnye Otnosheniia, 1975.
43. Foldi, T. and Kiss, Tibor (eds). *Socialist world market*

prices. Budapest: Akademiai Kiado, and Leiden: Sijthoff, 1969.

44. Fomina, Liudmila Pavlovna. *Pravo zemlepol'zovaniia v evropeiskikh sotsialisticheskikh stranakh*. Moscow: Nauka, 1975.
45. Freedman, R. O. *Economic warfare in the communist bloc*. New York: Praeger, 1970.
46. Garland, John S. *Financing foreign trade in Eastern Europe: problems of bilateralism and currency inconvertibility*. New York: Praeger, 1977.
47. Goriunov, V. P. (ed.). *Vneshnaia torgovlia evropeiskikh sotsialisticheskikh stran*. Moscow: Izdatel'stvo Mezhdunarodnye Otnosheniia, 1967.
48. Grzybowski, Kazimierz. *The socialist commonwealth of nations*. New Haven, Conn.: Yale University Press, 1964.
49. Hewett, Edward A. *Foreign trade prices in the Council for Mutual Economic Assistance*. New York and London: Cambridge University Press, 1974.
50. Hoffman, G. (ed.). *Eastern Europe: Essays in geographical problems*. London: Methuen, 1971.
51. Holzman, Franklyn D. *Foreign trade under central planning*. Cambridge, Mass.: Harvard University Press, 1974.
52. Ionescu, Ghita. *The reluctant ally; a study of Communist neo-colonialism*. London: Ampersand, 1965.
53. Jackson, W. A. Douglas. (ed.). *Agrarian policies and problems in Communist and non-Communist countries*. Seattle: University of Washington Press, 1971.
54. Jamgotch, Nish. *Soviet-East European dialogue; international relations of a new type*. Stanford, Calif.: Hoover Institution on War, Revolution and Peace, 1968.
55. John, Ieuan G. (ed.). *EEC policy towards Eastern Europe*. Farnborough, Eng.: Saxon House, 1975.
56. Karcz, J. F. (ed.). *Soviet and East European agriculture*. Berkeley: University of California Press, 1967.
57. Kaser, Michael. *Comecon: integration problems of the planned economies*. 2nd edn. London: Oxford University Press, 1967.
58. Kaser, Michael (ed.). *Economic development for Eastern Europe*. Proceedings of a conference held by the International Economic Association. London: Macmillan, 1968.

59. Kiss, Tibor. *Economic cooperation among socialist countries*. New York: 1968.
60. Kiss, Tibor. *International division of labour in open economies, with special regard to the CMEA*. Budapest: Akademiai Kiado, 1971.
61. Kiss, Tibor (ed.). *The market of socialist economic integration*. Selected conference papers. Budapest: Akademiai Kiado, 1973.
62. Kohler, Heinz. *Economic integration in the Soviet bloc, with an East German case study*. New York: Praeger, 1965.
63. Kormnov, Iu. *Mezhdunarodnaia spetsializatsiia proizvodstva; ekonomicheskie problemy na primere sotrudnichestva stran SEV v oblasti mashinostroeniia*. Moscow: Izdatel'stvo Ekonomika, 1968.
64. Kormnov, Iu. *Spetsializatsiia i kooperatsiia proizvodstva stran SEV v usloviakh sotsialisticheskoi ekonomicheskoi integratsii*. Moscow: Izdatel'stvo Ekonomika, 1972.
65. Kuznetsov, Valerii Ivanovich. *Economic integration: two approaches*. Moscow: Progress Publishers, 1976.
66. Ladygin, B. N. and Motorin, I. F. *Problemy sotrudnichestva stran SEV v razvitii toplivno-sogrevoi bazy; voprosy effektivnosti*. Moscow: Izdatel'stvo Ekonomika, 1968.
67. Lascelles, David. *Comecon to 1980*. London: Financial Times, 1976.
68. Lavigne, Marie. *Le Comecon: le programme du Comecon et l'intégration socialiste*. Paris: Editions Cujas, 1973.
69. Lavigne, Marie. *The Socialist economies of the Soviet Union and Europe*. London, 1974.
70. Lavrikov, Iurii Aleksandrovich. *Integratsiia sotsialisticheskogo proizvodstva i upravlenie*. Moscow: Mysl', 1976.
71. Lesechko, M. A. *Sovetskii soiuz v sisteme mezhdunarodnogo sotsialisticheskogo razdelennoe truda stran-chlenov SEV*. Moscow: Izdatel'stvo Ekonomika, 1970.
72. Loeber, Dietrich A. *East–West and intersocialist trade: a sourcebook of the law*. Dobbs Ferry, N.Y.: Oceana Pubs., 1976–7.
73. Luchkina, L. S. *Sovershenstvovania struktury promyshlennosti zarubezhnykh stran-chlenov SEV v usloviiakh nauchno-tekhnicheskogo progressa*. Moscow: Izdatel'stvo Nauka, 1972.
74. Lukin, Lev Ivanovich. *Organizatsiia statistiki v stranakh*

chlenakh SEV. Moscow: Izdatel'stvo Statistika, 1970.

75. Marczewski, J. *Socialist planning in communist countries; a comprehensive analysis of Eastern Europe and the USSR*. New York: Praeger, 1973.
76. Marer, Paul. *Postwar pricing and price patterns in socialist foreign trade (1946–1971)*. Bloomington, Ind.: International Development Research Centre, Indiana University, 1972.
77. Marer, Paul. *Soviet and East European foreign trade, 1946–1969; statistical compendium and guide*. Bloomington, Ind.: Indiana University Press, 1972.
78. Martynov, V. V. *Svodnye ekonomicheskie pokazateli stran sotsializma (Metody ischisleniia)*. Moscow: Statistika, 1971.
79. Mateev, E. *Mezhdunarodnoe sotsialisticheskoe razdelenie truda i narodnokhoziaistvennoe planirovanie*. Moscow: Izdatel'stvo Ekonomika, 1965.
80. Mazanov, G. *Mezhdunarodnye raschety stran-chlenov SEV*. Moscow: Izdatel'stvo Finansy, 1970.
81. Mellor, Roy E. H. *Comecon: challenge to the West*. New York: Van Nostrand, 1971.
82. Menson, M. S. N. *India and European socialist countries: an economic study*. New Delhi: Perspective, 1970.
83. Meshcheriakov, V. *et al. SEV – printsipy, problemy, perspektivy*. Moscow: Izdatel'stvo politicheskoi literatury, 1975.
84. *Mezhdunarodnye organizatsii sotsialisticheskikh stran. Pravovye voprosy organizatsii deiatel'nosti*. Moscow: Mezhdunarodnye Otnosheniia, 1971.
85. *Mezhotraslevoi balans i planirovanie v stranakh-chlenakh SEV*. Moscow: Izdatel'stvo Ekonomika, 1969.
86. *Mezhvedomstvennye sviazi i usloviiakh sotsialisticheskoi ekonomicheskoi integratsii*. Moscow: Iuridicheskoi Literatury, 1973.
87. Mikul'skii, K. *Problemy effektivnosti sotsialisticheskoi ekonomii; iz opyta khoziaistvennogo stroitel'stva v stranakh SEV*. Moscow: Izdatel'stvo Nauka, 1972.
88. Miroshnichenko, B. P. *et al.* (eds). *O kollektivnom opyte stroitel'stva sotsialisticheskoi ekonomiki*. Moscow: Izdatel'stvo Mezhdunarodnye Otnosheniia, 1968.
89. *Mnogostoronnee ekonomicheskoe sotrudnichestvo sotsialis-*

ticheskikh gosudarstv. 2nd edn. Moscow: Iuridicheskoi Literatury, 1972.

90. Montias, John M. *Economic development in Communist Romania*. Cambridge, Mass.: The MIT Press, 1967.
91. *The multilateral economic cooperation of socialist states: a collection of documents*. Moscow: Progress Publishers, 1977.
92. Neme, Jacques. *Economie européenne*. Paris: Presses universitaires de France, 1970.
93. North Atlantic Treaty Organization (NATO). Directorate of Economic Affairs. *Comecon: progress and prospects*. Colloquium held 16th–18th March 1977 in Brussels. Brussels: NATO, 1977.
94. Oleinik, I. P., and Sheviakov, F. N. *Ekonomicheskoe sotrudnichestvo, sotsialisticheskaia integratsiia i effektivnost' proizvodstva*. Moscow: Izdatel'stvo Mysl', 1972.
95. Os'mova, M. N. *Khoziaistvennye reformy i mezhdunarodnoe sotsialisticheskoe razdelenie truda*. Moscow: Izdatel'stvo Moskovskogo Universiteta, 1969.
96. Petushkov, Ivan Grigor'evich. *Ekonomika Kuby v sisteme mezhdunarodnogo sotsialisticheskogo razdeleniia truda*. Moscow: Nauka, 1976.
97. Pindak, F. *Comecon's programme of socialist economic integration*. Munich: Jahrbuch der Wirtschaft Osteuropas, 1974. Reprint edn.: Rotterdam: Erasmus Universiteit Rotterdam, 1974.
98. Pinder, J., and Pinder, P. *The European Community's policy towards Eastern Europe*. London: Chatham House – PEP, 1975. (European Series No. 25.)
99. Plotnikov, K., and Dostal', A. *Problemy ekonomicheskoi integratsii stran-chlenov SEV*. Moscow: Izdatel'stvo Ekonomika, 1970.
100. Poklad, B. *Council for Mutual Economic Assistance: its present and future*. Moscow: Novosti Press Agency, 1973.
101. Popov, I. V. *Osnovnye napravleniia tekhnicheskogo progressa v stranakh SEV*. Moscow: Izdatel'stvo Mysl', 1969.
102. Popov, K. *Razvitie ekonomicheskikh sviazei stran sotsializma*. Moscow: Izdatel'stvo Mysl', 1968.
103. Potemkin, P. N. *Problemy koordinatsii narodnokhoziaistvennykh planov stran SEV*. Moscow: Izdatel'stvo Mezhdunarodnye Otnosheniia, 1968.

104. *Problemy mezhdunarodnogo sotsialisticheskogo razdeleniia truda.* Leningrad: Izdatel'stvo Nauka, 1967.
105. *Proizvodstvennaia integratsiia SEV; kollektivnaia monografiia.* Moscow: Izdatel'stvo Nauka, 1972.
106. Prokhorov, G. M. *Vneshne-ekonomicheskie sviazi i ekonomicheskii rost sotsialisticheskikh stran.* Moscow: Izdatel'stvo Mezhdunarodnye Otnosheniia, 1972.
107. Pryor, Frederic L. *The Communist foreign trade system.* Cambridge, Mass.: The MIT Press, 1963.
108. Ransom, Charles. *The European community and Eastern Europe.* Totowa, N.J.: Rowman & Littlefield, 1973.
109. Robinson, W. F. *The pattern of reform in Hungary.* New York: Praeger, 1973.
110. Rudakov, E. V., *et al. Ekonomicheskaia reforma v sel'skom khoziaistva sotsialisticheskikh stran. Bolgariia. Vengriia. GDR. Pol'sha. Rumyniia. Chekhoslovakiia.* Moscow: Ekonomika, 1968.
111. Rumiantsev, Aleksei Matveevich. *O kategoriiakh i zakonakh politicheskoi ekonomii kommunisticheskoi formatsii; metodologicheskii ocherk.* Moscow: Mysl', 1965.
112. Salvi, Parasharam Ganapatarao. *Comecon and the emerging nations.* New Delhi: Writers and Publishers, 1971.
113. Schaefer, Henry W. *Comecon and the politics of integration.* New York: Praeger, 1972.
114. Selucky, Radoslav. *Economic reforms in Eastern Europe.* New York: Praeger, 1972.
115. Senin, M. *Socialist integration.* Moscow: Progress Publishers, 1973.
116. Seranne, Catherine. *L'intégration économique à l'est: le CAEM: Comecon.* Paris: 1976. (France. Direction de la Documentation. Notes et études documentaires, 4268–70).
117. Sergeev, V. P. *Problemy ekonomicheskogo sblizheniia stran sotsializma.* Moscow: Izdatel'stvo Nauka, 1969.
118. Shagalov, G. *Ekonomicheskaia effektivnost' tovarnogo obmena mezhdu sotsialisticheskimi stranami.* Moscow: Izdatel'stvo Mysl', 1966.
119. Shiriaev, Iurii, and Ladygin, B. *Problemy sovershenstvovaniia ekonomicheskogo sotrudnichestva stran-chlenov SEV.* Moscow: Izdatel'stvo Ekonomika, 1965.

120. Shiriaev, Iurii, and Ladygin, B. *Sotsialisticheskaia ekonomicheskaia integratsiia.* Moscow: Znanie, 1972.
121. Sirc, Ljubo. *Economic devolution in Eastern Europe.* London: Longmans, 1969.
122. Skripko, Vitalii Romanovich. *Okhrana prav izobretatelei i ratsionalizatorov v evropeiskikh sotsialisticheskikh stranakh.* Moscow: Izdatel'stvo Nauka, 1975.
123. *Sodruzhestvo sotsialisticheskoe; SEV.* Moscow: Izdatel'stvo Polit. Literatury, 1973.
124. Solov'eva, Klavdiia Fedorovna. *Ekonomicheskie problemy razvitiia mirovoi sotsialisticheskoi sistemy.* Moscow: Vysshaia Shkola, 1971.
125. Sorokin, G. M. *Mirovaia sotsialisticheskaia sistema khoziaistva.* Moscow: Izdatel'stvo Mysl', 1966.
126. Sorokin, G. M. *Problemy ekonomicheskoi integratsii stran-chlenov SEV.* Moscow: Izdatel'stvo Ekonomika, 1970.
127. *Sotsialisticheskaia integratsiia v oblasti kapital'nogo stroitel'stva.* Moscow: Stroiizdat, 1975.
128. *Sotsialisticheskoe gosudarstvo, pravo i nauchnotekhnicheskaia revoliutsiia.* Moscow: Iuridicheskaia Literatura, 1975.
129. *Sovershenstvovanie upravleniia ekonomikoi stran SEV.* Moscow: Izdatel'stvo Nauka, 1974.
130. *Sovet Ekonomicheskoi Vzaimopomoshchi: osnovnye pravovye problemy.* Moscow: Izdatel'stvo Nauka, 1975.
131. Stepanek, Jiri. *Chekhoslovakiia i ekonomicheskoe sotrudnichestvo so stranami-SEV.* Moscow: Progress Publishers, 1974.
132. Storozhev, V. I. (ed.). *Razvitie sel'skogo khoziaistva i sotrudnichestvo stran SEV.* Moscow: Izdatel'stvo Mysl', 1965.
133. Stupov, A. D. (ed.), *Ekonomicheskoe sotrudnichestvo i vzaimopomoshch' sotsialisticheskikh stran.* Moscow: Izdatel'stvo Akademii Nauk SSSR, 1962.
134. Suda, Z. *La division internationale socialiste du travail.* Leiden: Sijthoff, 1967.
135. Szasz, Ivan. *A uniform law on international sales of goods: the CMEA general conditions.* Leiden: Sijthoff, 1976. Revised and enlarged.

136. Tarnovskii, O. I., and Mitrofanova, N. M. *Stoimost' i tsena na mirovom sotsialisticheskom rynke*. Moscow: Izdatel'stvo Nauka, 1968.
137. Tokareva, Praskov'ia Alekseevna. *Uchrezhdenie mezhgosudarstvennykh ekonomicheskikh organizatsii stran-chlenov SEV: pravovye voprosy*. Moscow: Izdatel'stvo Nauka, 1976.
138. Triska, Jan (ed.). *Communist party states; comparative and international studies*. New York: Bobbs-Merrill, 1969.
139. United States Congress Joint Economic Committee. *Economic developments in countries of Eastern Europe; a compendium of papers*. Washington, D.C.: United States Government Printing Office, 1970.
140. United States Congress Joint Economic Committee. *East European economies post-Helsinki*. Washington, D.C.: United States Government Printing Office, 1977.
141. United States Congress Joint Economic Committee. *Re-orientation and commercial relations of the economies of Eastern Europe*. Edited by John Hardt. Washington, D.C.: United States Government Printing Office, 1974.
142. Usenko, Evgenii Trofimovich. *Formy regulirovaniia sotsialisticheskogo mezhdunarodnogo razdeleniia truda*. Moscow: Mezhdunarodnye Otnosheniia, 1965.
143. Vajda, Imre, and Simai, Michael (eds). *Foreign trade in a planned economy*. Cambridge: Cambridge University Press, 1971.
144. Vikent'ev, A. I. *Ekonomicheskie zakony sotsializma i planirovanie v stranakh SEV*. Moscow: Izdatel'stvo Mezhdunarodnye Otnosheniia, 1967.
145. *Vosproizvodstvo sovokupnogo obshchestvennogo produkta i metodologicheskie problemy mezhotraslevykh balansov stran chlenov SEV*. Moscow: Izdatel'stvo Moskovskogo Universiteta, 1970.
146. Wilczynski, Jozef. *The economics of socialism; principles governing the operation of the centrally planned economies in the USSR and Eastern Europe under the new system*. Revised edn. London: Allen & Unwin, 1972.
147. Wilczynski, Jozef. *Socialist economic development and reforms*. London: Macmillan, 1972.
148. Wilczynski, Jozef. *Technology in Comecon*. London: Macmillan, 1974.

149. Wiles, P.J.D. *Communist international economics*. New York: Praeger, 1968.
150. Zhelev, G. E. *Problemy vosproizvodstva mezhdunarodnogo razdeleniia truda v stranakh-chlenakh SEV*. Moscow: Izdatel'stvo Ekonomika, 1971.
151. Zhukov, V., and Ol'seviia, Iu. R. *Teoreticheskie i metodologicheskie problemy sovershenstvovaniia tsenoobrazovaniia na rynke SEV*. Moscow: Izdatel'stvo Nauka, 1969.
152. Zorgbibe, C. *L'Europe de l'Est face au Marché Commun*. Paris: A. Colin, 1971.
153. Zotova, N. A. *Torgovlia mezhdu stranami SEV v usloviiakh khoziaistvennykh reform*. Moscow: Izdatel'stvo Ekonomika, 1969.
154. Zubkov, A. *Mezhdunarodnoe razdelenie truda i razvitie metallurgii sotsialisticheskikh stran*. Moscow: Izdatel'stvo Nauka, 1968.

II. SHORTER STUDIES (ARTICLES, REPORTS AND OTHER DOCUMENTATION)

A. CMEA: General aspects

155. Alampiev, A., and Vorob'ev, E. 'Izmenenie otraslevoi struktury narodnogo khoziaistva stran SEV', *Voprosy Ekonomiki*, No. 7 (July 1976), 90–100.
156. Alampiev, P., and Shiriaev, Iu. 'Ekonomicheskoe sotrudnichestvo stran sotsializma (K 20-letiiu Soveta ekonomicheskoi vzaimopomoshchi)', *Voprosy Ekonomiki*, No. 1 (January 1969), 47–57.
157. Aleksic, M. 'Growing cooperation', *World Marxist Review*, XVII (July 1974), 110–16.
158. Alekseev, A., and Ivanova, L. 'Prospects of economic development before the CMEA countries', *International Affairs* (Moscow), No. 3 (March 1965), 18–25.
159. Alekseev, A., and Shiriaev, Iu. 'Problems of closing the gaps between economic levels of socialist countries', *International Affairs* (Moscow), No. 4 (April 1966), 8–13.
160. Alekseev, A., and Shiriaev, Iu. 'Voprosy sblizheniia ekonomicheskikh urovnei stran sotsializma', *Mezhdunarodnaia zhizn'*, No. 4 (April 1966), 10–18.

161. Arsic, Dragina. 'Certain problems of economic development and cooperation within the Comecon', *International Problems* (Belgrade), VIII (1967), 133–62.
162. Bakovestskii, O. 'Nekotorye voprosy sovershenstvovaniia organizatsionnykh form ekonomicheskogo sotrudnichestva sotsialisticheskikh stran', *Ekonomicheskie nauki*, No. 4 (April 1969), 45–53.
163. Banrevy, G. 'Legal problems related to the complex programme of the Council for Mutual Economic Assistance', *Acta Juridica* (Budapest), XVIII, fasc. 1–2 (1976), 149–62.
164. Baumer, Max, and Jacobsen, Hanns-Dieter. 'CMEA and the world economy: institutional concepts', in United States Congress Joint Economic Committee, *East European economies post-Helsinki*. Washington: United States Government Printing Office, 1977, pp. 999–1018.
165. Bautina, Ninel. 'International socialist production relations', *Soviet and Eastern European Foreign Trade*, IV (1968), 87–104.
166. Beliaev, Iu. 'CMEA cooperation today', *International Affairs* (Moscow), No. 12 (December 1968), 5–11.
167. Beliaev, Iu. 'Economic ties between the socialist countries', *International Affairs* (Moscow), No. 8 (August 1966), 16–22.
168. Beliaev, Iu. 'Voprosy khoziaistvennykh sviazei sotsialisticheskikh stran', *Mezhdunarodnaia zhizn'*, No. 8 (August 1966), 21–30.
169. Beloff, Nora. 'Comecon blues', *Foreign policy*, No. 31 (Summer 1978), 159–79.
170. Bogomolov, O. T. 'Economic cooperation among the Comecon countries', *Problems of Economics*, VII (January 1965), 39–46.
171. Bogomolov, O. T. 'New developments in socialist cooperation', *New Times* (Moscow), No. 45 (6 November 1966), 10–13.
172. Bogomolov, O. T., and Terechov, V. 'Lenin i razvitie mirovogo sotsialisticheskogo sodruzhestva', *Voprosy Ekonomiki*, No. 2 (February 1970), 3–15.
173. Bondarenko, E. L. 'Nekotorye voprosy sblizheniia ekonomicheskikh urovnei stran-chlenov SEV', *Vestnik Moskovskogo Instituta Ekonomiki*, No. 4 (April 1966), 57–67.

174. Brabant, Jozef M. P. van. 'Communism, international trade and the level of development', *Tijdschrift voor Economie* (Belgium), XV (1970), 317–36.
175. Brabant, Jozef M. P. van. 'The past decade's evolution of the CMEA: old or new problems', *Documentation sur l'Europe Centrale*, No. 4 (1972), 274–300.
176. Brabant, Jozef M. P. van. 'Planning and economic growth in a socialist economy', *Documentation sur l'Europe Centrale*, No. 1 (1972), 42–56.
177. Brabant, Jozef M. P. van. 'Trade creation and trade diversion in Eastern Europe: a comment', *The ACES Bulletin*, XIX (Spring 1977), 79–97. (Critique of Pelzman's article in *ACES Bulletin*, 1976.)
178. Broner, A. 'Autarky in centrally planned economies', *Journal of Common Market Studies*, XV (September 1976), 42–56.
179. Broner, A. 'Degree of autarky in centrally planned economies', *Kyklos*, XXIX (1976), 478–94; Discussion 31, No. 1 (1978), 86–99.
180. Buruguchov, G., and Rozenberg, M. 'CMEA general terms of goods delivery for 1968', *Foreign Trade* (Moscow), No. 5 (May 1969), 30–7.
181. Bykov, A. 'CMEA: international importance of its experience', *International Affairs* (Moscow), No. 2 (February 1965), 16–22.
182. Caire, G. 'Démocraties populaires: terres d'expériences', *Economie et humanisme*, No. 162 (July–August 1965), 22–36.
183. 'The CMEA', *Euromoney* (London), (January 1977), 14–15.
184. 'Comecon – les plans quinquennaux', *Moniteur du commerce international* (25 November 1971), 4771–4816.
185. 'Comecon; the wind is still in the West', *The Economist*, CCLXIII (16 April 1977), 92–94.
186. 'Comecon 1974', *European trends* (London), No. 38 (February 1974), 19–34.
187. 'Communiqué on the 31st session of the Council for Mutual Economic Assistance (held in Warsaw, Poland, 21–23 June 1977)', *Current Digest of the Soviet Press*, XXIX (20 July 1977), 7–8.

188. Dobriansky, Lev E. 'The institutional mould of Comecon', *Ukrainian Quarterly*, XXXI (Spring 1975), 13–26.
189. Dudinskii, I. 'O zakonomernostiakh mirovogo sotsialisticheskogo khoziaistva', *Voprosy Ekonomiki*, No. 3 (March 1968), 73–84.
190. Dutoit, B. 'La responsabilité contractuelle dans les pays de l'Est à la lumière des réformes économiques récentes', *Economies et Sociétés*, V (January 1971), 107–28.
191. 'Economic development in Eastern Europe', *Intereconomics*, No. 5/6 (1977), 158–64.
192. Faddeev, N. 'Leninskie idei i ekonomicheskoe sotrudnichestvo sotsialisticheskikh stran', *Mirovaia ekonomika i mezhdunarodnye otnosheniia*, No. 12 (December 1968), 3–14.
193. Faddeev, N. 'Plodotvornoe sotrudnichestvo (K 20-letiiu SEV', *Biulleten' ekonomicheskoi informatsii SEV*, No. 6 (June 1968), 3–14.
194. 'Future of the "socialist commonwealth": prospects for legal and institutional development in relations among the communist states: a panel . . .', American Society of International Law *Proceedings*, LXVII (November 1973), 47–70.
195. Galetskaia, R. 'Demographic situation in Comecon member nations', *Soviet Review*, XVI (Spring 1975), 34–55.
196. Grzybowski, Kazimierz. 'Foreign trade regime in the Comecon countries today', *Annuaire de l'U.R.S.S.* (Strasbourg), (1970–71), 99–122.
197. Heiss, Hertha W. 'The Council for Mutual Economic Assistance in the mid-1960s', in United States Congress Joint Economic Committee, Subcommittee on Foreign Economic Policy, *Economic developments in countries of Eastern Europe*. Washington, D.C.: United States Government Printing Office, 1970, pp. 528–42.
198. Hewett, Edward A. 'A gravity model of CMEA trade', in *Quantitative and analytical studies in East–West economic relations*, edited by J. Brada. Bloomington, Ind.: International Development Research Centre, 1976, pp. 1–16.
199. Hill, P. 'Long arm of Comecon multis', *Atlantic Community Quarterly*, XV (Autumn 1977), 310–15.

200. Holzman, Franklyn D. 'More on Soviet Bloc trade discrimination', *Soviet Studies*, XVII (1965), 44–65.
201. Holzman, Franklyn D. 'The operation of some traditional adjustment mechanisms in the foreign trade of centrally planned economies', *Economies et Sociétés*, II (1968), 407–44.
202. Hoya, Thomas. 'The Comecon general conditions – a socialist unification of international trade law', *Columbia Law Review*, LXX (February 1970), 252–305.
203. Hula, V. 'The CMEA is twenty-five years old', *Czechoslovak Economic Digest*, III (May 1974), 3–16.
204. Ivanov, I. O. 'O sblizhenii i vyravnivanii urovnei ekonomicheskogo razvitiia stran-chlenov SEV', *Voprosy Ekonomiki*, No. 3 (March 1974), 119–29.
205. Jagielski, M. 'Strategy of cooperation', *World Marxist Review*, XVII (November 1974), 30–7.
206. Kamecki, Z. 'L'avenir du Comecon', *Cahiers économiques de Bruxelles*, No. 47 (3e trimestre 1970), 321–30.
207. Khodov, L. 'Mezhdunarodnye ekonomicheskie organizatsii sotsialisticheskikh stran', *Voprosy Ekonomiki*, No. 10 (October 1966), 93–9.
208. Kohlmey, G. 'Productions dynamiques, structures de l'économie nationale, commerce extérieur socialiste', *Problèmes de Planification*, VIII (1971), 15–37.
209. Korbonski, Andrzej. 'The evolution of Comecon', in *International political communities; an anthology*. New York: Doubleday, 1966, pp. 351–404.
210. Kozma, Ferenc. 'A system of regional economic tables for analysing international economic cooperation', *Acta Oeconomica* (Budapest), VII (1971), 63–78.
211. Lamberg, Robert F. 'The Comecon: twenty years old and in its third crisis', *Swiss Review of World Affairs*, VIII (March 1969), 20–4.
212. Levcik, Friedrich. 'Migration and employment of foreign workers in the CMEA countries and their problems', in United States Congress Joint Economic Committee, *East European economies post-Helsinki*. Washington, D.C.: United States Government Printing Office, 1977, pp. 458–78. (Also published in *Eastern European Economies*, XVI (Autumn 1977), 3–33.)

213. Marer, Paul. 'Has Eastern Europe become a liability to the Soviet Union?', in *International Politics of Eastern Europe*, edited by Charles Gati. New York: Praeger, 1976.
214. Marer, Paul. 'The political economy of Soviet relations with Eastern Europe', in *Testing theories of economic imperialism*, edited by S. Rosen. Lexington, Mass.: Heath, 1974, pp. 231–260.
215. Menahem, H. 'Le marché commun de l'Est: le Conseil d'Assistance Economique Mutuelle', *Politique Etrangère*, XXX (1965), 410–44.
216. Michel, M. 'Le bloc oriental', *Europe Sud-Est* (Athens), No. 75 (March 1970), 17–29.
217. Mikheev, S. 'New stage in the economic cooperation of CMEA countries', *International Affairs* (Moscow), No. 3 (March 1972), 30–5.
218. Mikul'skii, K. 'Economic efficiency in the CMEA countries: 20 years of CMEA', *International Affairs* (Moscow), No. 3 (March 1969), 59–64.
219. Mikul'skii, K. 'Ekonomika stran SEV: faktory rosta i problema effektivnosti', *Mirovaia ekonomika i mezhdunarodnaia otnosheniia*, No. 10 (October 1971), 13–23.
220. Nesterov, L. 'National wealth estimation in socialist countries', *Review of Income and Wealth*, I (September 1972), 287–301.
221. Nikolaev, L. and Tarasov, L. 'Ekonomika stran-chlenov SEV v 1975–1976 gg.', *Voprosy Ekonomiki*, No. 5 (May 1976), 102–12.
222. Pelzman, Joseph. 'In defense of the gravity model with pooled cross-section and times-series observations: a reply to Jozef M. van Brabant', *The ACES Bulletin*, XIX (Spring 1977), 99–108.
223. Pelzman, Joseph. 'Trade creation and trade diversion in the Council for Mutual Economic Assistance: 1954–1970', *Economic Review*, LXVII (September 1977), 713–22.
224. Penkava, J. 'Theoretical problems of the world socialist market', *Czechoslovak Economic Digest*, IV (June 1974), 18–36.
225. Pinder, J. 'Comecon, an East European Common Market?', in *People's Democracies after Prague*, edited by Jerzy Lukaszewski. Bruges: De Tempel (Tempelhof), 1970, pp. 133–83.

226. Polienko, A. 'New stage in trade between the countries of the Council of Mutual Economic Assistance', *Problems of Economics*, VI (January 1964), 48–55.
227. Pritzel, C. '20 years of Comecon', *Central Europe Journal*, XXVII (9 September 1969), 251–8.
228. Ptichkin, N. 'The 19th session of the Council for Mutual Economic Assistance in Prague', *The American Review of Soviet and Eastern European Foreign Trade*, I (July–August 1965), 3–8.
229. Ptichkin, N. 'Novyi shag v ravnopravnom sotrudnichestve (k itogam XXXI zasedaniia sessii SEV)', *Vneshniaia torgovlia*, No. 10 (October 1977), 2–7.
230. Reutt, B. W. 'Planned partnership in the CMEA', *Polish Perspectives*, No. 5 (May 1969), 8–19.
231. Roucek, Joseph S. 'Changing aspects of the Comecon', *Central Europe Journal*, XV (August–September 1967), 223–37.
232. Roucek, Joseph S. 'Comecon's fateful twentieth anniversary', *Political Scientist*, VI (July–December 1969 and January–June 1970), 21–36.
233. Safari, H., and Kwiatowski, G. 'Equal rights, mutual assistance, economic advantage', *World Marxist Review*, XVII (June 1974), 92–101.
234. Senin, M. 'The USSR and the CMEA: steps of progress', Izvestiia, 14 March 1968, translated in *Current Digest of the Soviet Press*, XX, No. 1 (1 April 1968), 3–4.
235. Seranne, C. 'Les situations d'inégalité au sein du Conseil d'assistance économique mutuelle', *Etudes internationales*, II (June 1971), 250–96.
236. Shiriaev, Iu. 'Internatsional'nyi kharakter ekonomicheskoi sistemy sotsializma', *Voprosy Ekonomiki*, No. 10 (October 1977), 3–12.
237. Shmelev, N. 'Is the socialist economy autarkic? (a reply to bourgeois critics)', *Problems of Economics*, XIX (January 1977), 3–25.
238. Shmelev, N. 'Lichnoe podsobnoe khoziaistvo v stranakh SEV', *Voprosy Ekonomiki*, No. 7 (July 1978), 117–27.
239. Smith, Arthur J. 'The Council of Mutual Economic Assistance in 1977: new economic power, new political perspectives and some old and new problems', in United States Congress Joint Economic Committee, *East European*

economies post-Helsinki. Washington, D.C.: United States Government Printing Office, 1977, pp. 152–73.

240. Sokolov, A., and Shiriaev, Iu. 'Important trend in socialist countries' cooperation', *International Affairs* (Moscow), No. 1 (January 1966), 39–45.
241. Solodukhin, Iu. 'Ukreplenie bratskogo sotrudnichestva stran sotsializma', *Mezhdunarodnaia zhizn'*, No. 12 (December 1977), 65–76.
242. Sorokin, G. M. 'Lenin i ekonomicheskie problemy mirovoi sotsialisticheskoi sistemy', *Voprosy Ekonomiki*, No. 6 (June 1969), 3–16.
243. Sorokin, G. M. 'Leninskie printsipy sotrudnichestva sotsialisticheskikh stran', *Planovani Hospodarstvi* (CSSR), III (1969), 3–11.
244. 'The state of Comecon', *The Economist*, CCLVIII (17 January 1976), 78–9.
245. Stehr, Uwe. 'Unequal development and dependency structures in Comecon', *Journal of Peace Research*, XIV (1977), 115–28.
246. Stolte, Stefan C. 'Can Moscow hold Comecon together?', *Analysis of Current Developments*, No. 9 (1966–67), 1–5.
247. Stolte, Stefan C. 'Comecon at the crossroads', Institute for the Study of the USSR *Bulletin*, XVI (March 1969), 26–34.
248. Stolte, Stefan C. 'Comecon in the new decade', Institute for the Study of the USSR *Bulletin*, XVIII (March 1971), 24–38.
249. Stolte, Stefan C. 'Comecon on the threshold of the seventies', Institute for the Study of the USSR *Bulletin*, XVIII (July 1970), 5–24.
250. Stolte, Stefan C. 'Comecon through Soviet eyes', *Studies on the Soviet Union*, V (1966), 37–45.
251. Stolte, Stefan C. 'Comecon's nineteenth conference', Institute for the Study of the USSR *Bulletin*, XII (May 1965), 17–22.
252. Stolte, Stefan C. 'Economic developments in the Soviet bloc', Institute for the Study of the USSR *Bulletin*, XIV (October 1967), 29–35.
253. Storozhev, V. 'Intensifikatsiia sel'skogo khoziaistvo v evropeiskikh stranakh sotsializma', *Voprosy Ekonomiki*, No. 5 (May 1966), 90–8.

254. Strany SEV: ubeditel'nye itogi, vdokhnovliaiushchie perspektivy', *Kommunist*, No. 16 (1976), 74–84.
255. Strougal, Lubomir. 'International significance of socialism's economic achievements', *World Marxist Review*, XVII (September 1974), 8–14.
256. Szawlowski, Richard. *The system of the international organizations of the Communist countries*. Leiden: Sijthoff, 1976.
257. Szeker, Gyula. 'The comprehensive programme of CMEA, 1971–1975', *New Hungarian Quarterly*, XVIII (Spring 1977), 18–32.
258. Tarasov, L. 'Ekonomika stran-chlenov SEV v 1976–1977 gg.', *Voprosy Ekonomiki*, No. 5 (May 1977), 103–12.
259. Ulam, Adam. 'The destiny of Eastern Europe', *Problems of Economics*, XIII (January–February 1974), 1–12.
260. Uren, P. E. 'Economic relations among the Communist states', in *The Communist states at the crossroads between Moscow and Peking*, edited by Adam Bromke. New York: Praeger, 1965, pp. 199–218.
261. Uren, P. E. 'Patterns of economic relations', in *The Communist states in disarray, 1965–1971*, edited by Adam Bromke and Teresa Rakowska-Harmstone. Minneapolis: University of Minneapolis Press, 1972, pp. 307–22.
262. Ushkalov, I. 'Effektivnost' ispol'zovaniia trudovykh resursov v stranakh-chlenakh SEV', *Voprosy Ekonomiki*, No. 4 (April 1977), 123–31.
263. Ustor, Endre. 'Decision-making in the Council for Mutual Economic Assistance', Hague Academy of International Law *Recueil des cours*, III (1971), 163–295.
264. Utkin, E. 'Sotsialisticheskoe sorevnovanie i sotrudnichestvo proizvodstvennykh kollektivov stran SEV', *Voprosy Ekonomiki*, No. 5 (May 1977), 126–31.
265. Verner, P. 'Material basis of the socialist community', *World Marxist Review*, XX (January 1977), 74–82.
266. Viktorov, Felix. 'Economic Association of countries of socialism', *East European Quarterly*, I (1967), 261–75.
267. Virius, M. 'La division internationale socialiste du travail des pays du Conseil d'assistance économique mutuelle', *Commerce Extérieur Tchécoslovaque*, X (September 1970), 5–8.
268. Vladova, N. 'Material'noe stimulirovanie effktivnosti

truda v promyshlennosti evropeiskikh stran SEV', *Voprosy Ekonomiki*, No. 8 (August 1976), 95–105.

269. Vylev, N., *et al.* 'Five-year plan: confident start (results of 1976)', *International Affairs* (Moscow), (June 1977), 108–15.

270. Walz, Friedrich. 'Comecon: Partner with problems', *Prospects* (Swiss Bank Corporation), No. 3 (1975), 9–11.

271. Wiesel, I. 'The international socialist market', *Soviet and Eastern European Trade*, VII (Summer 1971), 109–118.

272. Wilczynski, Jozef. 'Comecon – success or failure?', *Australian Outlook*, XIX (April 1965), 47–61.

273. Zemelka, Stanley A. '20 years of Comecon: economic integration or disintegration?', *Central European Federalist*, XVI (December 1968), 35–43.

274. Zhukov, V., and Ol'senich, Iu. 'Internatsional'nye zatvaty i sotrudnichestvo stran SEV', *Voprosy Ekonomiki*, No. 3 (March 1967), 70–80.

B. CMEA: Theory of integration and political aspects

275. Abonyi, Arpad, and Sylvain, Ivan J. 'CMEA integration and policy options for Eastern Europe: a development strategy of dependent states', *Journal of Common Market Studies*, XVI (December 1977), 132–54.

276. Alampiev, Petr Martynovich. 'The structure of the national economy and integration of socialist countries', *Problems of Economics*, XVIII (June 1975), 16–36.

277. Alekseev, A., and Savenko, Iu. 'Problemy sotsialisticheskoi integratsii', *Mirovaia ekonomika i mezhdunarodnye otnosheniia*, No. 12 (December 1970), 3–14.

278. Barrera, M., and Haas, E. B. 'The operationalization of some variables related to regional integration; a research note', *International Organization* (Boston), XXIII (Winter 1969), 150–60.

279. Baumer, Max, and Jacobsen, Hanns-Dieter. 'Integration of Comecon into the world economy?', *Aussenpolitik* (1976).

280. Bautina, Ninel. 'The world socialist market and economic integration', *International Affairs* (Moscow), No. 1 (January 1970), 16–20.

281. Bird, Richard Miller. 'Comecon and economic integration

in the Soviet bloc', *Quarterly Review of Economics and Business*, IV (Winter 1964), 37–49.

282. Bogomolov, O. T. 'Integration of the CMEA countries and the Soviet Union', *Acta Oeconomica* (Budapest), XVI (1976), 71–8.
283. Bogomolov, O. T. 'Teoreticheskoe nasledie V. I. Lenin i ekonomicheskaia integratsiia stran sotsializma', *Mirovaia ekonomika i mezhdunarodnye otnosheniia*, No. 4 (April 1970), 55–67.
284. Bogomolov, O. T. 'Two types of international economic integration', *Problems of Economics*, XVIII (October 1975), 72–90.
285. Boll, Michael M. 'Soviet strategy in the Seventies: the complex integration program for East Europe', *Military Review*, LIV (April 1974), 59–69.
286. Brabant, Jozef M. P. van. 'The programme for socialist economic integration', *Osteuropa Wirtschaft*, XVII (December 1972), 272–290.
287. Brabant, Jozef M. P. van. 'Trade and integration of the centrally planned economies: a review', *Tijdschrift voor Economie*, XVII (1972), 82–99.
288. Bryson, Phillip J., and Klinkmuller, Erich. 'Eastern European integration: constraints and prospects', *Survey*, XXI (Winter–Spring 1975), 101–27.
289. Butler, W. E. 'Legal configurations of integration in eastern Europe', *International Affairs* (London), LI (October 1975), 518–30.
290. Cattell, David. 'Multilateral cooperation and integration in Eastern Europe', *Western Political Quarterly*, XIII (1960), 64–9.
291. Chalupsky, Zdenek. 'Management of the process of international socialist economic integration', *Czechoslovak Economic Digest* (June 1977), 27–50.
292. Chalupsky, Zdenek, and Tauchman, J. 'Integration in the Council of Mutual Economic Assistance', *Czechoslovak Economic Papers*, No. 14 (1974), 39–54.
293. Chukanov, O. 'Economic integration in the Comecon bloc: implementing the program of socialist economic integration', *Kommunist*, September 1972, translated in *Current Digest of the Soviet Press*, XXIV (13 December 1972), 13–15.

294. Dudinskii, I. V. 'Kompleksnaia programma sotsialisticheskoi integratsii v deistvii', *Voprosy Ekonomiki*, No. 7 (July 1972), 81–92.
295. East-West (Belgium). *Prospects of economic integration in Comecon*. Brussels: East–West Research and Advisory Service, 1971.
296. 'Economic integration and the world revolutionary process', *World Marxist Review*, XVII (September 1974), 39–62.
297. Fallenbuchl, Zbigniew M. 'Comecon integration', *Problems of Communism*, XXII (March–April 1973), 25–39.
298. Fallenbuchl, Zbigniew M. 'East European integration: Comecon', in *Reorientation and commercial relations of the economies of Eastern Europe*. United States Congress Joint Economic Committee. Washington, D.C.: United States Government Printing Office, 1974, pp. 79–134.
299. Fallenbuchl, Zbigniew M. 'L'intégration économique en Europe de l'Est', *Revue d'études comparatives est-ouest; économie, planification et organisation*, VIII (June 1977), 7–20.
300. Finley, David D. 'A political perspective of economic relations in the Communist camp', *Western Political Quarterly*, XVII (June 1964), 294–316.
301. Fischer, Lewis A. 'Comecon and the Brezhnev doctrine', *East Europe*, XXI (October 1972), 2–7.
302. Gehlen, Michael. 'The integrative process in East Europe: a theoretical framework', *The Journal of Politics*, XXX (February 1968), 90–113.
303. Ginsburgs, George. 'The implications of the 20-year Comprehensive Programme of economic integration', *American Journal of International Law*, LXVII (November 1973), 48–54.
304. Grebennikov, B., and Nikolaev, L. 'CMEA: integration year', *International Affairs* (Moscow), No. 10 (October 1972), 8–15.
305. Grebennikov, B., and Nikolaev, L. 'Strategy of integration (31st session of the CMEA)', *International Affairs* (Moscow), No. 9 (September 1977), 38–47.
306. Hamouz, F. 'Implementation of the Comprehensive Programme of socialist economic integration', *Czechoslovak Economic Digest*, VIII (December 1973), 3–46.

307. Hermann, Adolf. 'Can Comecon integrate?' *East Europe*, XVIII (May 1969), 15–18.
308. Holbik, Karel. 'Comecon and East European economic nationalism', *Zeitschrift für die gesamte Staatswissenschaft*, CXXII (October 1966), 721–40.
309. Isaev, B. L. 'A matrix balance of socialist economic integration', *Matekon*, X (Autumn 1973), 93–116.
310. Iskra, W. 'The mechanisms of integration', *Soviet and East European Foreign Trade*, VII (Summer 1971), 119–28.
311. Jaster, Robert S. 'The defeat of Khrushchev's plans to integrate Eastern Europe', *World Today*, XIX (1963), 514–22.
312. Kanet, Roger E. 'Integration theory and the study of East Europe', *International Studies Quarterly*, XVIII (September 1974), 368–92.
313. Karpich, V. 'CMEA countries' plan to develop integration', *International Affairs* (Moscow), No. 8 (August 1970), 8–13.
314. Kaser, Michael C. 'Comecon and integration: some remarks', *Economies et Sociétés*, V (1971), 277–80.
315. Kiss, Tibor. 'Integration of CMEA countries' national markets', *Acta Oeconomica*, V (1970), 209–224.
316. Korbonski, Andrzej. 'Theory and practice of regional integration: the case of Comecon', in *Regional integration: theory and research*, edited by Leon N. Lindberg and Stuart A. Scheingold. Cambridge, Mass.: Harvard University Press, 1971, pp. 338–73.
317. Kormnov, Iu., and Cheburakov, M. 'Improving the management of branch integration of Comecon member nations', *Problems of Economics*, XVI (January 1974), 69–90.
318. Kovaltsev, G. 'CMEA: new stage of integration', *International Affairs* (Moscow), No. 9 (September 1976), 75–80.
319. Kozma, Ferenc. 'Some theoretical problems regarding socialist integration and the levelling of economic development', *Trends in World Economy* (Budapest), No. 6 (1971).
320. Kraus, J. 'Socialist economic integration – objective necessity of further development of the Council for Mutual Economic Assistance (CMEA)', *Czechoslovak Economic Digest*, IV (June 1974), 37–68.
321. Kunts, V. 'Sotsialisticheskaia ekonomicheskaia integratsiia

i intensifikatsiia proizvodstva v stranakh SEV', *Voprosy Ekonomiki*, No. 7 (July 1977), 80–7.

322. Kuzinski, S. 'Integrating Eastern Europe', *Polish Perspectives*, No. 11 (November 1970), 11–19.
323. Ladygin, Boris. 'Socialist integration: achievement and prospects', *New Times* (Moscow), No. 2 (January 1976), 18–19.
324. Ladygin, Boris, and Rybakov, O. 'XXV s"ezd KPSS i uglublenie sotsialisticheskoi ekonomicheskoi integratsii', *Voprosy Ekonomiki*, No. 11 (November 1976), 76–84.
325. Lagneau, Janina. 'L'intégration socialiste ou le Marché Commun en Europe de l'Est', *Economies et sociétés*, V (1971), 263–76.
326. Lavigne, Marie. 'La XXIIe Session du Comecon et le problème de l'intégration des économies socialistes', *Revue de Défense Nationale* (April 1969), 611–25.
327. Lukaszewski, J. 'Le bloc communiste et l'intégration européenne', *Synthèses* (Brussels) (July–August 1966).
328. Marer, Paul. 'Economics and integration'. Paper prepared for the *Conference on Eastern Europe: Stability or Recurrent Crisis?*, Airlie House, Warrenton, Virginia, 13–15 November 1975.
329. Marsh, Peter. 'The integration process in Eastern Europe: 1968 to 1975', *Journal of Common Market Studies*, XIV (June 1976), 311–35.
330. Montias, John M. 'Economic nationalism in Eastern Europe: forty years of continuity and change', *Journal of International Affairs*, XX (1966), 45–71.
331. Montias, John M. 'Obstacles to the economic integration of Eastern Europe', *Studies in Comparative Communism*, II (July–October 1969), 38–60.
332. Montias, John M. 'Problems of integration', *World Politics*, XVIII (July 1966), 718–26.
333. 'Le nouveau programme d'intégration des pays du CAEM', *Courrier des Pays de l'Est*, No. 157 (November 1972), 7–18.
334. Nyers, R. 'Printsipal'nye i prakticheskie voprosy sotsialisticheskoi ekonomicheskoi integratsii', *Acta Oeconomica*, II (1969), 119–53.
335. Olsienkiewicz, Henryk. 'The problem of Comecon integration: integration by circuitous means', Institute for the Study of the USSR *Bulletin*, XI (August 1964), 3–13.

336. Olszewski, Kazimierz. 'Socialist economic integration and international relations', *World Marxist Review*, XX (May 1977), 63–73.

337. Pelzman, Joseph. 'Economic integration in CMEA', University of South Carolina *Working Papers in Economics* (November 1976).

338. Pelzman, Joseph. 'Trade integration in the Council of Mutual Economic Assistance: creation and diversion, 1954–1970', *The ACES Bulletin*, XVIII (Autumn 1976), 39–59.

339. Ptichkin, N. 'Further development of socialist economic integration', *Foreign Trade* (Moscow), No. 10 (1971), 2–11.

340. Reutt, B. W. 'Trade, cooperation and integration', *Handel Zagraniczy* (1970), 6–9.

341. Rohlicek, Rudolf. 'Integration: a new quality of the socialist economy', *Czechoslovak Economic Digest* (December 1976), 3–13.

342. Rybakov, O., and Khmelevskii, N. 'Certain methodological aspects in the planning of integration measures', *Problems of Economics*, XVII (September 1974), 3–19.

343. Ryschenkow, Zenia. 'Problems of economic integration in East and West Europe', *Studia Diplomatica*, XXVII (September–November 1974), 749–60.

344. Seifert, W., *et al.* 'Current legal problems of socialist economic integration', *Soviet and Eastern European Foreign Trade*, X (Summer 1974), 84–99.

345. Shaffer, H. G. 'Comecon integration', *Soviet and Eastern European Foreign Trade*, IX (Autumn 1973), 3–25.

346. Shiriaev, Iu. 'Novyi etap ekonomicheskoi integratsii sotsialisticheskikh stran', *Mirovaia ekonomika i mezhdunarodnye otnosheniia*, No. 9 (September 1971), 3–13.

347. Shiriaev, Iu. 'Socialist ownership under the conditions of economic integration of Comecon member nations', *Problems of Economics*, XVI (January 1974), 51–68.

348. Shul'man, A. 'Integration measures: a component part of national economic and branch plans', *Problems of Economics*, XVII (January 1975), 19–33.

349. Silpoch, Karel. 'The place and role of international economic organizations in the process of socialist economic integration', *Soviet and Eastern European Foreign Trade*, XI (Summer 1975), 36–51.

350. 'Socialist economic integration', *Problems of the Contemporary World* (Moscow), I (1973).
351. Soldaczuk, Jozef. 'Regional integration and East–West trade', *Polish Perspectives*, IX (January 1966), 10–17.
352. Soldaczuk, Jozef, and Giezgala, J. 'Economic integration of Comecon countries and the means and methods of hastening it', *Gospodarska Planova*, November 1968, translated in Radio Free Europe Research *Polish Press Survey*, 2170 (16 January, 1969).
353. Sorokin, G. M. 'Problemy ekonomicheskoi integratsii stran sotsializma', *Voprosy Ekonomiki*, No. 12 (December 1968), 77–86.
354. Stankovsky, Jan. 'Problems of integration in Comecon', *Soviet and Eastern European Foreign Trade*, VII (Autumn-Winter 1971–72), 306–19.
355. Stolte, Stefan C. 'Politics complicates the issue', Institute for the Study of the USSR *Bulletin*, XI (August 1964), 14–20. (Reply to Olsienkiewicz's article, listed above).
356. Wasowski, Stanislaw. 'Economic integration in the Comecon (Council for Mutual Economic Assistance)', *Orbis*, XVI (Autumn 1972), 760–79.
357. Zhamin, V., and Zhukov, V. 'Questions of economic integration of CMEA member-countries', *Voprosy Ekonomiki*, September 1970, translated in *Current Digest of the Soviet Press*, XXII (26 January, 1971), 23–4.

C. CMEA: Theory of the international socialist division of labour

358. Alampiev, Petr Martynovich, and Marnovskii, O. 'Vazhneishaia problema mezhdunarodnogo sotsialisticheskogo razdeleniia truda', *Voprosy Ekonomiki*, No. 2 (February 1966), 143–7.
359. Balassa, A. 'O putiakh dal'neishego razvitiia razdeleniia truda mezhdu stranami-chlenami SEV v oblasti mashinostroenie', *Acta Oeconomica*, Nos. 1 and 2 (1966), 89–106.
360. Bogomolov, O. T. 'The international socialist division of labour', *Problems of Economics*, III (June 1960), 44–50.
361. Bogomolov, O. T. 'Metodologicheskie problemy mezhdu-

narodnogo sotsialisticheskogo razdeleniia truda', *Voprosy Ekonomiki*, No. 11 (November 1963), 3–14.

362. Bogomolov, O. T. 'Osnovnye printsipy mezhdunarodnogo sotsialisticheskogo razdeleniia truda', *Voprosy Ekonomiki*, No. 11 (November 1966), 109–21.

363. Glikman, P. 'Economic effectiveness of capital investments associated with the international socialist division of labor', *American Review of Soviet and Eastern European Foreign Trade*, I (May–June 1965), 3–20.

364. Kovasznai, Gy., and Kozma, Ferenc. 'On the interrelations between the international division of labour and the efficiency of production', in *For the progress of Marxist economics*, edited by T. Foldi. Budapest: Akademiai Kiado, 1967, pp. 78–100.

365. Kozma, Ferenc. 'The effects of the international division of labour on national economies', *Acta Oeconomica*, IX (1972), 343–57.

366. Ladygin, Boris, and Kravsova, E. G. 'Kontsentratsiia proizvodstva i mezhdunarodnoe sotsialisticheskoe razdelenie truda', *Ocherki po sovremennom sovetskoi i zarubezhnoi ekonomike*, IV (1965).

367. Neuberger, Egon. 'International division of labor in CMEA: limited regret strategy', *American Economic Review*, LIV (May 1964), 506–15.

368. Oleinik, I. 'Forms of international division of labour in the socialist camp', *Problems of Economics*, IV (1961), 56–63.

369. Rybalkin, V. 'On certain indices of the international socialist division of labour', *Problems of Economics*, V (April 1963), 38–43.

370. Savin, V. 'Methods of evaluating a country's participation in the international division of labour', *Foreign Trade* (Moscow), No. 12 (December 1971), 33–7.

371. Sergeev, V. 'Razdelenie truda i tovaroobarot mezhdu stranami SEV', *Nauchnyi doklad vysshii shkoly: Ekonomiki nauki*, No. 5 (1965), 3–10.

372. Shiriaev, Iu. 'Razvitie mezhdunarodnogo sotsialisticheskogo razdeleniia truda', *Voprosy Ekonomiki*, No. 10 (October 1976), 3–13.

373. Shiriaev, Iu., and Sokolov, Anatolii I. 'The division of labour among CMEA countries: problems and prospects',

International Labour Review, CXVI (November-December 1977), 289–301.

374. Sorokin, G. M. 'Mezhdunarodnoe razdelenie truda, vazhnyi faktor ekonomicheskogo rosta', *Voprosy Ekonomiki*, No. 2 (February 1970), 108–19.
375. Sorokin, G. M. 'Some problems of the international socialist division of labour', *Problems of Economics*, V (April 1963), 28–37.
376. Streber, J. 'Relations among socialist international division of labor, national division of labor and production technology', *Soviet and Eastern European Foreign Trade*, VIII (Spring 1972), 3–24.
377. Tauchman, Josef, and Novozamsky, J. 'The nature of the international socialist division of labour under socialism', *Czechoslovak Economic Papers*, No. 11 (1969), 127–39.
378. Terekhov, V., and Shastitko, V. 'International socialist division of labour – criterion of effectiveness', *Problems of Economics*, VII (November 1964), 37–44.

D. Economic cooperation, plan coordination and product specialization in CMEA: General aspects

379. Askanas, Benedykt, *et al.* 'Economic development of the Comecon countries 1971 to 1975 and their plans until 1980', *Eastern European Economics*, XV (Spring 1977), 3–46.
380. Bartha, Ferenc. 'Some ideas on the creation of a multilateral clearing system among the Comecon countries', *Soviet and Eastern European Foreign Trade*, XII (Spring 1976), 19–33.
381. Blessing, H., and Thede, S. 'Structure of production and organization of international socialist specialization and cooperation', *Soviet and Eastern European Foreign Trade*, VIII (Spring 1972), 25–42.
382. Bogomolov, O. T. 'Aktual'nye problemy ekonomicheskogo sotrudnichestvo sotsialisticheskikh stran', *Mirovaia ekonomika i mezhdunarodnye otnosheniia*, No. 5 (May 1966), 15–27.
383. Bogomolov, O. T. 'Metodologicheskie voprosy koordinatsii planov stran SEV', *Voprosy Ekonomiki*, No. 2 (February 1968), 63–75.

384. Bogomolov, O. T. 'Nekotorye problemy spetsializatsii i kooperirovaniia proizvodstva mezhdu stranami SEV', *Mirovaia ekonomika i mezhdunarodnye otnosheniia*, No. 5 (May 1967), 73–81.
385. Bogomolov, O. T. 'Problems in production specialization and cooperation among CMEA countries', *Soviet and Eastern European Foreign Trade*, IV (Spring 1968), 68–90.
386. Bogomolov, O. T. 'Sotrudnichestvo stran SEV na vazhnom rubezhe', *Kommunist*, No. 18 (1966), 13–24.
387. Bogomolov, O. T., and Barkovsky, A. N. 'Economic cooperation among the Council for Mutual Economic Assistance (CMEA) countries', *Economic bulletin for Asia and the Far East* (Bangkok), No. 3 (December 1970), 11–30.
388. 'CMEA: new scope for cooperation', *World Marxist Review*, XXI (May 1978), 70–88.
389. Dobrescu, E. 'Principal bases of collaboration and socialist economic integration of Comecon countries', *Soviet and Eastern European Foreign Trade*, VIII (Autumn–Winter 1972–73), 325–34.
390. Dudinskii, I. 'Mutual benefits derived from socialist cooperation', in *The Soviet Economy*, edited by Harry G. Shaffer. New York: Appleton-Century Crofts, 1963, pp. 434–42.
391. Evstigneev, R. 'Kompleksnye programmy v ekonomike evropeiskikh stran SEV', *Voprosy Ekonomiki*, No. 8 (August 1977), 103–9.
392. Farkas, G. 'The role of the state in the establishment of international specialization and cooperation ventures', *Soviet and Eastern European Foreign Trade*, VII (Summer 1971), 135–57.
393. Fojtik, Frantisek. 'Some theoretical problems of joint planning in the CMEA countries', *Czechoslovak Economic Digest* (May 1976), 12–24.
394. Frolov, L. 'New targets for fraternal cooperation between CMEA countries', *Foreign Trade* (Moscow), No. 7 (August 1969), 8–12.
395. Gavrilov, V. 'Improving the economic collaboration of socialist countries', *Problems of Economics*, XVI (October 1973), 93–103.
396. Georgiev, E. K. 'K itogam konferentsii po spetsializatsii i kooperirovaniiu', *Vneshniaia Torgovlia*, No. 7 (August 1966), 16–18.

397. Glikman, Pavel, 'Ob effektivnosti spetsializatsii i kooperirovaniia proizvodstva stran chlenov SEV', *Voprosy Ekonomiki*, No. 2 (February 1967), 76–86.
398. Gorizontov, B., and Petukhova, S. 'The development of the international infrastructure of Comecon countries', *Problems of Economics*, XX (June 1977), 42–58.
399. Hamouz, F. 'Trends of future cooperation in the Council for Mutual Economic Assistance', *Czechoslovak Economic Digest*, III (May 1970), 55–63.
400. Hetenyi, I. 'Problems of long-term planning and the international coordination of national plans under CMEA', *Acta Oeconomica*, III (1968), 283–95.
401. Horvath, Janos. 'Grant elements in intra-bloc aid programs', *The ASTE Bulletin*, XIII (Autumn 1971), 1–17.
402. Ikonnikov, I. 'CMEA's role in cooperation between socialist countries', *International Affairs* (Moscow), No. 4 (April 1969), 65–70.
403. Inozemstev, N. 'Main tasks in the coordination of the national economic plans of Comecon countries', *Problems of Economics*, XVI (October 1973), 2–35.
404. Inozemstev, N., and Rybakov, O. 'Sovershenstvovanie planovykh osnov sotrudnichestva stran SEV', *Planovoe khoziaistvo*, No. 10 (October 1969), 13–23.
405. Ivanov, N., and Loshchakov, A. 'Sotrudnichestvo stran SEV i vyravnivanie urovnei ikh ekonomicheskogo razvitiia', *Voprosy Ekonomiki*, No. 6 (June 1977), 3–14.
406. Ivanov, P. 'Division of labor and coordination of economic plans', *American Review of Soviet and Eastern European Foreign Trade*, I (May–June 1965), 21–34.
407. Kazakevich, L., and Shishankov, V. 'Economic collaboration between the USSR and the socialist countries', *Problems of Economics*, XVI (October 1973), 72–92.
408. Kemenes, E. 'Rôle possible de l'entreprise multinationale dans l'économie des pays socialistes', *Problèmes Economiques*, No. 1260 (February 1972), 10–16.
409. Kiss, Tibor. 'International cooperation in planning within Comecon', *Eastern European Economics*, XIV (Summer 1976), 3–29.
410. Kohn, Martin J., and Lang, Nicholas R. 'The intra-CMEA foreign trade system: major price changes, little reform', in United States Congress Joint Economic Committee. *East*

European economies post-Helsinki. Washington, D.C.: United States Government Printing Office, 1977, pp. 135–51.

411. Kononenko, D. K. 'Razvitie form ekonomicheskogo sotrudnichestva stran SEV', *Vestnik Moskovskogo Universiteta: Seriia Ekonomiki*, No. 4 (April 1966), 63–77.
412. Kononenko, D. K. 'Spetsializatsiia i kooperatsiia proizvodstva osnova sotrudnichestva stran SEV', *Planovoe Khoziaistvo*, No. 4 (April 1966), 88–9.
413. Kormnov, Iu. 'Dolgorochnye tselevye programmy sotrudnichestva stran SEV', *Voprosy Ekonomiki*, No. 1 (January 1977), 86–94.
414. Kozlov, I., Lifshits, A., and Khakimov, V. 'Collaboration of Comecon countries in the key branches of industry', *Problems of Economics*, XVII (September 1974), 2–38.
415. Ladygin, Boris, and Shiriaev, Iu. 'Problems of improving economic cooperation between countries belonging to the Council of Mutual Economic Assistance (CMEA)', *American Review of Soviet and Eastern European Foreign Trade*, II (September–October 1966), 3–18.
416. Lavigne, Marie. 'The problem of the Multinational Socialist Enterprise', The Association for Comparative Economic Studies *Bulletin*, XVII (Summer 1975), 33–61.
417. Maly, Bohuslav. 'Outline of international specialization and cooperation within the framework of the Council for Mutual Economic Assistance', *Czechoslovak Economic Papers*, XVII (1977), 109–19.
418. Marer, Paul. 'Soviet economic policy in Eastern Europe', in *Reorientation and commercial relations of the economies of Eastern Europe* in United States Congress Joint Economic Committee. Washington, D.C.: United States Government Printing Office, 1974, pp. 134–63.
419. Matejka, Ladislav, and Bohm, Arnost. 'New forms of joint planning by Comecon member-countries', *Soviet and Eastern European Foreign Trade*, XI (Summer 1975), 3–18.
420. Mikulskii, K. I. 'Key problems of labour resources utilization in the Comecon countries at the present stage', *Soviet and Eastern European Foreign Trade*, XI (Autumn 1975), 54–76.
421. *Mnogostoronnee ekonomicheskoe sotrudnichestvo sotsialisticheskikh gosudarstv: dokumenty za 1972–1975 gg.*

Moscow: Iuridicheskaia literatura, 1976.

422. Morozov, V. 'Prospective forms of collaboration of Comecon member-nations', *Problems of Economics*, XVIII (May 1975), 57–75.

423. 'New stage of economic cooperation of CMEA countries: interview with Czechoslovak Prime Minister, Dr Lubomir Strougal', *Czechoslovak Economic Digest*, IV (September 1971), 3–10.

424. Pelzman, Joseph, 'Soviet-Comecon trade: the question of intra-industry specialization', *Weltwirtschaftliches Archiv/Review of World Economics*, Band 114 (1978), 297–304.

425. Ptichkin, N. 'The Comecon countries' bilateral arrangements', *Vneshniaia Torgovlia*, December 1964, translated in *Current Digest of the Soviet Press*, XVI, No. 52 (20 January 1965), 14–15.

426. Rybakov, O. 'Improvements in planning methods of collaboration among Comecon countries', *Problems of Economics*, XV (March 1973), 3–21.

427. Rybakov, O. 'Some organizational and methodological problems relating to the elaboration of long-range plans for collaboration between the USSR and socialist countries', *Problems of Economics*, XVI (October 1973), 3–19.

428. Rybakov, O. 'Sovmestnaia planovaia deiatel'nost stranchlenov SEV', *Mirovaia ekonomika i mezhdunarodnye otnosheniia*, No. 11 (November 1971), 3–12.

429. Rybakov, O. 'Strategy of cooperation: coordinated programme of CMEA multilateral integration measures', *New Times* (Moscow), No. 38 (September 1975), 21–2.

430. Shiriaev, Iu. 'Developing scientific foundations of joint planning activity of Comecon countries', *Problems of Economics*, XVI (October 1973), 55–71.

431. Simai, Mihaly, 'Coordination and cooperation in Council for Mutual Economic Assistance', in *International organization*. London: Frances Pinter Ltd., 1978, pp. 137–54.

432. Sokoloff, G. 'Les structures internes et les problèmes de coopération internationale des économies socialistes de l'Est', *Economies et Sociétés*, V (1971), 227–61.

433. Spulber, Nicolas. 'Economic problems of socialist cooperation', in *The Soviet economy*, edited by Harry G. Shaffer.

New York: Appleton-Century Crofts, 1963, pp. 423–33.

434. Strougal, Lubomir, 'New stage of economic cooperation between socialist countries', *Czechoslovak Economic Digest*, No. 6 (September 1971), 3–10.
435. Syomin, N. 'Cooperation between socialist countries in the new five-year period (1966–1970)', *International Affairs* (Moscow) (July 1966), 3–19.
436. Tiraspolsky, Anita. 'The development of terms of trade in the Eastern bloc', *Soviet and Eastern European Foreign Trade*, XIII (Spring 1977), 68–94.

E. Economic cooperation and product specialization in CMEA: Individual industries and products

437. Behr, O. 'CMEA and raw materials prices', *World Marxist Review*, XVIII (May 1975), 139–41.
438. Belovich, A. 'Cooperation in capital construction between the CMEA member-countries', *Foreign Trade* (Moscow), No. 5 (May 1973), 13–19.
439. Bukh, M. 'Razvitie sel'skogo khoziaistva v evropeiskikh stranakh SEV', *Voprosy Ekonomiki,* No. 5 (May 1976), 92–101.
440. Bychkov, G. 'Sotrudnichestvo stran SEV v oblasti sel'khozmashinostroeniia' *Voprosy Ekonomiki*, No. 1 (January 1976), 104–13.
441. Chermkov, L. 'Ekonomicheskie sviazi i razvitie transporta stran-chlenov SEV', *Voprosy Ekonomiki*, No. 6 (June 1966), 101–10.
442. Chupin, G. 'Integratsiia stran SEV v avtomobilestroenii', *Voprosy Ekonomiki*, No. 6 (June 1977), 71–8.
443. 'Comecon's energy problems', *The Economist*, CCLXIII (16 April 1977), 84–5.
444. 'Comecon's energy squeeze', *The Economist*, CCLXVII (6 May 1978), 88–9.
445. Dudinskii, I. 'The fuel and raw material problem of the countries of the Council for Mutual Economic Assistance and ways to solve it', *Voprosy Ekonomiki*, May 1966, translated in *Current Digest of the Soviet Press*, No. 18 (27 July 1966), 9–12.
446. Dudinskii, I. 'Puti pobyshleniia effektivnosti proizvodstva v

stranakh SEV', *Voprosy Ekonomiki*, No. 6 (June 1964), 74–86.

447. Ebel, Robert E. *Communist trade in oil and gas: an evaluation of the future export capability of the Soviet bloc*. New York: Praeger, 1970.

448. Fischer, Lewis A. *Agricultural product markets in the Comecon*. Ottawa: Agricultural Economics Research Council of Canada, 1969.

449. Frumkin, B. 'Sotrudnichestvo stran SEV v prodovol'stvennoi sfere', *Voprosy Ekonomiki*, No. 9 (September 1977), 98–107.

450. Gavrilov, V. 'Implementation of the CMEA Comprehensive Programme on the railways', *Foreign Trade* (Moscow), No. 7 (August 1973), 16–19.

451. Gavrilov, V. 'Razvitie khimicheskoi promyshlennosti stran SEV i sotsialisticheskoe mezhdunarodnoe razdelenie truda', *Nauchnyi doklad vysshii shkoly: Ekonomicheskie nauki*, No. 1 (1964).

452. Gorizontov, B. 'Transport i ego rol' v ekonomicheskom sotrudnichestve stran sotsializma', *Voprosy Ekonomiki*, No. 5 (May 1969), 69–78.

453. Gorizontov, B. 'Transport i mezhdunarodnoe sotsialisticheskoe razdelenie truda', *Voprosy Ekonomiki*, No. 1 (January 1968), 74–81.

454. Joyner, C. C. 'Energy situation in eastern Europe', *East European Quarterly*, X (Winter 1976), 495–516.

455. Kapitonov, V. 'Important instrument of the CMEA countries' economic integration re: transport system', *International Affairs* (Moscow) (May 1976), 105–13.

456. Kaser, Michael. 'Technology and oil in Comecon's external relations', *Journal of Common Market Studies*, XIII (1975), 161–72.

457. Kharitonov, V. 'Sotrudnichestvo stran SEV v pishchevom mashinostroenii', *Voprosy Ekonomiki*, No. 7 (July 1977), 88–97.

458. Klykov, V. 'Joint capital construction in Comecon countries and the determination of its economic effectiveness', *Problems of Economics*, XVI (January 1974), 91–104.

459. Koralka, Jaroslav. 'International division of labor in the agriculture of the member states of Comecon', *American*

Review of Soviet and Eastern European Foreign Trade, II (January–February 1966), 56–70.

460. Kormnov, Iu. 'Economic stimulation of the development of international production specialization', *Problems of Economics*, XI (January 1969), 45–54.

461. Kormnov, Iu. 'Effektivnost' mezhgosudarstvennyi spetsializatsii proizvodstva', *Planovoe Khoziaistvo*, No. 2 (February 1966), 12–19.

462. Kormnov, Iu. 'Ekonomicheskii effekt vnutriotraslevoi spetsializatsii proizvodstva stran SEV', *Voprosy Ekonomiki*, No. 4 (April 1966), 73–83.

463. Kormnov, Iu., and Frumkin, B. 'Agrarno-promyshlennaia integratsiia stran-chlenov SEV', *Planovoe Khoziaistvo*, No. 1 (January 1975), 84–93.

464. Krystev, Gancho. 'Osnovnye itogi sotrudnichestva stran-chlenov SEV v oblasti proizvodstva sel'skokhoziaistvennoi produktsii za 1971–1975 gg. i puti ego uglubleniia', *Ekonomicheskoe sotrudnichestvo stran-chlenov SEV*, No. 5 (1978), 72–9.

465. Kuligin, P. 'Principles underlying the division of labor and cooperation among Comecon countries of the fuel industry', *Eastern European Economics*, No. 4 (Summer 1964), 24–34.

466. Maliarova, M. G. 'O mezhgosudarstvennoi spetsializatsii i strukturnykh sdvigakh v proizvodstve evropeiskikh stran-chlenov SEV', *Vestnik Moskovskogo Universiteta: Seriia Ekonomiki*, No. 2 (February 1966), 78–86.

467. McMillan, C. H. 'Soviet specialization and trade in manufactures', *Soviet Studies*, XXIV (April 1973), 522–32.

468. Markov, I. A., and Skliarov, V. 'Cooperation between CMEA member countries over mineral resources', *Natural resources forum* (New York), I (July 1977), 337–45.

469. Os'mova, M. 'Nekotorye problemy podgotovki i ispol'zovaniia trudovykh resursov v stranakh SEV', *Voprosy Ekonomiki*, No. 1 (January 1966), 105–12.

470. Pomazanov, S., and Iakunin, A. 'Razvitie integratsionnykh protsessov v energetike stran SEV', *Voprosy Ekonomiki*, No. 6 (June 1976), 70–9.

471. Portiannikov, I., and Rakhutin, N. 'Koordinatsiia narodno-khoziaistvennykh planov stran-chlenov SEV', *Planovoe Khoziaistvo*, No. 11 (November 1976), 85-91.

472. Prybyla, J. S. 'Eastern Europe and Soviet oil', *Journal of Industrial Economics*, XIII (March 1965), 154–68.
473. Savostianov, V. 'The economic effectiveness of specialization in the socialist countries' engineering industry', *Foreign Trade* (Moscow), No. 7 (July 1969), 24–8.
474. Sawyer, Herbert L. 'Soviet oil and Eastern Europe', *The ACES Bulletin*, XIX (Spring 1977), 53–78.
475. Schmidt, S. C. 'Comecon wheat trade and prospects for the 1970s', *American Review of East–West Trade*, I (October 1968), 14–33.
476. Shanina, V. 'Transportno-ekonomicheskie sviazi stran SEV', *Voprosy Ekonomiki*, No. 5 (May 1977), 91–102.
477. United Nations. Department of Economic and Social Affairs. *Economic integration and industrial specialization among the member countries of the Council for Mutual Economic Assistance*. New York: United Nations, 1966.
478. Vais, T. 'The topic of an international symposium: labour resources in Comecon nations', *Problems of Economics*, XVI (July 1973), 77–86.
479. Vais, T., and Degtian, L. 'Collaboration of Comecon countries in the utilization of labour resources', *Problems of Economics*, XVII (June 1974), 24–34.
480. Varzin, N. 'Rost proizvoditel'nosti truda v stranakh SEV', *Voprosy Ekonomiki*, No. 1 (January 1973), 71–8.
481. Virius, Miroslav, and Balek, Jaroslav. 'Cooperation between CMEA countries in securing supplies of fuels and energy', *Czechoslovak Economic Digest* (May 1976), 25–44.
482. Yakushin, A. 'CMEA countries' cooperation in solving the fuel problem', *Foreign Trade* (Moscow), No. 1 (January 1971), 5–10.
483. Zemelka, Stanley A. 'The problem of specialization in Comecon', *East Europe*, XVIII (May 1969), 9–14.
484. Zubkov, A. 'Osobennosti mezhdunarodnoi kontsentratsii investishchii pri reshenii toplivno-syr'evoi problemy stran SEV', *Voprosy Ekonomiki*, No. 9 (September 1972), 52–60.
485. Zubkov, A. 'Proizvodstvennaia integratsiia stran SEV', *Voprosy Ekonomiki*, No. 3 (March 1975), 58–66.

F. Scientific-technical cooperation among CMEA member-countries

486. Alekseev, A., and Shiriaev, Iu. *Spravochnik mezhdunarodnye ekonomicheskie i nauchno-tekhnicheskie organizatsii sotsialisticheskikh stran*. Moscow: Izdatel'stvo Ekonomika, 1966.
487. Azarov, T. 'Problems in coordinating the scientific and technical research of Comecon countries', *Problems of Economics*, VII (January 1965), 47–52.
488. Campbell, Robert. 'Technology transfer among Communist countries', *The ASTE Bulletin*, XI (Winter 1969), 1–11.
489. Gertsovich, G., and Mikhailov, B. 'Ekonomicheskie problemy nauchnotekhnicheskogo progressa v stranakh chlenakh SEV', *Voprosy Ekonomiki*, No. 11 (November 1972), 87–97.
490. Kirillin, Vladimir. 'Aktual'nye problemy povyshenniia effektivnosti nauchno-tekhnicheskogo sotrudnichestva stran-chlenov SEV', *Ekonomicheskoe sotrudnichestvo stran-chlenov SEV*, No. 5 (1977),
491. Lagneau, Janina. 'Coopération scientifique et technique entre les pays membres du CAEM', *Economies et Sociétés*, V (1971), 281–309.
492. Medvedkov, Iu. 'The scientific-technical revolution and economic collaboration among the socialist countries', *Problems of Economics*, XIII (July 1970), 34–52.
493. Ordukhanova, T. 'Nekotorye tsifry i fakty v nauchno-tekhnicheskom sotrudnichestve stran-chlenov SEV', *Vestnik Statistiki*, No. 4 (April 1966), 45–50.
494. Popov, I. V. 'Nauchno-tekhnicheskaia informatsiia v stranakh chlenakh SEV', *Voprosy Ekonomiki*, No. 5 (May 1969), 109–118.
495. Schorcht, Josef and Zalud, Jiri. 'A system of joint scientific and technical progonostication of the CMEA countries', *Czechoslovak Economic Digest* (May 1976), 45–61.
496. Segal, G. 'Has Comecon missed the (scientific-technical) revolution?', *Scientist and Science Journal*, LI (5 August 1971), 310–11.
497. Sheetov, V. 'Scientific and technical integration of the

socialist countries', *International Affairs* (Moscow) (March 1976), 23–30.

498. United Nations, Economic Commission for Europe. *Review of the economic, scientific and technical cooperation of CMEA member countries.* New York: United Nations, 1968.

499. Vaks, A. 'Upravlenie nauchno-tekhnicheskim progressom v stranakh SEV', *Voprosy Ekonomiki*, No. 8 (August 1972), 65–73.

G. Foreign trade of CMEA member-countries

500. Caire, G. 'Les critères du choix du commerce extérieur au sein du Conseil d'entraide économique', *Annuaire de l'URSS* (1968), 401–25.

501. Caire, G. 'Economie et politique de l'énergie en URSS', *Annuaire de l'URSS* (Strasbourg), (1970–71), 227–54.

502. De Fiumel, Henryk. 'The Council for Mutual Economic Assistance in international relations', *Studies on International Relations* (Warsaw), No. 7 (1976), 60–78.

503. Dlugosz, Stanislaw. 'The evolution of foreign trade', *Soviet and Eastern European Foreign Trade*, XIII (Spring 1977), 35–54.

504. Esze, Zs. 'The modified system of export incentives for 1971–1975', *Acta Oeconomica* (1972), 61–75.

505. Faude, E. 'The organization of socialist foreign trade and the process of concentration', *Soviet and Eastern European Foreign Trade*, VII (Spring 1971), 24–49.

506. 'Foreign trade and the international division of labour', *Czechoslovak Economic Digest* (December 1977), 44–7.

507. Hertzfeld, G. 'Comecon and the Western trade of Comecon countries', *Common Market*, VII (December 1967), 309–12; and VIII (January 1968), 15–20.

508. Holzman, Franklyn D. 'Foreign trade behaviour of centrally planned economies', in *Industrialization in two systems*, edited by Henry Rosovsky. New York: Wiley & Sons, 1966, pp. 237–65.

509. Holzman, Franklyn D. 'Soviet foreign trade pricing and the question of discrimination: a "customs union" approach', *Review of Economics and Statistics*, XCIV (May 1962), 134–47.

510. Holzman, Franklyn D. 'La théorie du commerce extérieur des économies centralement planifiées', *Revue de l'Est*, III (1972), 5–36.
511. Ivanov, Y. 'The CMEA and world economic relations', *International Affairs* (Moscow) (February 1968), 30–9.
512. Kamecki, Z. 'The problems of foreign trade monopoly in a socialist economy', in *International trade and development – theory and policy*, edited by J. Soldaczuk. Warsaw: PWM, 1966, pp. 11–36.
513. Kaser, Michael. 'The East European economic reforms and foreign trade', *World Today*, XXIII (December 1967), 512–22.
514. Katona, P. J. 'The international sale of goods among member states of the Council for Mutual Economic Assistance', *Columbia Journal of International Law and Politics*, IV (Summer 1971), 183–211.
515. Kormnov. Iu. 'International economic organizations and their role in the collaboration of Comecon countries', *Problems of Economics*, XVI (October 1973), 36–54.
516. Lawson, C. W. 'An empirical analysis of the structure and stability of Communist foreign trade 1960–68', *Sóviet Studies*, XXVI (April 1974), 224–39.
517. Marer, Paul. 'Foreign trade', in *Comparative socialist systems: essays on politics and economics*, edited by C. Mesa-Lago and C. Beck. Pittsburgh: University Center for International Studies, University of Pittsburgh, 1975, pp. 367–96.
518. Mendershausen, H. 'Terms of trade between the Soviet Union and smaller Communist countries', *Review of Economics and Statistics*, XCI (May 1959), 106–18.
519. Mendershausen, H. 'The terms of trade of Soviet satellite trade: a broadened analysis', *Review of Economics and Statistics*, XCII (May 1960), 152–63.
520. Montias, John M. 'Structure of Comecon trade and the prospect for East–West exchanges', in *Reorientation and commercial relations of the economies of Eastern Europe*. United States Congress Joint Economic Committee. Washington, D.C.: United States Government Printing Office, 1974, pp. 134–63.
521. Morozov, V. 'Mnogostoronnie mezhdunarodnye ekonomi-

cheskie sviazi stran SEV', *Voprosy Ekonomiki*, No. 9 (September 1977), 108–15.

522. Nykryn, Jaroslav. 'International production cooperation in the system of external economic relationships', *Soviet and Eastern European Foreign Trade*, XI (Summer 1975), 19–35.
523. Olszewski, Jerzy. 'Strategies in the development and management of foreign trade', *Soviet and Eastern European Foreign Trade*, XIII (Spring 1977), 55–67.
524. Prokhorov, G. 'Optimization of the foreign economic relations of socialist countries', *Problems of Economics*, XIII (August 1970), 63–80.
525. Selucky, Radoslav. 'The impact of the economic reforms on the foreign economic relations of the socialist countries', *Soviet and Eastern European Foreign Trade*, IV (Autumn 1968), 72–86.
526. Sergeev, V. P. 'Economic principles of the foreign trade of socialist states', in *International trade theory in a developing world*, edited by R. F. Harrod. London: Macmillan, 1963, pp. 277–96.
527. Staller, G. J. 'Patterns of stability in foreign trade: OECD and Comecon 1950–1963', *American Economic Review*, LVII (September 1967), 879–88.
528. Vajda, I. 'Le problème de l'élasticité de la demande et des termes de l'échange dans le commerce extérieur des pays socialistes', *Problèmes de Planification*, VIII (1971), 35–54.
529. Walz, Friedrich, 'Comecon: a trading partner?', *Prospects* (Swiss Bank Corporation), No. 2 (1977), 2–5.
530. Wong, J. 'Southeast Asia's growing trade relations with socialist economies', *Asian Survey*, XVII (April 1977), 330–44.
531. Zauberman, A. 'The criterion of efficiency of foreign trade in Soviet-type economies', *Economica* (1964), 5–12, reprinted in *Aspects of Planometrics*, edited by A. Zauberman. London: Athlone Press, 1967, pp. 203–18.
532. Zhuravlev, Iu. 'Mezhdunarodnye sviazi Soveta Ekonomicheskoi Vzaimopomoshchi', *Vneshniaia Torgovlia*, No. 1 (January 1978), 2–9.

H. Financial aspects of CMEA

533. Alekseev, A. 'Some aspects of the further improvement of

prices in CMEA trade', *Vneshniaia Torgovlia*, No. 11 (November 1967), 26–32.

534. Allen, Mark. 'The structure and reform of the exchange and payments systems of some East European countries', International Monetary Fund *Staff Papers*, XXIII (November 1976), 718–39.
535. Ausch, Sandor, and Bartha, Ferenc. 'Theoretical problems relating to prices in trade between the Comecon countries', *Soviet and Eastern European Foreign Trade*, IV (Summer 1968), 35–71.
536. Bird, Richard. 'The possibility of fiscal harmonization in the Communist bloc', *Public Finance*, XIX (1964), 201–24.
537. Borozin, Iu. 'Nauchno-tekhnicheskii progress i tseno-obrazovanie v stranakh-chlenakh SEV', *Voprosy Ekonomiki*, No. 8 (August 1972), 114–23.
538. Botosh, K. 'Nekotorye finansovye voprosy sovmestnogo preprinichatel' stva v ramkakh SEV', *Acta Oeconomica*, XVII (1976), 301–20.
539. Bozyk, Pawel. 'Domestic and foreign trade prices in the process of integration in Comecon countries', *Soviet and Eastern European Foreign Trade*, VI (Summer 1970), 125–37.
540. Brabant, Jozef M. P. van. 'Possible reforms of intra-CMEA prices', *Osteuropa Wirtschaft*, No. 1 (March 1971), 31–50.
541. Brabant, Jozef M. P. van. 'Socialist world market prices; content and controversy', *Osteuropa Wirtschaft*, No. 3 (October 1970), 168–90.
542. Bryson, P. J., and Brabant, Jozef M. P. van. 'Non-market pricing in the socialist world market', *Kyklos*, XXVIII (1975), 309–36.
543. Chvojka, Petr. 'International monetary relations in the development of Comecon integration: the prospects and prerequisites for bringing national currencies into the system', *Soviet and Eastern European Foreign Trade*, XIII (Summer 1977), 3–27.
544. 'Comecon borrowing on international credit markets', *Financial Market Trends* (OECD) (December 1977), 51–84.
545. 'The Comecon debt mountain . . . ', *The Economist*, CCLXV (29 October 1977), 75–6.
546. D'Iachenko, V. 'Main trends in improving prices among

Comecon members', *Problems of Economics*, XI (June 1968), 40–9.

547. Frank-Ossipof, Z. 'Problèmes monétaires et financiers du CAEM', *Revue de pays de l'Est* (Brussels), XIII (1972), 7–23.
548. Garbuzov, Vasilii F. 'The development of currency and financial relations of Comecon member-nations', *Soviet and Eastern European Foreign Trade*, IX (Summer 1973), 74–82.
549. Garbuzov, Vasilii F. 'Mezhdunarodnaia valiutno-finansovaia sistema stran-chlenov SEV na sovremennom etape', *Ekonomicheskoe sotrudnichestvo stran-chlenov SEV* (Moscow), No. 3 (1977), 70–4.
550. Gilhodes, P. 'Les prix dans les relations économiques entre états socialistes', *Revue française de science politique*, XX (August 1970), 735–53.
551. Haase, Herwig. 'The Comecon foreign trade price system', *Soviet and Eastern European Foreign Trade*, XII (Summer–Autumn 1976), 81–108.
552. Hermann, Adolf. 'Monetary problems of Comecon; concerning proposals for the replacement of the presently strictly bilateral settlement of accounts by a universally acceptable currency', *Banker*, CXIX (March 1969), 236–7.
553. Indruch, Antonin. 'The further development of socialist economic integration and foreign currency financial relations in the Comprehensive Programme', *Soviet and Eastern European Foreign Trade*, XIII (Summer 1977), 28–36.
554. Ivanov, I. A. 'Improving foreign exchange relations of Comecon member-nations', *Problems of Economics*, XVII (September 1974), 39–49.
555. Karpich, V. 'The development of currency and financial relations among Comecon countries', *Soviet and Eastern European Foreign Trade*, VI (Summer 1970), 103–25.
556. Kaser, Michael. 'Comecon report – East European cross rates', *International Currency Review*, V (January–February 1973), 42–4.
557. Kaser, Michael. 'Le mécanisme des paiements internationaux dans l'Europe de l'Est', *Economie Appliquée*, XXIII (1970), 123–37.
558. Kohlmey, G. 'Monetary theory and foreign economic

theory, monetary planning and foreign economic planning', *Soviet and Eastern European Foreign Trade*, V (Spring–Summer 1969), 74–80.
559. Konstantinov, Iu. 'Currency and financial relations between the CMEA countries', *Foreign Trade* (Moscow), No. 10 (October 1972), 2–8.
560. Krulis, Zdenek. 'International socialist money and development of socialist economic integration of the CMEA member countries', *Czechoslovak Economic Digest*, No. 7 (November 1975), 63–86.
561. Kurilin, N. 'Valiutno-finansovye otnosheniia stran-chlenov SEV v usloviiakh ekonomicheskoi integratsii', *Voprosy Ekonomiki*, No. 4 (April 1974), 75–83.
562. Marczewski, J. 'La zone rouble et les problèmes d'unification monétaire des pays du Comecon', *Revue d'économie politique*, LXXX (July–August 1970), 608–27.
563. Masnata, A. 'Problèmes monétaires en rapport avec les pays du Comecon', *Revue d'économie politique*, LXXX (July–August 1970), 628–9.
564. McMillan, C. H. 'The bilateral character of Soviet and Eastern European foreign trade', *Journal of Common Market Studies*, XIII (1975), 1–20.
565. Mescheriakoff, H. 'Les règlements monétaires au sein du Comecon', *Annuaire de l'URSS* (Strasbourg) (1970–71), 255–69.
566. Meynell, Charles. 'Moscow's views on world banking', *Euromoney* (January 1978), 29– .
567. Mitrofanova, N. 'Tendentsii dvizheniiá kontraktnykh tsen v torgovle stran SEV', *Voprosy Ekonomiki*, No. 8 (August 1978), 101–6.
568. Nove, Alec. 'Inflation, integration and convertibility in Eastern Europe', *International Currency Review*, III (November–December 1971), 15–20.
569. Pechi, K. 'K razvitiiu mezhdunarodnoi sotsialisticheskoi valiutnoi sistemy', *Acta Oeconomica*, XVI (1976), 267–82.
570. Reese, K. 'The Soviet ruble and Comecon countries', *South African Journal of Economics*, XLI (June 1973), 134–45.
571. Rotleider, A. 'The convertible ruble: the international socialist currency of Comecon countries', *Problems of Economics*, XV (November 1972), 83–96.

572. Salusinszky, Istvan. 'Financing investments in the East European countries', *Marketing in Hungary*, No. 4 (1975), 25–8.

573. Savost'ianov, V. 'Pricing of imported machinery and equipment', *Soviet and Eastern European Foreign Trade*, XII (Summer 1976), 109–24.

574. Schaefer, Henry W. 'An East European Payments Union?', *East Europe*, XV (March 1966), 14–21.

575. Schonfield, A. 'Changing commercial policies in the Soviet block', *International Affairs* (London), XLIV (January 1968), 1–13.

576. Suliaeva, L. K. 'Novoe v praktike raschetno-kreditnykh otnoshenii stran-chlenov SEV', *Uchenyi zapiski Moskovskii finansovyi instituta* (1965), 26–37.

577. Suliaeva, L. K. 'Currency and financial cooperation among Comecon members', *Problems of Economics*, X (October 1967), 45–50.

578. Tarnovskii, O. 'Price formation in the world socialist market', *Problems of Economics*, XII (October 1969), 42–57.

579. Valek, Vratislav. 'Price setting within the framework of joint enterprises of Comecon member nations', *Eastern European Economics*, XV (Summer 1977), 29–49.

580. Valyi, Peter. 'Financial cooperation within CMEA', *Hungarian Quarterly*, XI (Summer 1970), 44–54.

581. Vit. Jan. 'Methods employed by Comecon members in drawing up their balance of payments', *Soviet and Eastern European Foreign Trade*, XII (Summer–Autumn 1976), 66–80.

582. 'Who Comecon's negotiators are', *Euromoney* (January 1978), 19.

583. Wiles, P. 'On purely financial convertibility.' in *Banking, Money and Credit in Eastern Europe* (Main Findings of Colloquium held from 24 to 26 January 1973 in Brussels), Brussels: NATO Information Service, 1973, pp. 119–25.

584. Zhelev, G. 'On using a proper base of price formation on the international socialist market', *American Review of Soviet and East European Trade*, II (July–August 1966), 3–22.

585. Zlobin, I. 'The world socialist market – its prices, currency and system of settlements', *Problems of Economics*, V (November 1962), 12–21.

586. Zukal, R. 'Currency convertibility and external economic relations', *Soviet and Eastern European Foreign Trade*, IV (Autumn 1968), 58–71.
587. Zwass, A. 'Convertibility in the Comecon region? Proposals and reverses', *Soviet and Eastern European Foreign Trade*, VIII (Summer 1972), 99–132.
588. Zwass, A. 'Currency in the foreign trade of CMEA countries', *Soviet and Eastern European Foreign Trade*, X (Autumn–Winter 1974–5), 46–96.

I. The International Bank for Economic Cooperation and the International Investment Bank

589. Babitchev, Eugene. 'The International Bank for Economic Cooperation', in *Money and plan: financial aspects of Eastern European economic reforms*, edited by G. Grossman. Berkeley: University of California Press, 1968, pp. 129–52.
590. Bednarik, Mojmir K. 'The Moscow Bank: the International Bank for Economic Cooperation', *American Review of Soviet and Eastern European Foreign Trade*, II (January–February 1966) 3–8.
591. Brabant, Jozef M. P. van. 'The CMEA investment bank: organization and purposes', *Documentation sur l'Europe centrale*, No. 3 (1970), 215–219.
592. Francusz, H. 'The International Bank for Economic Cooperation', International Monetary Fund *Staff Papers*, III (1969), 489–503.
593. Hermann, Adolf. 'Comecon's credit needs: how the West could respond', *Banker*, CXXII (March 1972), 297–9.
594. Lavelle, M. J. 'The international bank for economic cooperation', *Osteuropa Wirtschaft*, XVIII (December 1973), 222–33.
595. Marczewski, J. 'Le rôle du système bancaire dans les pays de l'Est', *Problèmes Economiques*, No. 1284 (9 August 1972), 21–6.
596. Mazanov, G. 'International settlements of CMEA countries: improvement problems', *International Affairs* (Moscow), No. 4 (April 1969), 71–7.
597. Meynell, Charles. 'Rivalry between Comecon and Russia's foreign trade bank', *Euromoney* (November 1977), 62–3.

598. Osiecki, Zdzislaw. 'The international banks of the COMECON countries', *Soviet and Eastern European Foreign Trade*, XII (Spring 1976), 12–18.
599. 'Socialist international organizations: specialized institutions and agreements', *Soviet Statutes and Decisions*, XI (Summer 1975), 339–477.
600. Vorob'ev, V. A. 'A comprehensive programme of socialist economic integration and the International Investment Bank', *Problems of Economics*, XVIII (December 1975), 56–69.
601. Wilen, K. 'The International Investment Bank of Comecon', *Soviet and Eastern European Foreign Trade*, VII (Spring 1971), 68–74.
602. Zahalka, V. 'Banks and foreign trade', *Soviet and Eastern European Foreign Trade*, VIII (Summer 1972), 155–73.
603. Zwass, A. 'The international investment bank and the Council for Mutual Economic Assistance', *Soviet and Eastern European Foreign Trade*, IX (Spring 1973), 3–50.
604. Zwass, A. 'CMEA monetary institutions and steering instruments', *Soviet and Eastern European Foreign Trade*, X (Autumn–Winter 1974–75), 97–158.

J. Individual member-countries of CMEA and associated states

605. Apro, Antal. 'Hungarian economy and cooperation within CMEA', *International Affairs* (Moscow), No. 7 (July 1967), 27–33.
606. Bass, L., and Keremidchiev, V. 'Uchastie Bolgarii v spetsializatsii i kooperirovanii proizvodstva stran SEV', *Voprosy Ekonomiki*, No. 7 (July 1976), 101–8.
607. Chernyshev, V. 'Ekonomicheskie sviazi mezhdu SSSR i SFRIU', *Voprosy Ekonomiki*, No. 10 (October 1977), 113–19.
608. Csikos-Nagy, B. 'Perfectionnement des mécanismes économiques en Hongrie', *Economies et Sociétés*, V (January 1971), 51–70.
609. Csikos-Nagy, B. 'La politique économique de la Hongrie. Ses objectifs et ses moyens', *Revue de l'Est*, III (January 1972), 5–29.
610. Davadorzh, Tsedevsuren. 'How CMEA membership

benefits Mongolia', *World Marxist Review*, XIX (October 1976), 105–12.

611. Dobrescu, E., *et al.* 'Comecon-Romanian views', *Soviet and Eastern European Foreign Trade*, VIII (Autumn–Winter 1972), 325–34.
612. Fekete, Janos. 'Monetary policy in Hungary: interdependencies with the CMEA and the western world', *Three Banks Review* (September 1977), 3–20.
613. Filipov, Grisha. 'Cornerstone of the party's economic policy (Bulgaria)', *World Marxist Review*,. XX (August 1977), 32–42.
614. Filipov, Grisha. 'Bulgaria in the international division of labour', *International affairs* (Moscow), No. 4 (April 1978), 13–19.
615. Henys, Otta. 'Coordination of five-year national economy plans of Czechoslovakia and the CMEA countries in 1976–1980', *Czechoslovak Economic Digest* (May 1976), 3–11.
616. Iumin, M. N. 'The Mongolian People's Republic in the system of international socialist economic integration', *Chinese Economic Studies*, VII (Winter 1973–74), 92–105.
617. Iumin, M. N. 'Mongol'skaia Narodnaia Respublika i Sovet Ekonomicheskoi Vzaimopomoshchi', *Narodny Azii i Afriki* (Moscow), No. 3 (1977), 17–28.
618. Jovanovic, M. 'Yugoslav trade with EEC and Comecon countries', *Law and contemporary problems*, XXXVII (Autumn 1972), 586–91.
619. Kanet, R. E. 'Hungarian views of CMEA integration', *Problems of Communism*, XXVI (January 1977), 67–9.
620. Korbonski, Andrzej. 'Poland and the Council of Mutual Economic Assistance 1949–1971', *Central European Federalist*, XIX (July–December 1971), 40–51.
621. Kostal, M. and Vesely, Z. 'The Czechoslovak Socialist Republic and the Council for Mutual Economic Assistance', *Czechoslovak Economic Digest*, V (August 1973), 25–43.
622. Kovalevski, Iu. 'Pol'sha v mezhdunarodnom promyshlennom sotrudnichestve', *Voprosy Ekonomiki*, No. 3 (March 1976), 123–32.
623. Kresta, Joromir. 'Problems of exchanging consumer goods with the Comecon countries (Czechoslovakia's relations

with Comecon)', *Soviet and Eastern European Foreign Trade*, IV (Autumn 1968), 44–57.

624. Marai, L. 'Uchastie Vengrii v mezhdunarodnom sotsialisticheskom razdeleni truda', *Planovoe Khoziaistvo*, No. 3 (March 1965), 56–63.
625. Montias, John M. 'Background and origins of the Rumanian dispute with Comecon', *Soviet Studies*, XVI (October 1964), 125–51.
626. Mosoczy, Robert. 'Development of Hungary's economic cooperation with the Comecon countries', *Soviet and Eastern European Foreign Trade*, XII (Winter 1976–77), 3–18.
627. Pertot, V. 'Yugoslavia's economic relations with Eastern European countries', *Coexistence*, IV (1967), 7–13.
628. Pindak, F. 'Czechoslovakia and Comecon', *The Economist*, CXVII (September–October 1969), 516–42.
629. Prochazka, Milos. 'Long-term trade agreements between Czechoslovakia and the CMEA member-countries for the years 1976–1980', *Czechoslovak Economic Digest* (November 1976), 53–62.
630. Puchmeltr, Zdenek. 'The share of Czechoslovak science and technology in the development of socialist integration', *Czechoslovak Economic Digest* (September 1975), 77–89.
631. Ramerie, Louis. 'Tensions au sein du Comecon: le cas roumain', *Politique Etrangère*, XXVIII, 249–57.
632. Sheinin, E. 'Ekonomika Kuby v sisteme mezhdunarodnogo sotsialisticheskogo razdeleniia truda', *Voprosy Ekonomki*, No. 8 (August 1978), 107–16.
633. Sivov, V. 'Sotsialisticheskaia integratsiia i razvitie proizvodstva v Bolgarii, *Voprosy Ekonomiki*, No. 2 (February 1976), 91–8.
634. Tabacek, J. 'Trade relations between Czechoslovakia and the Soviet Union', *New Trends in the Czechoslovak Economy*, VII (November 1969), 37–64.
635. Trzeciakowski, W. 'Evolution de la planification et de la gestion du commerce extérieur en Pologne', *Revue de l'Est*, II (1971), 5–38.
636. Valyi, Peter. 'Hungary and international economic integrations', *New Hungarian Quarterly*, XIII (Winter 1972), 22–32.

637. Vitkova, Marie. 'Changes in the system of planned management of foreign trade in the Bulgarian People's Republic since January 1, 1976', *Soviet and Eastern European Foreign Trade*, XIII (Summer 1977), 55–68.
638. Wandycz, P. S. 'Recent traditions of the quest for unity: attempted Polish-Czechoslovak and Yugoslav-Bulgarian confederations, 1940–1948', in *The people's democracies after Prague*, edited by J. Lukaszewski. Bruges: De Tempel (Tempelhof), 1970, pp. 35–93.
639. Wyschka, Gerhard, and Konig, Helmut. 'The GDR within the Council for Mutual Economic Assistance – prospects, problems and tasks of the foreign economy', *German Foreign Policy* (East Germany), VII (1969), 83–91.

K. CMEA and the European Economic Community

640. Akademiia nauk. Institut ekonomiki. *Problemy ekonomi cheskikh sotrudnichestva mezhdu vostokom i zapadom evropy*. Moscow: 1973.
641. Bergthun, O. L. and Nielsen, T. T. 'Comecon and EEC: a comparative analysis', *Res Publica*, X (1968), 407–32.
642. Binns, Christopher A. P. 'The development of the Soviet policy response to the EEC', *Coexistence*, XIV (1977), 240–65.
643. Brabant, Jozef M. P. van. 'En marge d'un colloque sur la politique économique de la CEE et du CAEM', *Documentation sur l'Europe Centrale*, No. 1 (1972), 63–9.
644. Brown, J. F., *et al.* 'Eastern Europe and the Common Market', *Communist Affairs*, VI (March–April 1968), 11–15.
645. Bogomolov, O. T. 'East–West economic relations: economic interests of the socialist and capitalist countries of Europe', in *World economy and East–West trade*, edited by F. Nemschak. Vienna and New York: Springer-Verlag, 1976.
646. Bogomolov, O. T., and Shmelov, N. P. 'Economic basis of European cooperation', in *All-European economic cooperation*, edited by Oleg Bogomolov and N. P. Shmelov. Moscow: 1973.
647. Bot, B. R. 'EEC-CMEA – is a meaningful relationship

possible?', *Common Market Law Review*, XIII (1976), 335–66.

648. Bykov, A. 'Two systems of integration and economic ties in Europe', *International Affairs* (Moscow) (February 1976), 12–21.
649. Cannucciari, Carl. 'Trade between the European Economic Community and the Eastern bloc: the development of a common external commercial policy for the EEC', *Syracuse Journal of International Law and Commerce*, II (Spring 1974), 79–98.
650. Ciamaga, L. 'Remarques sur la coopération économique entre l'Europe de l'Est et de l'Ouest', *Revue de l'Est*, V (April 1974), 41–3.
651. Djokanovic, Tihomiv. 'EEC-CMEA contacts', *Review of International Affairs* (Belgrade), XXVI (5 March 1973), 21–3.
652. Dobroczynski, Michal. 'Eastern Europe and Western Europe: prospects for economic cooperation', *Studies on International Relations* (Warsaw), No. 5 (1975), 35–47.
653. Dryer, H. Peter. 'EEC states cling to East deals', *New York Journal of Commerce* (11 December 1974).
654. Dumesnil, Claude. 'Les relations entre la CEE et les pays de l'Est', *Revue du Marché Commun*, No. 182 (February 1975), 57–61.
655. 'EEC-Comecon relations: a turning point', *East–West trade: the international yearbook 1975*. Oxford: Pergamon Press, 1975, pp. 113–38.
656. Ehrhardt, Carl A. 'EEC and CMEA tediously nearing each other', *Aussenpolitik*, XXVIII (1977), 162–77.
657. 'Eurocrats and commissars are inching closer', *The Economist*, CCLVI (30 August 1975), 26–29.
658. Feld, W. 'The utility of the EEC experience for Eastern Europe', *Journal of Common Market Studies*, VIII (March 1970), 236–61.
659. Forte, D. F. D. 'The response of the Soviet Union to the Common Market', *Soviet Studies*, XIX (1967–68), 373–86.
660. Groom, A. J. R. 'The functionalist approach to East–West cooperation in Europe', *Journal of Common Market Studies*, XIII (1975), 21–60.
661. Hanson, P. 'The European Community's commercial re-

lations with the CMEA countries: problems and prospects', in *Changing perspectives in East–West commerce*, edited by Carl H. McMillan. Lexington, Mass.: Lexington Books, D.C. Heath & Company, 1974, pp. 31–58.

662. Hewett, Edward A. 'Recent development in East–West European economic relations and their implications for US–East European economic relations', in United States Joint Economic Committee, *East European economies post-Helsinki*. Washington, D.C.: United States Government Printing Office, 1977, pp. 174–98.

663. Inotai, A. 'Some aspects of the economic relations between the Federal Republic of Germany and the CMEA', *Acta Oeconomica*, XVII (1976), 61–80.

664. Iskra, Wieslaw, 'CMEA and EEC: opportunities for cooperation', *World Marxist Review*, XIX (June 1976), 64–71.

665. Kaser, Michael. 'Comecon and the new multilateralism', *World Today*, XXVIII (April 1972), 162–9.

666. Kaser, Michael. 'The EEC and Eastern Europe: prospects for trade and finance', *International Affairs* (London), XLIX (July 1973), 402–13.

667. Kaser, Michael. 'Soviet trade turns to Europe', *Foreign Policy*, No. 19 (Summer 1975), 123–35.

668. Kaser, Michael, and Ransom, Charles. 'Relations with Eastern Europe', in *Economic integration in Europe*, edited by G. Denton. London: Weidenfeld & Nicholson, 1969, pp. 83–117.

669. Laroussilhe, Olivier de. 'Stop-go between EEC and Comecon', *Vision* (Paris) (June 1978), 27–8.

670. La Serre, Françoise de. 'La CEE et l'Europe de l'Est', *Revue française de science politique*, XXIV (December 1974), 1237–48.

671. Lukaszewski, J. 'The European Community and Eastern Europe', *The Round Table*, No. 249 (January 1973), 41–50.

672. Luttikholt, Harry. 'The Soviet Union and the European Communities', *Coexistence*, XIV (1977), 79–99.

673. Maentakanen, Erkki. 'Western and Eastern Europe in Finnish trade policy, 1957–1974: towards a comprehensive solution?', *Cooperation and Conflict*, XIII (1978), 21–41.

674. Mayer, Otto G. 'Comecon Ante Portas', *Intereconomics*, No. 3 (1976), 67.

675. Mensonides, Louis J., and Kuhlman, James A. (eds). *The future of inter-bloc relations in Europe*. New York: Praeger, 1974.
676. Morissens, L., *et al*. 'Politiques économiques de la CEE et du Comecon', *Cahiers économiques de Bruxelles*, No. 54 (2e trim. 1972), 157–276.
677. Mouskhely, Michel. 'Le bloc communiste et la Communauté Economique Européenne', *Revue d'économie politique*, LXXIII (1963), 406–38.
678. Nemschak, F. (ed.). *World economy and East–West trade: East–West European economic interaction* (Workshop Paper No. 1). New York: Springer-Verlag, 1976.
679. Ovchinnikov, K. 'Evropa: dalgorochnye soglasheniia v torgovlo-ekonomicheskikh otnosheniiakh mezhdu Vostokom i Zapadom', *Vneshniaia Torgovlia*, No. 6 (June 1974), 22–9.
680. Patolitchev, N. 'Coopération économique mutuellement avantageuse entre l'Est et l'Ouest européen', *Revue de la Société d'Etudes et d'Expansion* (Liège), No. 259 (January–February 1974), 66–70.
681. Pinder, John. 'The Community and Comecon: what could negotiations achieve?', *World Today*, XXXIII (May 1977), 176–85.
682. Pinder, John. 'A Community policy towards Eastern Europe', *World Today*, XXX (March 1974), 119–28.
683. Pinder, John. 'Economic integration and East–West trade: conflict of interest or comedy of errors?', *Journal of Common Market Studies*, XVI (September 1977), 1–21.
684. Pinder, John. 'EEC and Comecon', *Survey*, No. 58 (January 1966), 101–17.
685. Portier, J., and Seranne, C. 'Les deux intégrations et les relations économiques Est-Ouest', *Revue française de science politique*, XXIV (1974), 1219–29.
686. Ransom, Charles. 'The future of EEC-Comecon relations', *World Today*, X (1971), 438–45.
687. Scharpf, Peter. 'Les relations entre la Communauté Economique Européenne et la République Démocratique Allemande', *Revue du Marché Commun*, No. 178 (October 1974), 422–9.
688. Schiavone, G. 'The EEC-Comecon Dialogue: Towards a Recognition of Realities in Europe?', *Comunita*

internazionale, 1976, No. 2, pp. 311–20.

689. Shishkov, Iu. 'The Council for Mutual Economic Assistance and the Common Market – some comparisons', *American Review of Soviet and Eastern European Foreign Trade*, I (July–August 1965), 9–29.

690. Singleton, F. 'Finland, Comecon and the EEC', *World Today*, XXX (February 1974), 64–72.

691. Smole, Janko. 'Yugoslav-EEC relations', *Review of International Affairs* (Belgrade), No. 672 (1978), 1–4.

692. Soviet Committee for European Security. *All-European economic cooperation.* Moscow: Akademiia Nauk, 1973.

693. Suto, Otto. 'The problem of relationship between Comecon and EEC in the European policy of security and cooperation', *Studia Diplomatica*, XXVII (September–November 1974), 765–77.

694. Szita, J. 'Intra-European economic cooperation and East–West trade', *Acta Oeconomica*, XIII (1974), 275–94.

695. Turgeon, Lynn. 'Common Market and Comecon: their internal contradictions and common interests', *American Review of Soviet and Eastern European Foreign Trade*, I (March–April 1965), 3–12.

696. Wilson, Duncan. 'Soviet Westpolitik', *The Round Table*, No. 258 (April 1975), 127–38.

697. Wipf, L. J. 'The impact of West European trade strategies on exports to Eastern Europe', *European Economic Review*, VI (1975), 155–71.

698. Wolf, Thomas A. 'East–West European trade relations', in United States, Joint Economic Committee. *East European economies post-Helsinki.* Washington, D.C.: United States Government Printing Office, 1977, pp. 1042–54.

III. TEXTS OF CMEA AGREEMENTS AND CMEA PUBLICATIONS

A. CMEA agreements and documents

699. 'Alfavitnyi ukazatel' k edinoi tovarnoi nomenklature vneshnei torgovli stran-chlenov SEV, standardtnoi mezhdunarodnoi torgovloi klassifikatsii OON i Brussel'skoi tamozhen-

noi nomenklatury', *Biulleten' inostrannoi kommercheskoi informatsii prilozhenie*, XI (1967). Entire issue.

700. 'Comprehensive programme for the further intensification and improvement of collaboration and the development of socialist economic integration of Comecon member-nations', *Soviet and Eastern European Foreign Trade*,VII (Autumn-Winter 1971), 187–305.

701. East–West (Belgium). *Comecon statistical survey*. Brussels: Research and Advisory Service, 1971.

702. Russia (1923– USSR) Verkhovnii Sovet. 'Agreement concerning multilateral settlements in transferable rubles and organization of the International Bank for Economic Cooperation', *American Review of Soviet and Eastern European Foreign Trade*, II (January–February 1966), 9–36.

B. CMEA Publications

703. Sovet Ekonomicheskoi Vzaimopomoshchi. Sekretariat. *Agreement on cooperation between the Council for Mutual Economic Assistance and the Republic of Finland.* Moscow: CMEA Secretariat, 16 May 1973. Mimeographed.

704. Sovet Ekonomicheskoi Vzaimopomoshchi. Sekretariat. *Collected reports on various activities of bodies of the CMEA in 1973.* Moscow: CMEA Secretariat, April 1974.

705. Sovet Ekonomicheskoi Vzaimopomoshchi. Sekretariat. *Comprehensive Programme for the further extension and improvement and cooperation and the development of socialist economic integration by the CMEA member-countries.* Moscow: CMEA Secretariat, 1971.

706. Sovet Ekonomicheskoi Vzaimopomoshchi. Sekretariat. *The Council for Mutual Economic Assistance: 25 years.* Moscow: CMEA Secretariat, 1974.

707. Sovet Ekonomicheskoi Vzaimopomoshchi. Sekretariat. *Ekonomicheskoe sotrudnichestvo stran-chlenov SEV.* Spetsial'nyi vypusk Mai 1974 g. Bi-monthly from 1975–

708. Sovet Ekonomicheskoi Vzaimopomoshchi. Sekretariat. *General conditions of delivery of goods between organizations of the member-countries of the Council for Mutual Economic Assistance.* Moscow: CMEA Secretariat, 1968.

709. Sovet Ekonomicheskoi Vzaimopomoshchi. Sekretariat. *Information about CMEA countries' economic and technical cooperation with developing countries of tropical Africa.* Moscow: CMEA Secretariat, January 1974.
710. Sovet Ekonomicheskoi Vzaimopomoshchi. Sekretariat. *Information about CMEA countries' economic and technical cooperation with ESCAP developing countries.* Moscow: CMEA Secretariat, 1974.
711. Sovet Ekonomicheskoi Vzaimopomoshchi. Sekretariat. *Information on multilateral cooperation in the framework on CMEA in the field of industry.* Moscow: CMEA Secretariat, March 1974.
712. Sovet Ekonomicheskoi Vzaimopomoshchi. Sekretariat. *Information on the activities of member-countries of the Council for Mutual Economic Assistance in coordinating national economic plans within the framework of the CMEA bodies.* Moscow: CMEA Secretariat, 1967.
713. Sovet Ekonomicheskoi Vzaimopomoshchi. Sekretariat. *Information on the activities of the Council for Mutual Economic Assistance in 1975.* Moscow: CMEA Secretariat, 1976.
714. Sovet Ekonomicheskoi Vzaimopomoshchi. Sekretariat. *Obzor deiatel'nosti SEV.* Moscow. Annual. 1968?-
715. Sovet Ekonomicheskoi Vzaimopomoshchi. Sekretariat. *Sbornik informatsii o deiatel'nosti organov SEV.* Moscow. 1973?–
716. Sovet Ekonomicheskoi Vzaimopomoshchi. Sekretariat. *Standarty SEV i rekomendatsii SEV po standartizatsii: ukazatel'.* Moscow. Annual. 1975?–
717. Sovet Ekonomicheskoi Vzaimopomoshchi. Sekretariat. *Statisticheskii ezhegodnik stran-chlenov SEV.* Moscow. Annual. 1970–
718. Sovet Ekonomicheskoi Vzaimopomoshchi. Sekretariat. *Survey of CMEA activities in 1968.* Moscow: CMEA Secretariat, 1969.
719. Sovet Ekonomicheskoi Vzaimopomoshchi. Sekretariat. *Survey of CMEA activities in 1969.* Moscow: CMEA Secretariat, 1970.
720. Sovet Ekonomicheskoi Vzaimopomoshchi. Sekretariat. *A survey of 10 years of the CMEA.* Moscow: CMEA Secretariat, 1969.

MAJOR SOURCES OF INFORMATION

Brabant, Jozef M. P. van. *Bilateralism and structural bilateralism in intra-CMEA trade*. Rotterdam: Rotterdam University Press, 1973.

Business Periodicals Index. New York: H. W. Wilson Co.

Economic Abstracts. The Hague, Netherlands: Nijhoff.

Journal of Economic Literature. Menasha, Wisc.: American Economic Association.

Lavigne, Marie. *Le Comecon*. Paris: Editions Cujas, 1973.

McMillan, Carl H. *Aspects of Soviet participation in International Trade*. PhD. Thesis, John Hopkins University, 1972.

New Serial Titles. New York: Bowker.

Public Affairs Information Service. *Bulletin*. New York: H. W. Wilson Co.

Public Affairs Information Service. *Foreign Language Index*. New York: H. W. Wilson Co.

Social Sciences Index. New York: H. W. Wilson Co.

Tsagalov, Nikolai Aleksandrovich. *Bibliografiia po voprosam politicheskoi ekonomii: 1917–1966*. Moscow: Izdatel'stvo MGU, 1979.

United Nations. Dag Hammarskjold Library. *Current bibliographical information*. Geneva.

United Nations. Dag Hammarskjold Library. *Monthly checklist of new accessions*. New York.

Voprosy Ekonomiki. Moscow: Akademiia Nauk, Institut Ekonomiki.

Subject Index

Author Index